Also by Ivor Noël Hume

HERE LIES VIRGINIA (1963)

1775: ANOTHER PART OF THE FIELD (1966)

HISTORICAL ARCHAEOLOGY (1969)

These are Borzoi Books,
published in New York by Alfred A. Knopf

A GUIDE TO

ARTIFACTS
OF COLONIAL
AMERICA

Frontispiece. *Upper left*: glass wine bottle with seal of Samuel Cobbs of Williamsburg, c. 1735; another wine bottle, c. 1755; brass candlestick with inverted baluster and knopped stem and turned foot, c. 1720; and inverted-baluster stemmed wine glass with waisted bowl and folded foot, c. 1730. *Lower left*: small delftware plate with a stylized floral pattern in blue, c. 1745; latten spoon with trifid handle terminal, no rat tail, maker's mark TS and three spoons, late 17th century; two-tined steel fork with pistol-grip wooden handle, first half of 18th century; small white saltglaze plate with barley pattern on the rim (*see also* Fig. 35, No. 3), c. 1750; brass tobacco box engraved with pictorial designs on top and bottom, Dutch, first half of 18th century; and clay tobacco pipe with 13-inch stem, c. 1720–60. *Center*: yellow slipware cup decorated with horizontal brown combing, third quarter of 18th century; delftware bowl with polychrome floral decoration, c. 1740; and pewter spoon, late 18th century. *Upper right*: delftware mug decorated with figures and a landscape painted in purple, c. 1760; and Westerwald gray stoneware mug decorated with sprigged GR medallion and incised geometric and scroll devices adorned with blue, and with "4" capacity mark in blue below the handle, c. 1740. *Bottom*: delftware plate with chinoiserie decoration in blue, c. 1725; two-tined steel fork with riveted plate bone handle, mid-18th century; and table knife with plain bone handle, third quarter of 18th century. All are English, unless otherwise stated, and were found in excavations at Williamsburg, Virginia. Exceptions are the latten spoon, tobacco pipe, and tobacco box, which were found in the River Thames at London.

Delmore Wenzl

A GUIDE TO

ARTIFACTS OF COLONIAL AMERICA

IVOR NOËL HUME

ALFRED A. KNOPF
1970
NEW YORK

THIS IS A BORZOI BOOK
PUBLISHED BY ALFRED A. KNOPF, INC.

Library of Congress Catalog Card Number: 76–79314

Manufactured in the United States of America

For AUDREY

who has no need of it

PREFACE

Beware the self-professed expert, for he has ceased to learn; and look closely at the man who bestows that distinction on another, for it means only that the recipient is less ignorant than he.

There is a widely held belief that to write is to be right, and therefore anything published must be infallible. Would that it were so.

These two thoughts were uppermost in my mind when I began to put this book together, and for a while they almost frightened me into abandoning it. I was fearful that the novice would hail me as an expert on everything, while specialists in fields outside my own would condemn me for not being able to tell them something that they did not already know. These are the dangers of attempting any compilation of an encyclopedic nature. It is difficult enough when one is dealing only in facts; but in the world of the past, fact and fiction, theory and countertheory, research and rebuttal, ensnare us at every turn.

I confess that there was a time, a good many years ago, when if I heard someone introduce me as an expert on English glass or pottery, I was inclined to believe him. I have since learned better. Many of the rules and criteria that once seemed safe and infallible have been revealed to be so qualified by variants and exceptions that yesterday's certainties have been diminished to today's tentative possibilities. In short, there is truth in the adage that the more one learns, the more one needs to learn, and that among antiquaries there can be no experts—only elderly students. Nevertheless, this student has been toiling in the archaeological wilderness of the seventeenth and eighteenth centuries for twenty years, and it is reasonable to suppose that he may have emerged knowing a little more than those who are just setting out. Had some gentle mentor thrust this book into my hand when first I girded on my trowel, I would probably have done better and gone further. In writing it now, I do so in the hope that it may help my successors to do both.

Williamsburg   INH
June 1968

ACKNOWLEDGMENTS

Giving credit where it is due is one of an author's more satisfying duties—provided he is confident that he has left no one out. In this instance I approach the task with no such confidence. The information collected here has been garnered over a period of some twenty years and is the product of scores of excavations, my own and other people's. When they were mine, they were by no means mine alone, for I was helped by scores of assistants both amateur and professional. I have learned from countless reports, articles, and books by heaven knows how many writers, and I have benefitted from advice and suggestions from conversations and correspondence with specialists in many fields. I am in the debt of each and every one of them.

More specifically I am indebted to numerous friends and colleagues who have answered questions and who have provided illustrations specifically for this book. Their names are as follows: John C. Austin, curator of ceramics, Colonial Williamsburg; R. J. Charleston, keeper of ceramics, Victoria and Albert Museum, London; V. Clain-Stefanelli, curator of numismatics, Smithsonian Institution; John M. Graham, curator of collections, Colonial Williamsburg; Jacob L. Grimm, curator, Fort Ligonier Memorial Foundation; J. C. Harrington of Richmond, Virginia; J. Paul Hudson, curator, United States National Park Service, Jamestown; Sir Anthony Jenkinson, Port Royal, Jamaica; Robert Marx, submarine archaeologist, Institute of Jamaica; Ralph Merrifield, deputy keeper, Guildhall Museum, London; Arnold Mountford,

ix

Acknowledgments

director, Hanley Museum, England; Richard Muzzrole, department of cultural history, Smithsonian Institution; Eugene T. Peterson, director of historic projects, Mackinac Island State Park Commission, Michigan; Hugh de S. Shortt, curator, Salisbury Museum, England; Stanley South, archaeologist, North Carolina Department of History and Archives; Donald Streeter, Iona, New Jersey; Ross E. Taggart, curator of ceramics, Nelson-Atkins Gallery of Art, Kansas City, Missouri; and C. Malcolm Watkins, curator of cultural history, Smithsonian Institution.

The photographs have been generously provided from negatives in the following collections: Colonial Williamsburg, Inc., Frontispiece and Figures 1, 14, 29–31, 36–9, 49, 65, 53, 54, 59, 60, 66, 68, 82–5, 91, and 93; Guildhall Museum, London, Figures 6, 27, and 52; Fort Ligonier Memorial Foundation, Figure 3; Nelson-Atkins Gallery of Art, Kansas City, Figure 40; Smithsonian Institution, Figures 18, 48, and 61; and the United States National Park Service, Figure 28. All other photographs are my own, as are all the drawings, with the exception of Figures 2, 73, and 99b by Daniel Barber and Figure 23, which was drawn and provided by Stanley South. The tile typology illustrated in Figure 94 is derived in part from Korf Dingeman: *Dutch Tiles* (New York: Universe Books, Inc.).

The illustrated artifacts are drawn from the following private and public collections: The City of Alexandria, Virginia, Figure 48; Sir David Burnett of Tandridge Hall, Surrey, England, Figure 74 (No. 1); Colonial Williamsburg, Inc., Frontispiece (with the exception of the pipe, tobacco box, and latten spoon) and Figures 7, 16, 20 (Nos. 5, 9, and 11), 21, 25, 29, 30 (right), 31 (Nos. 3 and 4), 32, 34, 36–9, 49, 51, 53, 54, 58 (except No. 4), 64 (except Nos. 1–4), 66, 68, 70–3, 74 (Nos. 4–8), 75–7, 77b (Nos. 3 and 4), 79 (No. 1), 79 (Nos. 2, 3, and 4), 82–5, 87 (Nos. 7 and 8), 91, 92 (Nos. 2 and 3), 93 (Nos. 1 and 2), and 100 (Nos. 3–5); Fort Ligonier Memorial Foundation, Figure 3; Guildhall Museum, London, Figures 4–6, 27, 52, 55–7, and 98; Hanley Museum, England, Figure 48; Institute of Jamaica, Figures 20 (Nos. 1 and 2), 58 (No. 3), 99b, and perhaps also 79 (No. 2); Nelson-Atkins Gallery of Art, Kansas City, Figure 40; Audrey Noël Hume, Figure 19; Smithsonian Institution, Figures 18 and 61; Donald Streeter, Figures 77a (Nos. 1, 2, 10, and

Acknowledgments

11) and 80; United States National Park Service, Jamestown, Figures 28, 50, and 78 (No. 1); L. B. Weber, Newport News, Virginia, Figures 14, 60 (Nos. 1–3), 74 (Nos. 2 and 3), 77 (No. 2), and 87 (Nos. 3–5). The remaining individual items (as opposed to type drawings) are in my own collection. Not included in the foregoing list are the wine bottles shown in Figures 8–13, the whereabouts of some of which are not now known.

CONTENTS

Contents

ILLUSTRATIONS

Illustrations

Illustrations

Illustrations

xviii

A GUIDE TO

ARTIFACTS
OF COLONIAL
AMERICA

SIGNPOSTS
TO THE PAST

There are some words in the dictionary that one just cannot warm to, and the term *artifact* happens to be among my pet aversions. It is one of those cold, new, pushy words that are in constant use, but which mean everything and nothing at the same time. It seems to have been born in the mid-nineteenth century, and *The Shorter Oxford English Dictionary* dismisses it in a suitably brief line: "... [f. L. *arti-* + *factus*.] An artificial product." While the word is much more used in the United States than in England, the Oxford dictionary is sufficiently sporting to refrain from trying to pass it off as an American creation. It is, however, doubtless significant of something or other that American dictionaries treat it with considerably more respect. *The Random House Dictionary of the English Language* offers the following: "... 1. an object made by man, esp. with a view to subsequent use. 2. *Biol.* a substance, structure, or the like, not naturally present in tissue but formed by artificial means. as chemicals." It is left to Messrs. Littler and Ives in their *Webster Dictionary* (1957 edition) to get to the nub of the matter in the following pungent passage: "... [1. artifis; 2. artifaekt], fr. Lat. *ars, art-* (*em*), 'art,' & *fact-us*, 'made'. See artifice & fact. (archaeol.) Object, such as early palaeolithic flint, made and shaped by human art and skill, as opposed to natural object, shaped by weather, water &c." Why they chose to select an "early palaeolithic" flint instead of a late one, or flint instead of quartzite, is one of the world's minor mysteries; but the important fact is that the definition emphasizes the term's archaeological usage.

Littler and Ives's definition of *archaeology* stresses its close relationship with prehistory and ignores its use in the study of the classical, Dark Age, medieval, or post-medieval eras. It is hardly surprising, therefore, that this dictionary should think of an artifact as being a manmade object from remote antiquity. For my part, if I have to think of it at all, I prefer the all-embracing definition of the *OED*—"an artificial product"; in short (or almost as short) anything made by man at any time. Providing that it is used within the limiting brackets of archaeological parlance, the word serves a useful purpose, describing something that has been unearthed. Only rarely is it used to describe an object that has simply survived; normally those are classed as antiques or sometimes as bygones. However, the law places limitations on the meaning of *antique*, requiring an object so described to have been manufactured before a certain date. The word *artifact* has not been dignified by legislation, and it can embrace any artificially manufactured object from something as ancient and once-important to man as a stone ax, to something as recent and useless as a discarded LBJ button.

In England, objects, or parts of objects found in the ground are termed "finds," a word that at least has the merit of suggesting discovery and therefore exciting interest. *Artifact*, on the other hand, seems to have the dead hand of the museum upon it and does, indeed, evoke the mental image of rows of palaeolithic flints in dusty cases, mute, save for their faded and curling labels. Nevertheless, when you get down to it, a word is no more than an assemblage of letters or sounds meaning whatever the writer or speaker wants them to mean—providing that the person who reads or hears them accepts that interpretation. For this reason it is imperative that we agree (if only for the duration of this book) on what the term *artifact* shall embrace. It is equally important to agree on what I mean by "Colonial America." If we want to be precise, *agree* is not the right word; it is merely a euphemism for *accept*, and so I ask you to accept the fact that I intend to restrict the content of the book largely to objects that have been, or could be, dug up on British American sites inhabited during the seventeenth and eighteenth

4

centuries. With very few exceptions they are identical to those that are unearthed on English sites of the same period. In some instances, such as the sections on coins and furniture fittings, I have discussed and illustrated examples that were minted or manufactured much later than 1775. I have done so because it is often as useful for the archaeologist (and the collector, for that matter) to know when an object is *not* of the colonial period as when it is.

To the archaeologist, the recovery of artifacts is not, or should not be, the object of the exercise. Just like the digging, artifacts are a means to an end, that of teaching us something new about the past. They are three-dimensional additions to the pages of history. Similarly, the dedicated collector of antiques sees beyond the mere acquisition of rarities to the world of which they were part. By carefully studying one item the collector learns about others; in the same way the archaeologist obtains knowledge from fragments that teach him about the intact objects. The latter is also true of the museum curator and, for that matter, of the collector.

The fragments that an archaeologist digs up make him acutely conscious of small details; for example, the structure of pottery, something that neither the curator nor collector has a chance to observe unless he has the misfortune to let a prized specimen slip through his fingers. I have frequently found that both collectors and museum personnel are unable to identify from fragments objects with which they are well acquainted when intact. I venture to hope, therefore, that this book's archaeological approach to looking at antiques will open new vistas for those of us who have neither the opportunity nor the desire to dig. I also hope that it will help both amateur and professional excavators to see beyond the fragments to the whole and thence to the life of which that whole was a part.

The connoisseur will look, say, at a long-case clock and judge it first as an entity, as an aesthetic whole, and then proceed to date it on the basis of mechanical and stylistic details. The archaeologist, on the other hand, will probably look at the same clock and see it not as a splendid marriage of the clock- and casemakers' arts but rather as an assemblage of hinges, brass capitals, lock, escutcheon, latches, weights, pulley wheels, dial, spandrels, hands, bell, and mechanical parts, any or all of which he may expect to find in the ground and need to be able to identify and date. He will look at

5

other furniture in the same way, seeing metal escutcheons, locks, and drawer pulls held together with pieces of wood. Were he digging in Egypt where wooden objects are frequently unearthed, he would doubtless see with eyes that were differently educated. The antique collector's initial reaction to this seemingly Philistine approach may be scathing, but if he will give it a little thought he may find that it has something to offer him.

Much of what we know about the age of antiques is derived from surviving dated examples and from theories and counter-theories put forward by collectors and dealers. These researches often result in broad generalizations that, in fact, are only true of fairly small regions and narrow periods. For example, the collectors of cream-colored earthenware tend to believe that it was all made either at Leeds or in the factory of Josiah Wedgwood. In truth, there were scores of English factories producing that ware, but little or nothing is known about them because many were small and their records have not survived. Archaeological excavations on those lesser factory sites can provide the only means of determining what they made, and until that digging is done their surviving products will continue to be attributed to Wedgwood or to Leeds.

In the past ten years excavations in Virginia have thrown new light on colonial cabinetmaking, potting, brass casting, gunsmithing, and swordsmithing, none of which information was to be derived from the study of documentary records or from surviving antiques. Digging in Philadelphia has yielded exciting new information about the products of the Bonnin and Morris porcelain factory, while excavations on the site of the New Bremen glass manufactory in Maryland have added enormously to our knowledge of both the glass of John Frederick Amelung and of eighteenth-century glass technology in general. In all these instances the new information was derived from small fragmentary artifacts which only tell their full story when compared with intact pieces and in relation to the extant documentary record. The study of the past through its antiques should be a combination effort by archaeologists, social historians, and students of the useful and decorative arts. Ideally, of course, (and certainly most economically) all three roles should be played by the same person. I have contended elsewhere that there is no such thing as an archaeologist per se, for to do his job properly he must be fully conversant with both the history and the objects of the period whose site he is digging—which makes him a social historian. However, as digging is merely a technique whereby one takes the ground apart in a meaningful manner, it is a simple matter for a historian to learn to dig in the earth for his information as competently as he does in the library.

I have made a distinction between the historian and the student of the useful and decorative arts, knowing that there is often only the finest of lines between them. The latter cannot escape being a social historian, though the social historian can, and often does, ignore the testimony of surviving objects. It is unfortunate that we live in a world that has to pin labels on everything, and that in the smaller academic sphere those labels create almost unsurmountable barriers. Archaeology has been bracketed with anthropology and was—and frequently still is—shunned by historians, the same historians who contemptuously dismiss the potential contributions to be made by objects or artifacts as "pots and pans" history.

It so happens that pots and pans, both in trade and in use, were the very stuff of history, and, as the Minnesota Historical Society has demonstrated, a collection of copper kettles or a cloth bag full of files recovered by divers can bring portage history to life in a way that no document can ever achieve. The same is also true of many another submarine archaeological site—providing that the diving excavators know what they are doing. The lost city of Port Royal in Jamaica is a classic example of what I mean. Wrecked and partially submerged in the earthquake of 1692, the site remains the most important potential source of late-seventeenth-century English artifacts in the western hemisphere. But because much of it lies beneath ten feet of silt and twenty feet of water, its archaeological story must be told largely through its artifacts and not through the normal study of the relationship between those artifacts and the stratigraphy of the ground in which they lie.

In 1688, Port Royal possessed approximately five thousand European inhabitants and as many Negro and Indian slaves, living and working in about fifteen hundred houses—six hundred of them brick—many of which, though built on sand, were four stories high, "Cellard, covered with Tiles and glazed with Sash Windows."[1]

---

[1] John Taylor: "History of His Life and Travels in America" (1688); manuscript in the archives of the Institute of Jamaica.

There were a governor's mansion, church, market, prison, forts, courthouse, ordinaries, a coffee house, and "many Taverens, and aboundance of Punch houses, or rather may be fittly called Brothel Houses." Not only were there many merchants living there "to the Hight of Splendor,"[2] there were also goldsmiths, tailors, carvers, armorers, hatters, tanners, combmakers, upholsterers, cabinetmakers, joiners, turners, smiths, and many other tradesmen. In an instant most of their homes and possessions were swallowed by the water or the heaving sand, while those buildings that survived were destroyed in a fire that "consumed all ye Town"[3] in January 1702/3.

Had this been the end of Port Royal, it would be reasonable to conclude that any diver could bring up artifacts from the silt and feel reasonably certain that they dated before the earthquake or at the latest, prior to the fire of 1703. However, that was by no means the end of Port Royal; on the contrary it was rebuilt again and again, suffering through disastrous hurricanes, more earthquakes, and another all-consuming fire in 1815. That section of the town that had sunk in 1692 became an anchorage for British ships through the eighteenth and nineteenth centuries and a repository for their trash. In 1817 a large naval hospital was built over part of the old town and fronted onto the submerged area; thus, sick sailors and their attendants contributed their share of artifacts tossed into the silt over pre-earthquake Port Royal. When one dives there now it is immediately apparent that the twentieth century is equally well represented on the bottom, in the shape of Coke bottles, automobile tires, and a miscellany of old iron, much of which is carried by the tide down into the holes dredged by diving archaeologists. Visibility is rarely more than a couple of feet, and when you put out your hand to pick up a potsherd, a cloud of silt rises up and reduces vision to nil. Nevertheless, one does catch tantalizing glimpses of stratified layers with their artifacts imbedded in them.

It is quite possible to pluck Port Royal's "goodies" out of the banks like plums from a cake, but that is simply treasure hunting. The trick is to keep the material from each layer separate, even

[2] Ibid.
[3] Eye-witness account by Christian Lilly; quoted in Frank Cundall: *Historic Jamaica* (London, 1915), p. 60.

though it may never be possible to relate those layers one to another. Because, in archaeology, one dates each layer by the most recent artifact found in it, it is essential that the diving archaeologist be capable of recognizing and dating the artifacts even before he brings them to the surface. Only then can he be sure that he is dealing with a bona-fide pre-earthquake layer unsullied by the intrusive British naval chamber pot thrown away in the mid-nineteenth century.

In 1967 a large quantity of Spanish silver coins was brought up from a single location in the course of diving work at Port Royal, and along with the coins were silver spoons, a curiously shaped brass weight, and a filigree-decorated brass plate. These last items attracted far less interest than the hoard of commercially valuable coins; yet to me they were the most important. The filigree ornament was part of the crown from a typical, brass lantern clock of the seventeenth century, while the weight could well have come from a clock of the same type. (Fig. 58, No. 3) Although the decorative crown plates were often anchored to the clock by steel screws, it is extremely unlikely that they would have parted in the earthquake, and therefore, even if the iron had subsequently corroded away, the crown would have been lying beside the rest of the clock, almost all of which would have been of brass. The diver was certain that there were no more pieces close by, and therefore it is reasonable to conclude that the crown plate and weight were simply parts stored in the same building as the silver treasure. Now it so happens that clockmakers, goldsmiths, and silversmiths were often one and the same, and so it is reasonable to suggest that the coins and the related artifacts came from the shop of a clockmaker and worker in precious metals. Without the two momentarily worthless brass objects, the silver treasure would have been just that, with no clue as to whom it belonged at the time of the earthquake.

Vast quantities of artifacts have already been salvaged from the submerged area of Port Royal, but most of them retain no associations one with another. Delftware pottery of the 1680's lies cheek by jowl with wine bottles of the 1720's; Rhenish stoneware of the 1700's shares the same boxes as pieces of the mid-nineteenth century; and tobacco pipes of the earthquake period are mixed with those tossed away by British sailors of Nelson's time. The information necessary to prevent this sort of thing happening does exist,

9

but it is scattered through countless books, magazines, journals, and even newspaper articles, copies of which are virtually impossible to obtain even if one knows of their existence. I dare to hope that the contents of the present book will do something to fill the terrestrial and submarine archaeologists' need for a concise guide to colonial artifacts.

Most of us are not fortunate enough to have submerged or buried cities to play with, or even to have the time or money to undertake the total excavation of a single historical site, but there are thousands of people who actually live on sites that have been occupied ever since the colonial period, and for them, every digging of the garden or laying of a utility is likely to bring something of the past to the surface. Immediately the questions are asked: What is it? and How old is it? With luck the answers to both questions will be found between these covers. It is obviously impossible, however, to include everything that was manufactured by Western man in the seventeenth and eighteenth centuries. Furthermore, many of the less artistically attractive objects have received little or no study by curators or collectors. Some of those objects must have been quite common, and yet even after considerable study we are still unable to so much as identify their purpose. There are at least two small iron objects found on most eighteenth-century colonial sites that are familiarly known to us in Williamsburg as "another one of *them!*"

Although collectors collect all sorts of extraordinary things, there are some objects that are found on early American sites that would probably be spurned even if they were recovered intact. I am thinking of such objects as bricks, roofing tiles, windowpanes, nails, and such like builders' debris. Nevertheless, they *are* artifacts, and they were among the most common items of their periods. Consequently, they have their place in the present book. Besides, they are the stuff of life to the practitioners of a new and growing profession, that of the restoration architect. As a rule such people realize the need for experienced archaeological assistance, but it is not uncommon for architects to undertake excavations of their own—usually without any understanding of the importance of artifacts in interpreting the structural remains they are seeking.

Although I am not writing another archaeological textbook, I should explain that, in the absence of documentary evidence, the only way that a building can be closely dated is by means of the artifacts that are associated with it.[4] It is true that such factors as house plans, brickbonds, and mortar components provide broad dating criteria (though generally with regional limitations), but they can never be as informative as closely datable domestic artifacts. For example, a Liberty penny of 1793 found in the original backfilling of a builder's construction trench would provide irrefutable evidence that the wall standing in that trench could not be of colonial date. Almost any artifact, be it an old bottle neck, a scrap of Staffordshire pottery, or the handle of a decayed pewter spoon, has a date to tell us—providing we have the wit to interpret it. It is the date after which that type of bottle neck, that type of pottery, or that handle design was first used. In archaeological parlance that date is known as a *terminus post quem*, the date after which the object must have found its way into the ground. It may have been *any* time after, from then until now, but not before. This simple logic is, incidentally, the cornerstorne of all archaeological reasoning. The trick is to be able to date the artifacts, and that can only be learned through lengthy experience or through knowing in which book to look to find the answers.

The relationship between the collector of American antiques and the historical archaeologist is rapidly becoming closer. Each is learning that the other has much to offer him—or her. The digger in the ground rarely unearths artifacts sufficiently well preserved for them to be of commercial value as antiques, but the fragments recovered from tightly dated archaeological contexts such as abandoned well shafts and domestic rubbish pits can often provide dating evidence that the collector might be unable to obtain from any other source. Thus it was that the discovery of the waste products from the Bonnin and Morris porcelain kilns in Philadelphia revealed unrecorded information about the shapes, fabric, and decoration of one of the first American quality ceramic factories. Similarly, the excavation of the Geddy family's mid-eighteenth-century brassworking shop in Williamsburg yielded information about the range and quality of their products that was only hinted at in the

[4] This thesis is explored at length in the author's *Historical Archaeology* (New York, 1969).

11

written sources. In addition, the archaeological study of the James Geddy House site led beyond Williamsburg to provide new thinking about clockmaking in Philadelphia. This is one of the most important contributions that archaeology makes, the provision of unexpected catalysts to activate new research in other fields. The Geddy discovery is sufficiently dramatic and intriguing to merit a place as a classic example of the way in which archaeologist's reasoning carried him into research in the field of the decorative arts that he might never otherwise have considered.

James Geddy, Sr., was a gunsmith and brassfounder who settled in Williamsburg, Virginia, in the 1730's. He died in 1744, leaving a widow, three daughters, and four sons, David, James Jr., William, and John. David and William carried on their father's business after his death in a factory building whose foundations and operating debris were found in excavations there in 1967. In 1760 the widow sold the property to her son James Geddy, Jr., who was then recorded as being a silversmith, though he subsequently called himself a goldsmith. His advertisements showed him to be a jeweler and also a watch repairer. What became of David and William is not clear from the surviving records, though the archaeological evidence suggests that William continued to work on the same lot until the Revolution. In the course of the digging, the rough casting for an ornamental spandrel for a clock was found in a context of about 1765. (Fig. 58, No. 2) As an unfinished fragment from another spandrel of a different type had already been found, there was little doubt that both examples had been cast in the Geddy workshop. This raised a number of questions: Which Geddy made the spandrels? Did the caster design them himself? What was the date of the design, and which of the Geddy family was a clockmaker?

The small fragment comprised only the head of a cherub and was not large enough to be traceable. Besides, cherubs were used on spandrels from the late seventeenth century to at least the third quarter of the eighteenth century. The almost complete example, on the other hand, was of an unusual form, its principal feature being a crown topped by a large cross and supported by a pair of wingless cherubs whose legs trailed out into foliate scrolls. Nothing quite like it could be found on English clocks, and in its horological ignorance Williamsburg's archaeological team began to think that this motif must have been one of the Geddy's own creations. Scores of American clockfaces were studied, most of them from New England, without any success. Eventually, however, a Philadelphia clock made by John Wood I (d. 1761) was encountered with what might be identical spandrels. What, then, was the relationship between the Wood clock and the spandrel from the Geddy site? While trying to learn more about John Wood, we heard of two more clocks having the same type of spandrels, and careful comparative study left us almost certain that at least one spandrel from one of those clocks came from the same pattern as did the Geddy example. The clock in question was made by Peter Stretch of Philadelphia, who died in 1746. His shop, known as "Peter Stretch's Corner" was subsequently bought by John Wood I and given to his son, John Wood II, who was also a clock- and watchmaker. It is possible, therefore, that John Wood I also bought some of Peter Stretch's tools—including the spandrel pattern. In any case, there was a connection between Wood and Stretch. As yet, however, no connection has been found between them and the third clockmaker, Isaac Pearson of Burlington, New Jersey, who was the proprietor of the Mount Holly Ironworks and who died in 1749.

Wood, Stretch, and Pearson were working in the Philadelphia area (Burlington being only a short distance upstream on the other side of the Delaware River from Philadelphia) at much the same time. Wood was advertising as early as 1734, making him a contemporary of both Stretch and Pearson, who died within three years of each other. It must therefore be concluded that the crown and cherub spandrels are a Philadelphia characteristic established prior to 1746, or before the death of Peter Stretch. The Geddy spandrel, on the other hand, coming as it does from a context of c. 1765, appears to have been made some fifteen years later, when the Geddy shop was owned by James Geddy, Jr., goldsmith and watch repairer. But appearances can be deceptive, and in archaeology they frequently are.

The evidence of the Philadelphia and Burlington clocks leaves no doubt that the crown-and-cherub spandrel was popular before 1750, and it is therefore entirely possible that the Geddy example was also made in the same period. As I have already explained, an artifact can have been thrown away any time after its type came into being, but not before. Thus the Geddy spandrel could have been cast in the 1740's and have remained on the site until it was buried in the 1760's. It is, of course, more than a little tempting to associate this and other clock parts found on the site with James Geddy, Jr., the watch repairer. However, it is not clear whether he actually *made* watches; and, furthermore, craftsmen who made clocks and watches normally advertised themselves as doing both. None of James Geddy, Jr.'s, advertisements made any such claim, nor, for that matter, did the very few surviving advertisements of his father or of his brothers David and William. James Geddy, Sr., had unquestionably been a gunsmith and brassfounder; but could he also have been a clockmaker? One might be forgiven for supposing that gunsmithing and clockmaking had little in common. Nevertheless, Burlington's Isaac Pearson was both an ironfounder and a clockmaker. Furthermore, James Geddy, Sr.'s, inventory made at the time of his death included founder's patterns, an old clock, and a clock dial.

Even if the Geddy spandrel was cast by the first James, we still have not explained how the same pattern was used both in Philadelphia and in Williamsburg. Even if we supposed that the patternmaker who served Wood, Stretch, and Pearson also supplied James Geddy, Sr., that still does not explain why the Williamsburg spandrel has the same flaws in it as one of those used by Stretch. The most logical explanation would seem to be that a Stretch clock was brought into the Geddy shop and that one of its spandrels was taken off and used as a pattern to shape the mold for the excavated example. This conclusion is strengthened by the fact that the details of the Williamsburg spandrel are blurred as they would tend to be when cast from a pattern once removed from the original.

If the pattern came from a Stretch clock that had been brought to Williamsburg, the dating evidence provided by Stretch's working life would be invalidated, for the copy could have been made years after his death. Then again, if the archaeological context of c. 1765 is actually close to that of the casting, we would be back in James Geddy, Jr.'s, period. It may or may not be a coincidence that earlier excavations at Anthony Hay's cabinetshop (c. 1757–76) only four or five minutes' walk away had produced considerable evidence relating to the making or repairing of cases for clocks. Perhaps there is still to be heard in some quiet American home the ticking of a long-case clock with crown and cherub spandrels cast by a Geddy and housed in a case by Anthony Hay.

Thus, the finding of a discarded brass casting at the James Geddy House promoted a chain of inquiry that tells us something completely unexpected about a Williamsburg craft and, at the same time, provides collectors of Early American clocks with something new to consider.

In many instances the new lines of thought are new only to the thinkers. I believe it was Will Rogers who said that everyone is ignorant—about something. Both archaeologists and collectors are likely to be ignorant about periods and objects outside their immediate fields of specialization, and when they venture beyond the safety of their knowledge they are likely to be as green as the rawest novice. This unhappy fact was brought home to me some little while ago in a way that I am not likely to forget. It is possible, however, that had I had this book in my hand at the time I might have escaped—though under the circumstances I doubt whether I would have thought to make use of it.

My own special field during the past fifteen years or so has been English ceramics and glass, a pasture broad enough for an individual to spend a lifetime exploring without ever reaching the other side. Nevertheless—touch wood—I think I have learned enough not to get caught, at least not too often. At the time of which I am writing, I knew very little about guns; I knew the names of the parts and of the differences between lock mechanisms, but I was totally unschooled in the matter of model variations and in the nuances of dating by fitting shapes or by proof marks. It so happened that I had, for years, wanted to own a regulation British Brown Bess musket and, as I had just finished work on a book about the American Revolution in which the musket played a losing role, my desire to possess an example of that period was not to be denied. So, realizing how little I knew about the subject, I decided that the only safe course was to go to a reputable dealer and tell him what I wanted, and be prepared to pay through the nose for it. I accordingly went to a firm in London who had been specialists in antique firearms since 1928 and who had a world-wide reputation in the field. I explained what I wanted, admitted that I was there because

I did not know enough to use my own judgment, and so threw myself on their mercy. They sold me what they described on the receipt as a Brown Bess musket of c. 1780. After the gun had been wrapped I asked whether they had a bayonet of the same period that would fit it. They said they did, and I bought that too. Both gun and bayonet then went to the shippers, and I did not see either for three months. When they arrived, I immediately discovered that the bayonet did not fit the musket and that its socket was only 3 1/16″ long instead of the standard British length of 4″. That jarring discovery sent me hastening to the appropriate books, where more unpleasant surprises were in store. The lock was certainly made in the eighteenth century and it still bore its Tower arsenal inscription, but the GR and crown of George III had been ground off and replaced by another crown—and an ordnance mark introduced in 1841. The barrel was stamped with view and proof marks dating no earlier than 1813, and the brass side plate belonged to what is termed the New Land Pattern and which was introduced no earlier than 1802. Neither the trigger guard nor the butt plate were of types used on regulation muskets; and, to cap it all, a gunsmith specializing in the study of antique weapons said that he thought that whatever the gun was, it had been restocked in the not too distant past.

I naturally wrote to the dealer and explained what I had discovered about the gun and asked for an explanation. He replied that he had bought it at auction and that the sale catalog had called it "A Tower musket 12 bore with Tower markings and crown & GR [which it did not have], XVIIIth century." He therefore saw no reason to call it anything else and ended by claiming that "the law of England on antiques is 'Caveat Emptor.' " It was an expensive lesson, but from it I learned something about "reputable" antique dealers and rather more about muskets.

I asked myself: What should I have known to have avoided the trap?—apart from not throwing myself on the mercy of a dealer. What small, readily learned piece of expertise could I have memorized that would have made me suspect that I was being taken? The answer lay in the gun's brass fittings, which happen also to be parts that an archaeologist is most likely to encounter in the ground. Measurement discrepancies are not readily detected unless one has a ruler to hand or is able to compare the right with the wrong. Similarly, there are too many mark variations for the novice to learn them, and besides, later marks were sometimes stamped on older guns. No; in my case the easiest guide should have come from the brass side plate which, on the standard Revolutionary-period Brown Bess, was anchored by only two screws, one at the fore end and the other at the crest of a bow approximately two thirds along its length. (Fig. 70) Without this my musket could not possibly have been a fully fitted regulation Brown Bess. In the India Pattern musket which followed, the side plate screws remained in the same position, but the plate was shortened and terminated at the rear screw, eliminating what had previously been a purely decorative tail. The Land Pattern that followed in 1802 added a third screw in the midsection of the India-style plate. There are other variations in side plate styles which are discussed on p. 217; my purpose here is simply to indicate the kind of insights to the dating of antiques that can be derived from an archaeological approach to them. By this I mean a concentration on details and particularly upon the techniques employed in the manufacture of those details.

I confess to knowing very little about furniture woods or cabinetmaking techniques, but I do know something about furniture hardware because that survives in the ground and is fairly easily recognized and dated. I have also learned a bit about window glass and the way it was made—and window glass was used in the doors of china cabinets and cupboards. Consequently, if someone offers me an eighteenth-century corner cupboard in allegedly original condition and yet the glass in the doors is an even thickness, devoid of bubbles, and slightly blue in color, I leave my checkbook in my pocket until I have obtained a second, more knowledgeable opinion. Until the last quarter of the century, most quality window glass of the 1700's was made by the crown process, which involved the spinning of an opened glass bubble into a circular disc. This glass was rarely free of bubbles or stress marks, both of which followed the curvature of the disc as it was rotated. Any glass without bubbles or stress marks is liable to be late, at least post-colonial, while any lines of stress, or groups of bubbles that do not curve, however slightly (the discs or crowns were usually about five feet in diameter), are unlikely to have been made by the crown process. Realizing that early glass invariably had flaws in it, firms reproducing old glass have often added spurious stress marks by adding wiggles and lines to sheet glass while still in the plastic state. However, as the marks in the original crown glass followed the curvature of the discs and were the product of the manufaturing technique, it is a simple matter to spot the reproduction panes whose "flaws" are added by craftsmen who do not really understand what their antiquing is supposed to represent.

There is, of course, all the difference in the world between reproductions and deliberate fakes. The principal distinction stems from the fact that the faker has generally been to considerable trouble to learn *how* an original object was made so as to be able to include some of those reassuring touches of authenticity in his spurious product. On the other hand, the man making a reproduction is not trying to cheat anyone and so is not concerned with the copying of the effects of the original manufacturing process unless they have some obvious bearing on the form or style of the reproduction. He would not, for example, bother to remove from the underside of a seventeenth-century-type table the marks of his circular saw—a tool not invented until the third quarter of the eighteenth century. When reproducing an eighteenth-century brass candlestick, the modern manufacturer would see no need to weld together a shaft made in two separately cast halves, when he could produce a stick of the same form in one operation. After all, he will argue, why reproduce two unsightly seams down the sides, seams that the original candlestickmaker tried to conceal.

While it is true that the manufacturer of reproductions is not trying to pass off his products as originals, the fact remains that those reproductions often find their way into antique shops where they age remarkably quickly. The transition from reproduction to bogus antique is becoming increasingly easy as more and more antique dealers augment dwindling supplies of original items by stocking reproductions. While the distinction is normally made clear by the dealer, there is always the chance that the "green" customer may make a mistake and even that the dealer may inadvertently put the "wrong" piece on the right shelf. The possibility of such errors increases when the dealer knows little about his stock. It has become common practice for would-be antique dealers to open a shop having bought their entire stock from a supplier. I recall one such "kit" that stressed "Willow-Pattern," transfer-printed ironstone china and other comparable wares, a considerable part of which comprised reproductions made by the descendants of famous name manufacturers in the present century. Among the original pieces was what appeared to be a most unusually proportioned ironstone teapot. It turned out that the end of its spout had been knocked off and the truncated remains had been carefully filed down and shaped to a new mouth. The dealer was genuinely unaware that the teapot had been doctored or that all the "Willow-Pattern" glistering on her shelves was not old.

In contrast to the honest mistakes that every dealer must inevitably make, there are those errors that are made by the customer alone. It is by no means unknown for unscrupulous dealers to file off the modern manufacturer's identifying marks from reproductions and to sell them as originals. This is not, however, a new practice; it has been going on ever since there were reproductions of anything. In the second half of the nineteenth century, for example, many excellent reproductions and style adaptations of seventeenth-century Rhenish stonewares were made by one Hubert Schiffer. He was not making fakes, only continuing in the Rhineland's renowned ceramic tradition and supplying a large Victorian market with a taste for the baroque. His pieces were stamped on the underside with his initials, and even during his lifetime examples were turning up in shops and salesrooms with the HS carefully filed off and posing as original pieces. So common did this practice become that nowadays a piece with a slightly dished, smooth area on its base is recognized as Schiffer's as readily as it would be were his mark intact. As it happens, one does not need to look at the bottoms to see that they are not right; the originals were thrown on the wheel while the reproductions were cast, leaving mold marks that could rarely be entirely concealed.

Although ornamental pottery had been slip-cast in molds as long ago as the first century A.D., the casting of pottery vessels (as opposed to figures) died out and was not widely used again until the second quarter of the eighteenth century, when alabaster and later plaster molds became available in England. Rhenish potters continued in the old tradition up to the end of the eighteenth century, throwing the pot on the wheel and then luting separately cast decoration to the body. Thus anyone remembering even this simple and very general scrap of know-how can avoid being misled by a piece of mold-made Rhenish stoneware.

The fact that some modern reproduction manufacturers neither know nor care how the originals were made was brought graphically home to me a few years ago when I visited a reconstructed glass factory that purported to demonstrate how seventeenth-century glass was blown. At the same time it made, among other items, reproduction wine bottles of the period for sale to visitors. Thinking that it would be amusing to own one but being anxious that it should be as authentic as possible, I took along an original from my own collection to ask the blower to get as close to the early style as possible. I had previously noticed that to make the reproductions acceptable to the modern customer, care was taken to round off the mouths, rather than leaving them irregular as were those that were struck straight from the blowing iron. Although this refinement changed the character of the bottle, I imagine that it was dictated by the fact that modern lead glass is hard and sharp while the seventeenth-century soda glass used in bottlemaking was much softer.

The glass blower was sure that I was mentally awry, but he reluctantly agreed not to tool the mouth of the bottle. My attempts to explain that anything else would not be a true reproduction merely added to the blower's conviction that I might become dangerous if not humored. I had also noticed that his products had a myriad of bubbles deliberately added to make them pretty. The originals inevitably had some bubbles, but only because they could not be avoided. I explained that I would like my bottle made with no extra bubbles.

The man's reaction was almost as though I had impaled him on his own pontil iron. His jaw sagged, his cheek hollowed, and then chokingly he gasped, "No bubbles?"

"No bubbles," I replied.

"But everybody likes bubbles! Nobody wants no bubbles. I wets my paddle, stick it in the batch, and then I stir, stir, stir. Everybody wants bubbles."

"Except me," I added. I repeated that I wanted this to be like the original, with no more bubbles than are created by rotating the blowing iron to pick up the gather. I watched the bottle made (without bubbles and struck directly from the iron without any additional tooling) and then saw the glass seal applied bearing the initials of my wife and myself—a "personalizing" touch that is as popular today as it was in the seventeenth and eighteenth centuries. I was told by the blower that my bottle would take a day to anneal and that I could come back for it the following weekend. I duly did so, paid my $7.00 or whatever the price was, and being in a hurry did not open the box until I got home. Then followed the ceremonial unwrapping of yards of tissue paper and the revealing of our very own genuine reproduction, seventeenth-century glass wine bottle—complete with rounded mouth and a billion bubbles.

I never went back to the factory to find out what happened. I can only suppose that my idiotic request to have a bottle made to resemble the originals had resulted in such a travesty of the modern glass blower's art that he killed it at birth and substituted what he knew I would have wanted had I had more sense.

It is entirely possible that after I am gone, my bottle will turn up in some antique shop masquerading as a bona-fide seventeenth-century item—complete with original but unknown owner's seal. I can only hope that this book will also survive and that the section on glass bottles will deter anyone from buying it—the bottle, not the book.

The artifactual products of digging in the ground are principally valuable as evidence of when and where certain types of objects, particularly common objects, were in use. It is the same evidence that we can expect to find in the documentary records but is much more unequivocally and graphically presented. Two examples will serve as illustrations. The inventory of Williamsburg cabinetmaker Anthony Hay made at the time of his death in 1770 listed "two coloured stone teapots" valued at one shilling and sixpence.[5] The inventory did not tell us how large the teapots were, how they were decorated, or what color or colors were used. It was

---

[5] Wills and Inventories, York County (Va.), Number 22 (1771–83), pp. 19–24. Hay's inventory was recorded on January 21, 1771.

left to excavations on Hay's home site to reveal fragments of two "Littler's blue" teapots that well fitted the inventory description. (Fig. 39) Inventories are normally made prior to the disposal and dispersal of property, in which case it is unlikely that the actual cataloged items would find their way into the ground of the site where the inventory was made. In the Hay instance, however, his widow continued to live on the property for sixteen years after his death, thus making it possible, and even likely, that teapots listed in the inventory were subsequently broken and buried on the site. Yet even when this favorable chronology does not exist, the similarities between excavated artifacts and inventory listings can be revealing. If a creamware eggcup is found on a home site in a context of 1780 and a 1782 inventory of that home lists "6 Queen's ware eggcups" it is reasonable to suggest that the excavated example may be of the same shape and quality. It cannot be proved, but it is still a valuable guide for anyone wanting to put appropriate eggcups back in the house.

My second example of the potential relationship between artifacts and inventories also comes from Williamsburg. Digging on the already discussed Geddy House property, a large quantity of scrap iron was found in a shallow pit behind the house. This waste material dated from the early years of the Revolution, and from the presence of numerous unfinished or dismantled gun parts it was clearly the residue of gunsmithing. There was little doubt that the craftsmen had been repairing and refitting muskets for use by the patriot forces. This was not in itself particularly surprising, though it was certainly interesting to see such evidence of the kind of work the gunsmith was doing. But what was very surprising indeed was the age of some of the guns that he had been repairing; at least one of the more complete locks was of a type common in about 1640, more than 130 years earlier. While we have no inventory directly relating to this gunsmith's work, we frequently find others that list "1 old gun" or "2 old muskets," and we usually think of them simply as not being new, perhaps thirty or forty years old at most. Now, however, we have evidence to indicate that some of the guns that were around at the beginning of the Revolution were very old indeed—but still not too old to be refitted and put back into service.

The evidence of archaeology is particulary important in America, where we have such a dearth of contemporary illustrations to show us how homes were furnished. The concept of the "period room," so beloved of museums and architectural restorations, is becoming increasingly under attack as thinking people realize that very rarely did anyone furnish a house or even a room totally to one period. Furniture, paintings, ornaments, and any other durable household items were passed down from generation to generation, making the contents of a house a hotch-potch of periods, mirroring the taste and economic status of both the owner and his forebears. Unfortunately, this kind of information is generally missing from household inventories, though it can sometimes be deduced by inference. Thus, for example, a reference to "1 old oak table" in an inventory of 1760 would suggest, on the grounds that oak was not popular in the eighteenth century, that the table was either an eighteenth-century country piece or was a survival from the previous century. There can, of course, be no denying that such items did survive through the eighteenth century, otherwise there would be none to grace the showrooms of the antique shops of today. Because wood does not normally survive in the ground, it is unusual for archaeology to be able to contribute to such arguments when they relate specifically to furniture. There are exceptions, however, and the Anthony Hay cabinetshop was one of them. Although the shop was not in operation into 1759, the majority of the brass drawer pulls, handle plates, and escutcheons found in the excavations dated from the late seventeenth century and from the first half of the eighteenth. In fact, very few examples of the Chippendale styles of the Hay period were found. Consequently, it can be deduced that the earlier brasswork came from old furniture brought into the shop to be repaired or modernized. If this archaeological evidence is valid, it would seem that old furniture styles were the norm in the colonial home rather than the exception. Documentary support for this conclusion is not uncommon, and one can sometimes follow the progress of a piece of furniture as it was passed down through a family in the wills of successive generations.

Coupled with the uncertainty as to what furnishings did continue in use in American homes over a long period of time, there is

23

also the question of the alleged time lag between the advent of new styles in England and their becoming generally available in the colonies. It seems reasonable to conclude that seventeenth-century Americans were more concerned with the creation and development of the colonies than they were with being fashionable. That came with the degeneration of the generations that followed and was confined to the wealthy urban middle class and to the plantation gentry. These were the people who wrote to agents in England ordering, as did George Washington, "Silver Spur's of the new'r Fashn,"[6] or who sent blanket requests for chinaware of whatever styles happened to be fashionable, without any apparent concern as to whether or not they would like what they received. These people were in the minority, but because they held positions of prominence and owned the more handsome houses, it is they who are remembered as the nation's founding forefathers, and it is their houses that are restored and reconstructed into national shrines. This gives us an extremely lopsided impression of what life was like in colonial America, and we tend to forget that without the continuing stream of immigrants imbued with the pioneer spirit the country would have decayed on the east coast without ever reaching the west. It was the constant transfusion provided by the hungry and hopeful that pushed the colonial frontiers farther and farther inland as each new family had to carve out its future in the Indians' wilderness. These pioneers, like their seventeenth-century predecessors, had little time or inclination to worry about fashion.

For these reasons it is dangerously misleading to make blanket statements about the place of fashion and taste in colonial America, for each colony had its two cultures, those of the prosperous and of the penurious. The same was true in England, of course, with one important exception—there was no free land to reward any man with a heart big enough and a back broad enough to reach it and work it. Our knowledge of the life and possessions of the colonial pioneer is woefully inadequate. He left few written legacies, and his home was rarely of any architectural merit. Indeed, if he prospered,

[6] John C. Fitzpatrick, ed.: *Writings of George Washington from the Original Manuscript Sources, 1745–1799* (Washington, D.C., 1931), III, 92. Invoice of goods to be shipped by Robert Cary & Co., July 15, 1772.

he would probably tear it down himself or convert it into servants' or slaves' quarters, leaving it to them to let it fall down. The only way that we can hope to get to know the pioneers is through careful archaeological studies of their home sites and the artifacts recovered from them. As yet very little has been done in this field, and we have little knowledge of how long it took the settler on the Ohio to acquire, say, the same kind of teapot that a Philadelphia tailor first purchased in 1750.

Personally, I am inclined to believe that once the merchandise reached the colonies, there was no appreciable time lag between its acceptance in the coast and its availability in the frontier settlements. The mid-eighteenth-century pioneer housewife who wanted a teapot would not have bought it from the Indians, nor would she have been likely to find a local potter with the skill to make it. She would have obtained it when her husband traveled to one of the coastal towns or would have bought it from an itinerant trader. Thus the time lag was only as long as it took husband or trader to journey to the town and back again.

During excavations for the study and reconstruction of the French and British fort at Michilimackinac at the Straits of Mackinac in northern Michigan, large quantities of fragmentary English pottery were uncovered: saltglaze, creamware, Whieldon wares, Chinese export and English porcelains, more or less anything that was in general use in the 1760's and 1770's. So surprised by this was one historian that he wrote to a friend describing the fort as a "Williamsburg on the frontier," an undreamed-of cultural phenomenon. In truth, there was nothing surprising about it at all; the fort was manned by British officers and men and they were not about to abandon their way of life simply because they happened to be stationed in one of the outer outposts of empire. One of the officers even brought his own billiard table with him, so the presence there of English teapots, wine glasses, punch bowls, or wine bottles should astound no one. On the contrary it is possible that contemporary English taste may have manifested itself at Michilimackinac before it became the vogue in Williamsburg. An officer destined for a tour of colonial duty would have been likely to equip himself with the essential comforts of England before setting out. Consequently, he would buy his tea ware from a fashionable

London china shop and carry it with him, the arrival on the frontier of the current London taste taking just as long as that officer took to get there. On the other hand, there were no china shops in Williamsburg, ceramics being sold by all sorts of tradesmen from milliners to a blacksmith. These retailers bought their stock through agents in London (who did the best they could for the money) or from ships' captains who carried speculative cargoes. Either way, the shopkeepers would not be buying the most expensive and fashionable products, for these would be hardest to market. It was left to wealthy Virginians returning from England with new styles in their baggage to promote the latest fashions, and only then would the market for them be created in Williamsburg.

The supposed parallel between Michilimackinac and Williamsburg is a poor one, for Williamsburg was not a wealthy town when compared, say, to Philadelphia, Charleston, New York, or Boston. It has acquired its popular status by accident or, more correctly, as a result of John D. Rockefeller, Jr.'s, interest in it. Thus, today, little Williamsburg, with its normal, eighteenth-century white population of about 750 souls, has become the average American's embodiment of all that was colonial. It is just about as valid a view as the Englishman's belief that the Plymouth pilgrims were the first to establish a British colony in America.

A comparably distorted idea of value and importance has developed around the artifacts that have survived from the seventeenth and eighteenth centuries. In the field of ceramics, for example, those that were pretty tended to be better looked after than those that were not. But prettiness was not necessarily synonymous with value. Such things as mid-eighteenth-century agateware cats were made for sale at country fairs, where they could be purchased for a few pence. Nowadays they are looked upon as major manifestations of the potter's art and fetch hundreds of dollars in shops and salesrooms. Rarity in anything tends to create value, sometimes legitimately, as in the case of a unique painting, but often misleadingly when an object's original scarcity was occasioned not by its high value or intentionally limited availability but by the public's rejection of it. The potter who produced a new glaze combination that failed to attract popular favor would have been foolish to have persevered with it. Consequently, only a comparatively small number of pieces with that glaze would have been manufactured, and an even smaller number would survive to become antiques. Because anything that is old and uncommon is now considered a collector's prize (no matter how hideous it may be), archaeologists are easily tricked into believing that finding an example of an unpopular ware on a colonial site is evidence of the wealth or high taste of its owner; whereas, in fact, by eighteenth-century standards, the reverse may have been true. Rejected in England, the pottery may have been shipped to the colonies to unload it onto a less discerning market.

Regardless of these potential pitfalls, there can be no denying that the best way to study the artifacts of the past is through finding them in archaeological contexts, for they are there related to each other both in time and space. The broken cups, the wine bottles, the gun parts, buckles, tobacco pipes, and whatnot were all thrown away together, probably by one person at one time, and came from a single household. Museum and private collections built up through individual purchase and gifts have no such unity; the specimen artifacts are simply examples of their type. Desirable and helpful though archaeological associations undoubtedly are, they, too, have real limitations. The excavator generally only sees the objects after they have been taken from their normal contexts and placed in others that tell us little about the artifacts' previous existence. It is akin to going to a graveyard and unearthing the bones of a man in the hope that they will reveal the story of his life. They may tell us something about the cause of his death and a little about his appearance at the moment of interment, but that is all. The cracked glass decanter found in a colonial rubbish pit can reveal why and when it was discarded, but it has nothing to say about where it was kept before it was broken. That is the kind of information that can only be derived from written or pictorial records.

This brings us back to the vexing question of the "period rooms" that museums and the furnishers of historic houses put together to show us what it was like to live in the world of earlier generations. These creations represent the most ambitious use of artifacts that we are likely to see. No longer are we asked to admire them for their alleged artistic excellence, for their quaintness, or for their present-day monetary value—we are seeing them restored to life. The door of the past has been opened, and we are invited to step through it—as far as the velvet rope barrier will permit. In theory, this should be the most exciting experience imaginable, and yet as a rule it is depressingly disappointing. Why?

There are a variety of reasons, the most obvious being that artifacts never had a life of their own, and therefore they cannot be expected to live now; at best they were the settings and props within and with which the drama of life was played. Once these things are removed from their original location they are no more evocative than a folded tent is of a circus. The sense of intimacy with the past that Howard Carter felt as he opened the tomb of Tutankhamen could not be successfully reproduced in a Cairo museum any more than it can in, say, the reconstructed birthplace of an American hero, furnished with antiques of the sort with which he might or might not have grown up.

The task of re-creating the past is even more difficult when the curator is not trying to show us the home or room of an individual but merely a vague interpretation of what an unnamed somebody's room or house might have looked like—if he had had the same taste and imagination as the curator. The difficulty is further increased by the fact that most curators are generally thinking in terms of presenting the "decorative arts" to a cretinous public, and that is not at all the same thing as showing *the past* to the public, cretinous or otherwise. As I have already contended, the very idea of a "period" room is an anachronism, because nine tenths of the people who lived in the seventeenth and eighteenth centuries accumulated their possessions through generations of gifts and bequests and purchased what they wanted when they needed it, regardless of style. Furniture and furnishings were relatively more durable than they are today, and once settled, people did not move about as often as they do in our own time. Consequently, one would be much more likely to find a 1960's "period room" than one would one of the 1760's.

Even if the curator possesses sufficient imagination to include pieces of furniture and crockery that are fifty or a hundred years older than the date of the room he is portraying, it is still unlikely to fire the imagination of the visitor. "Period rooms," no matter how well stocked with artifacts, invariably fail to look lived in.

Some theatrical-minded curators have inserted wax dummies, a few of which even wink and move their limbs, but the result is liable to cause any precocious child to ask: "Hey, Dad, what's the funny wax figure who winks his eye doing in the 'period room'?"

One of my more curious friends once confessed that whenever he was a guest in a strange house, he made a point of visiting the bathroom before leaving and while there peeping in the closet. He explained that this was one place the average hostess never cleaned up before a party and it revealed her in her true colors, dust, outdated prescriptions, sloppily squeezed toothpaste tube, curlers, and all. There, he contended, he could expect to come face to face with the life of that household. Looking at my own bathroom closet I can see precisely what he meant; but if you open the closet door of a "period room," how much life comes tumbling out? It is liable to be empty save for a modern fire extinguisher and a vacuum cleaner. Had it really been a room from the past, opening the closet door would be like lifting the lid of an overstuffed Pandora's box. Take, for example, the closets of William Blaikley of Williamsburg, the contents of which were inventoried when he died in 1739:

In the closet upstairs

1 old deal box with no lid
1 childs wicker cradle and basket

In the chamber closet

1 copper tea kettle
1 copper chocolate pot
1 coffee pot
1 old coffee mill with a small stone jar
1 copper pot
1 warming pan
3 Indian baskets
1 meal barrel, 1 old search [sieve]

In Mrs. Blaikley's Closet

1 Hamburg chest
1 old clock
1 looking glass, a little box
1 old box, 3 new hilling hoes
1 new hatchet, 1 tin lamp

1 pr. pistols, holster, sword, gun
2 baskets, 1 parcel of watchmakers things
An iron crow with other lumber
A mans cain in the desk, some raisers and
    other small things.[7]

Not only would it be a miracle to find a museum curator with a sufficiently wild imagination to put a hatchet or hoes in a lady's closet, it is equally unlikely that he would leave the door open for the public to see inside. An open closet door with the artifactual debris of eighteenth-century life peeping out would ruin the symmetry of the display. In the same way, a half-burned candle with the wax cascaded onto the candlestick would cause tarnish, while dregs of tea in the bottoms of cups on the tea table would stain the porcelain. As a result, the unburned candles increase the shrinelike effect of the "period room," while the absence of tea within reach of the tea service makes the latter a display of the porcelain and not an arrested moment in tea drinking.

I have often looked at my own living room after it has been groomed to receive visitors and have noted with some dismay how quickly and totally my presence has been irradicated. The closet doors are shut, the scatter of papers and books that normally litter the floor have gone, the ashtrays are empty, and the cushions are all puffed up; even the ashes under the log fire have been brushed into shape. Nobody lives there any more, and you begin to doubt whether anyone ever did. How much more difficult it is, therefore, for the museum curator to capture so illusive a quality in a setting that is, in any case, largely fictitious. On the other hand, if I walk out of my living room at night, leaving it exactly as it was when I ceased to do whatever I was doing, I can return in the morning and continue where I left off, and only the hands of the clock and the position of the sun (or rather the world to the sun) bear witness to any appreciable lapse of time. It is reasonable to conclude, therefore, that if, having walked out, I did not return and the room remained untouched for a century, at the end of it the sense of my

[7] Wills and Inventories, York County (Va.), Number 18 (1732–40), pp. 312–16. Blaikley's inventory was recorded on June 30, 1736.

presence would be just as strong. It is the hope of such a confrontation with the past that makes the average tourist visit historic houses, castles, battlefields, or archaeological sites, and as long as the artifacts of that past remain *in situ* something of that hope is realized.

This desire to reach into the past is by no means a twentieth-century fad, it has existed ever since man left anything behind to look back at. A classic example occurred in London in 1802 when one Nathaniel Bentley was evicted from his house and shop in Leadenhall Street. He was the son of a goldsmith and inherited the business in 1761; according to legend he was then a young man of fashion in London and was due to be married. On the day chosen for the engagement banquet his intended bride died; Bentley was so overcome by the loss that he closed up the house, leaving the meal still laid, and proceeded to live alone in part of the building for more than forty years. During that time the principal rooms were kept locked, and both Bentley and his house sank into abject squalor. When his lease expired, his ground landlord evicted him and became the first person from the outside world to enter the building in forty years. A contemporary account describing what Mr. Gossling, the landlord, saw revealed that "he now indulges his customers and the public with a view of the apartments; and we will venture to say that they have now been honoured with more company (we hear by 2000 persons, the first fortnight) than have ever entered them for half a century past."[8] The unhappy and eccentric Mr. Bentley was known as "Dirty Dick," and there is still a London pub of that name whose landlord allegedly bought up the contents of Bentley's banquet room—including the skeletons of rats and mice—which are to this day displayed to a gasping and bibulous clientele. Unfortunately, the validity of these relics is somewhat diminished by the presence of other alleged "dirty dickery," including a mummified crocodile that can hardly have figured in the story. Nevertheless, the point is simply that Bentley stopped the clock for forty years and the public flocked to see the phenomenon. The dramatic experience was not soon forgotten, and as late as 1852

[8] William Granger: *The New Wonderful Museum and Extraordinary Magazine* (London), II (1804), 945.

a poem entitled "The Dirty Old Man" described the sight. One of the verses read as follows:

> Cup and platter are masked in thick
>   layers of dust,
> The flowers fallen to powder, the wine
>   swath'd in crust.
> A nosegay was laid before one special
>   chair,
> And the faded blue ribbon that bound
>   it is there.[9]

As a poetic gem the lines leave something to be desired, but as an evocative use of artifacts to re-create the scene at No. 46 Leadenhall Street they are extremely successful. Indeed, it may have been these that gave Dickens the idea for Miss Havisham's petrified wedding breakfast in *Great Expectations*.

It is a sad fact that the past is more successfully re-created in our imagination by means of the written word than it is through any curator's three-dimensional reconstruction. But just as a computer's responses are only as good as the data that is fed into it, so our imagination's ability to "see" the past is dependent on our knowledge of it and particularly on our knowledge of its artifacts. If a novelist writing of the Wars of the Roses described his heroine as "Watching at the window as Sir Thomas rode down the snow-cleansed lane and out of her life," it is useful to know that her teeth were probably chattering loud enough to drown the pounding of her heart. In the fifteenth century very few windows were glazed with anything but horn or waxed paper, and those that did have glass were not sufficiently clear to be seen through with any clarity. Consequently, the poor girl would have had to open the window to watch her lover leave her. Thus it is that a knowledge of the evolution of window glass helps to fill in such essential little details.

Just as a knowledge of artifacts can enliven a written picture of the past, so words surviving from earlier times can teach us about artifacts and their place in it. I have already illustrated the value of

---

[9] William Kent, ed.: *An Encyclopaedia of London* (London, 1937), p. 638.

household inventories, and there can be no better source to reveal who owned a pistol and where he kept it. Such inventories were part of the county court records, and, although many of the volumes have since been destroyed by accidents and the attrition of war, large numbers still survive, many of them unstudied and unpublished.

Inventories are not necessarily solely domestic, for they included more or less everything that a man owned when he died. If he happened to be a blacksmith, the inventory would include his forge, his tools, and even his supply of scrap iron. If he were a shopkeeper, it would contain a listing of his stock and its value. This, of course, is extremely helpful, not only for what it tells us about one man's business but for what it reveals about the taste and needs of his customers. The latter information can also be gleaned from the colonial shopkeepers' newspaper advertisements. An excerpt from one such notice inserted into the *Virginia Gazette* (Purdie and Dixon) for July 25, 1766, by the Norfolk merchants Balfour and Barraud will serve as an example. The following represents the range of ceramic items that this firm had just imported:

> . . . china bowls of all sorts, plates, dishes, chocolate cups and saucers, coffee and tea cups and saucers, tea and milk pots, mugs, &c. Earthen ware, chamber and spitting pots, mugs, coffee cups, butter tubs and stands, colliflower do. tea and cream pots, enamel, tortoise, and white sets of childrens toys complete, Dutch jugs, egg cups, salts, pepper castors, punch strainers, childrens chair pans, potting pots, white, green, and blue candlesticks, patty pans, shapes for fruit and salad, baskets, delft bottles and basons, nappy dishes, white stone wash hand basins, Italian lamps with floats, plates and dishes, gallipots, vials, baking dishes, Dutch tiles, pickled leaves and stands, glass funnels, sauce boats, sugar basons, mustard pots, blomange cups, English china of all sorts, dessert plates, blue glass and gilt cannisters. Figures for ornament, harlequins, sailors, boys, flowers, birds, squirrels, lambs, dogs, sheep, &c. &c. carboys, smoking basons, fish strainers, stone bottles, butter pots, stone jugs . . .

Some of the items are hard to identify, but one thing is certain; if that cargo were to be recovered from a wreck today, it would be worth a president's ransom. It leaves little doubt that there was a

Virginia market for a wide range of "genteel" items from patty pans to ceramic sailors. As so often happens, it is not always possible to determine which items belong in what category. The first group is presumably of Chinese export porcelain, but thereafter we get into trouble. Does "Earthen ware" mean a group of common, but unspecified, kitchen wares, or is it used as an adjective to describe the items that follow? These could, in fact, be of cream-colored earthenware, as this was the body used for the "colliflower" shape and the "tortoise"-glazed wares that were listed a few items further along. Then again, "Dutch jugs" almost certainly meant Rhenish stoneware (shipped out of Dutch ports); but were the "egg cups, salts, pepper castors," and "punch strainers," also of blue and gray stoneware? If they were, no surviving examples are known. Very often, no amount of research or erudition will resolve these questions. There are many instances where it is obvious that the man writing the advertisement was not sure what he was describing, and there are doubtless many more cases where his ignorance is not so obvious but is there just the same.

Not only do advertisements tell us what people possessed, they also reveal what they called them and how they pronounced the names. Derby porcelain occurs as "Darby" while Rouen faïence appears as "Roan," "Roen," or "Rhoan." The products of the German Rhineland drift from "Deutch" to "Dutch"—which can be very confusing indeed—and items manufactured in the colonies when nonimportation agreements were in effect were referred to as "country made," a term that made no distinction between town and country. Determining how to describe an artifact can be almost as difficult as identifying it. Where possible, it is best to employ the same name given the object by the people who knew and used it—though there is clearly nothing to be gained by calling Rouen faïence "Roan ware," or German stoneware "Dutch." Unfortunately, the field of antiques is abloom with misleading and improper terminology, most of it coined by nineteenth- and twentieth-century collectors. Chinese export porcelain is still widely known as "Oriental Lowestoft"; cream-colored earthenwares from Staffordshire and elsewhere are collectively called "Leeds"; and the mottled-brown Rhenish stonewares of the sixteenth and seventeenth centuries are called "tigerware," a term presumably coined by someone who did not know the difference between a tiger and a leopard. All this, and much, much more, serves to confuse the novice out of his wits and sometimes right out of collecting. I can but hope that the appropriate sections of this book will help him avoid some of the pitfalls and also assist him in translating when confronted by an "expert" who uses these well-entrenched terms.

Just as difficult as finding the right name for a complete object is the problem of finding the proper term for a part of something. Both are frequently to be learned from contemporary salesmen's catalogs, for these generally illustrated the item being offered, giving its name, size and style variations, and prices. It is true that most of these catalogs tend to be of nineteenth-century date, but one or two go back to the sixteenth and seventeenth centuries, and there are a surprising number that survive from the latter part of the eighteenth century. Most of those that have a bearing on the artifacts of colonial America are of English origin, and the Victoria and Albert Museum in London has a large collection ranging through Leeds cream-colored earthenwares, teapots, and coffin furniture, to harness and saddler's ironmongery, brassfounders' wares, and furniture fittings. There is similar source material in the library of the British Museum, and in some cases long-established companies, such as Josiah Wedgwood Ltd., still retain their early catalogs and pattern books. Any and all of these are likely to be able to provide names and descriptions of artifacts that are vastly more authentic than anything cooked up by imaginative collectors.

The person who collects without any thought as to how his acquisitions were manufactured or used belongs in much the same bracket as the archaeological pot hunter who digs only to possess. Not only is such information necessary to an understanding of an artifact's or antique's place in the past, it can also help to distinguish between an original object and its modern copy. As far as the eighteenth century is concerned, there is no finer source than Denis Diderot's monumental *L'Encyclopédie, ou Dictionnaire Raisonné des Sciences, des Arts et des Métiers* issued between 1751 and 1765, and which remains the most elaborately illustrated contribution to the history of technology ever published. The idea stemmed from a publisher's request for the preparation of a French translation of Ephraim Chambers' *Cyclopaedia: or, an Universal Dictionary of*

Arts and Sciences, which was first printed in London in 1728. Although but thinly illustrated, this, too, is an important source for data on manufacturing processes, and it has the advantage of relating specifically to the work of English craftsmen. The same advantage applies to Joseph Moxon's *Mechanick Exercises: or the Doctrine of Handy-works* (1677) and to Richard Neve's *City and Country Purchaser's and Builder's Dictionary: or, The Complete Builder's Guide* (1703), though the latter is not illustrated. There are a handful of other works devoted to specific crafts, such as Antonio Neri's *L'Arte vetraria* (1612), which was translated into English and published in London in 1662; in addition there are many useful but isolated nuggets to be mined from collected essays on husbandry and trade like Gervase Markham's *The Way to Wealth, The English Housewife* (before 1637) and John Houghton's *A Collection for the Improvement of Husbandry and Trade*, 1681–3 and 1692–1703. Other gems are buried in even more unlikely corners such as Randle Holme's *An Academie or Store House of Armory & Blazon* (first published in 1682), which was ostensibly a book on heraldry but which also contains much fascinating data on mid-seventeenth-century domestic objects and manufacturing processes. I can imagine that some professional historians may blanch at my use of the adjective *fascinating*, but I can think of no more suitable word to describe the information contained in the following extract from Holme's section on combs and combmaking:

> The combe to be distinguished from the single tooth combe is often termed a double tooth combe, and a head combe, or a close and narrow tooth combe . . . it is a thing by which the haire of the head is layd smooth and streight, and kept from growing into Knotts and Arslocks. . . .
> Of what combs are generally made.
> Wood combs, made of light
>   and close wood as black thorn.
> Box combs, made of Box tree.
> Horn combs, made of oxe and cows horns.
> Ivory combs, made of Elephants teeth.
> Bone combs, made of the shank bones of
>   Horses and other large beests.
> Tortois combs, made of the sea and land

Tortois shell, the counterfeit combs
of this sort are Horn stained with
Tortois shell colours.
Cocus combs, made of cocus wood.
Lead combs, used by such as haue red hair,
   to make it of another colour.

The passage ends with a paragraph on women's hairpins:

> The Bodkin is a thing usefull for women to bind vp their haire
> with and aboute, they are usually made of siluer and gold the
> inferiour haue them of Brasse, but the meanest content them selues
> with a scewer or sharp pointed stick. Of these there are seuerall
> coates Armour composed, as Gules 3 Bodking, Argent, borne by the
> name of Kennardy.[1]

As one moves into later periods, so the literature becomes more
plentiful; at the same time it is clearly both more precise and more
reliable, and—equally important—it had become more readily available to contemporary craftsmen. Thus, the country joiner of the
seventeenth and early eighteenth centuries whose furniture hewed
close to rural tradition was able to develop into a cabinetmaker
keeping pace with fashion, thanks, in some measure, to the publication of such guides and catalogs as Thomas Chippendale's *The
Gentleman and Cabinet-Maker's Director* (1754), and *The Universal System of Household Furniture* (c. 1762) by William Ince and
Thomas Mayhew that contained designs for scores of items from
canopy beds to china shelves. Two years earlier the Society of Upholsterers and Cabinet-Makers published the first edition of its
Genteel Household Furniture in the Present Taste. Shortly after
the death of George Hepplewhite in 1786, the company continued
by his widow (A. Hepplewhite & Co.) issued *The Cabinet-Maker
and Upholsterer's Guide*, which, like the earlier publications of
Chippendale, and Ince and Mayhew, was really a trade catalog.
Then, at the close of the century, Thomas Sheraton published *The
Cabinet Maker and Upholsterer's Drawing Book* (1791), which
quickly went through three printings. While all of these books are
of inestimable value to the collector of furniture and to the student

[1] Randle Holme: *An Academie or Store House of Armory &
Blazon* (Roxburghe Club, London, 1905), p. 13.

37

of design history, none of them can substitute for a glimpse of the pieces in their original settings. For that we must turn to those seventeenth- and eighteenth-century substitutes for the modern camera, the genre painters, who captured life on canvas and unwittingly provided legacies for the future that could have been handed down in no other way.

As far as English genre art of the eighteenth century is concerned, one name immediately comes to mind, that of William Hogarth (1697–1764). His drawings, paintings, and engravings are filled with an enormous variety of domestic artifacts, but unfortunately the accuracy with which he depicted them is sometimes open to debate—a debate to which I propose to return in a moment.

There were actually very few English painters of the contemporary scene in the eighteenth century, and Hogarth was by far the most celebrated of them, though we are prone to underestimate the importance of his contemporary, Joseph Highmore (1692–1780), whose twelve illustrations for Samuel Richardson's *Pamela* (1743) and other genre pieces are rich in carefully observed detail. In his own way and in his own time Thomas Rowlandson was as good, and certainly as informative, as Hogarth. His drawings span the period 1774–1825, the majority of them devoted to rural, sporting, and tavern scenes. To the same era (but to a different class) belong the elegant conversation pieces painted by John Zoffany between 1769 and 1810; so, too, do the celebrated satirical drawings between 1778 and 1811, of James Gillray which contain many scenes of tea and liquor drinking.

Although Hogarth and Rowlandson conveniently spanned most of the eighteenth century, the fact remained that, prolific though these men were, the English scene lacked the differing artistic viewpoints needed to properly gauge the accuracy of what survives. Furthermore, there were no comparable English artists at work in the seventeenth century. On the other hand, across the Channel in Europe the Dutch and Flemish schools produced scores of painters who reveled in depicting every facet of daily life. Fortunately, at least in the first half of the seventeenth century, English and British colonial artifacts were often identical to those in use in Europe, so the Continental paintings provide splendid dating evidence for everything from baskets to watering cans.

The first artist whose works may be of use to the collector and student of Early American artifacts is undoubtedly Pieter Bruegel the Elder, who was born in about 1527 at Breda and whose working life was confined to a few extraordinarily productive years between 1552 and 1568. During that time he produced scores of pictures of Flemish life, macabre allegories reminiscent of Hieronymus Bosch (d. 1516), series of sin and virtue, as well as biblical and other subjects, nearly all of them containing a mass of meticulously delineated artifactual evidence. His son, Pieter Bruegel the Younger, continued in the same manner until his death in 1637. It is impossible and pointless to attempt to list all the genre painters who were working in the Netherlands in the seventeenth century; many well-illustrated books have been devoted to them, and anyone interested in European stoneware, maiolica, glass, costume, hardware, architectural details, and the like, can expect to learn more from them than from any other source. For the benefit of anyone new to this approach, however, I would note that I have found the following painters particularly helpful: for vigorous tavern scenes there was no one to beat Adriaen Brouwer (d. 1638), though similar settings on somewhat more tranquil occasions were favorites of Adriaen van Ostade (d. 1684), Richard Brakenburgh (d. 1702), and Cornelis Dusart (d. 1704). Van Ostade also specialized in peasant interiors and portraits of the lower classes surrounded by the paraphernalia of their trades. Jan Steen (d. 1679) was particularly good at convivial groups and interiors, as was Jan Miensz Molenaer (d. 1668), whose careful rendering of Rhenish stonewares is enormously valuable. Ferdinand van Kessel (d. 1696) had a penchant for interiors peopled with cats and monkeys and liberally scattered with every conceivable type of domestic artifact. Both Teniers, David "the Elder" (d. 1649) and David "the Younger" (d. 1690?), had a corner in alchemical subjects and showed many glass flasks, bottles, and phials; while Jan Siberechts (d. 1704) has much to tell us about farmyards and milkmaids—with appropriate equipment, of course. For the homes and artifacts of the merchant classes there was no one to equal the work of Jan Vermeer (d. 1675)—Han van Meegeren notwithstanding.

In addition to these and many other Flemish and Dutch genre painters of the seventeenth century, there were numerous painters

Fig. 1. Scene III (the Rose Tavern scene) from *The Rake's Progress* series by William Hogarth, engraved 1735. The plate differs from the original painting in minor details including the presence of an additional wanded bottle on the table. This detail, partially painted out, is visible in an unsigned painting of the same scene, now in the Nelson-Atkins Gallery of Art in Kansas City.

of still life whose dated canvases provide a pictorial catalog of the small domestic artifacts of the period: tobacco pipes, knives, drinking glasses, porcelain and earthenware dishes, stonewares, plate, musical instruments, and scores of comparable items from playing cards to watches. Here again the list of painters is astonishingly long, but the names of Willem Kalf (d. 1693), Jan Davidsz. de Heem (1684), and Jacob van Es (d. 1666) immediately come to mind.

There is rarely any doubt that the painters of still life had those objects in front of them as they worked, but there is always the question of whether the genre painters were copying "from the life" or whether they drew their subjects from memory and imagination. By and large it is fair to assume that Dutch artists had both the people and the artifacts in front of them, and as proof of this one may cite the self-portrait of Josse van Craesbeeck (d. 1662), who is seen at his easel drawing a rather glum group of models in poses of petrified conviviality.

To the student of the past's artifacts, the Dutch and Flemish artists' faithful copying of the people and things of their time is enormously helpful and satisfying, but to William Hogarth it was an anathema. In his autobiographical notes he wrote of their "tedious repetition of hackneyed, beaten subjects";[2] as for still life painting, he declared that it "ought to be held in the lowest estimation."[3] He went on to explain why:

> Whatever is, or can be perfectly fixed, from the plainest to the most complicated object, from a bottle and glass to a statue of the human figure, may be denominated *still life*. Ship, and landscape

[2] John Ireland: *Hogarth Illustrated* (London, 1798), III, 32.
[3] Ibid., p. 37.

painting ought unquestionably to come into the same class; for if
copied exactly as they chance to appear, the painters have no occasion of judgement; yet with those who do not consider the few tal-
ents necessary, even this tribe sometimes pass for *very capital artists*.[4]

It is evident from Hogarth's own writings and from those of
people who knew him (or claimed to know him) that most of his
creations came from memory or were assembled from sketches made
in the course of his daily life, then stored away until an opportunity
arose to make use of them. In all probability, therefore, having
drawn, say, a rat trap two or three times, Hogarth knew what a rat
trap looked like and thenceforth extracted it from his memory
"prop room" whenever he needed it. Consequently, every trap he
drew looked more or less the same, no matter whether it had been
outmoded by new and better rat traps developed later on in his
life.

[4] Ibid.

Much has been written about "Hogarth glasses" with hexagonal bowls, which allegedly appear on the table in his *Midnight Modern Conversation,* but in fact when those details are considerably enlarged it is evident that the angular appearance results from somewhat eccentric shading of a conical form. Efforts have been made to see the evolution of artifacts mirrored in Hogarth's artistic progress, but careful scrutiny suggests that we are on firmer ground if we take each picture at its face value, deducing only that artifacts of the types shown therein existed before it was penciled, burined, or brushed. But even this is no mean contribution. Take, for example, Hogarth's famous third plate from his *Rake's Progress* series (Fig. 1); it shows the rake being entertained (and robbed) by a covey of whores in a room at the celebrated Rose Tavern in Drury Lane. It was painted in 1735 and published as a print in the same year. Thus, chairs, table, sword, shawls, caps, plates, and so forth are examples of types that were common in or before 1735. Had this cultural capsule been buried intact by some Pompeian catastrophe, a surprisingly large percentage of those objects would be likely to survive as identifiable archaeological artifacts. Reading from left to right in the engraving (the reverse of the painting), one might expect to recover the curtain hooks and rings (both probably of brass), the watch, drinking glasses, tin lantern frame, sword and metal scabbard parts, buttons, shoe buckles, brass upholstery tacks, beads, sconces, mirror plate, candlestick, English wine bottles, French wanded bottles, table knife, bell pull, trumpet, harp parts, punch bowl, pewter plate engraved with the name of the tavern, a dagger (?), chamber pot, plates, table forks, chicken bones, and, of course, the bones of the revelers themselves. If, instead of being buried *in situ,* the whole lot had been thrown down a well or interred in some similarly waterlogged location, a great deal more could survive, including the wood of the furniture, paneling, and picture frames, the canvases of the twelve Caesars, the curtains and dress fabrics, the leather shoes, and even the patches that the ladies stuck to their faces in pursuit of a spot of beauty.

It is evident from surviving antiques and from the evidence of archaeology that most of the objects in Hogarth's tavern orgy were of types that really existed at that time, though whether they were actually part of the Rose Tavern's furnishings is another matter.

We do know, however, that large oval tables were common in taverns and that portraits of the twelve Caesars did decorate their walls both in England and in colonial America. We know, too, that taverns frequently had their names engraved on their pewter to prevent thievery; chamber pots were not foreign to dining and other public rooms; and French straw- or wicker-covered bottles were much used in England and her colonies at that time. There is one disturbing item, however, that makes us treat the whole picture with caution; it is the knife being brandished by the girl on the far side of the table. Its strange scimitar-shaped blade would make one suppose that it was some sort of jackknife were it not for the fact that in another drawing Hogarth shows a knife having a similar blade, together with a spoon, fork, tobacco pipe, bottle, and glass, as the symbols of conviviality. The Rose Tavern knife is therefore almost certainly intended to be a table knife, but so curious is its shape that in 1791 Hogarth's biographer John Ireland identified it as a razor.

Hogarth's treatment of bottle necks and wine-glass stems tended to be equally eccentric, though as wholes, both bottles and glasses expressed the general shapes of the period. It would seem, too, that Hogarth had never given much thought to brickwork; he simply drew rows of rectangles, ignoring the bonds used in eighteenth-century walls, and he invariably omitted the "closers" that figured at the ends of alternating courses to ensure that the joints between the bricks were staggered from row to row. In short, therefore, it is evident that Hogarth drew many of his artifacts from a somewhat faulty memory, eschewing the preciseness of detail that was so common in the Dutch and Flemish schools of the previous century. But although this may be a fair assessment of Hogarth's famous satirical or "moral" works, it does not necessarily apply to his family groups. Here the sitters are shown with their favorite possessions around them, and it is reasonable to assume that Hogarth painted those things with as much care as he devoted to the faces of his patrons. Proof of the reality of the "props" is provided by his portrait of the Strode family drinking tea. On the floor in the foreground is a rectangular wooden tea caddy with brass or gilt fittings, and, according to the London National Gallery, that caddy is still in existence.

43

Hogarth did not enjoy painting portraits or conversation pieces, but they were his principal source of income, at least in the early years of his career. But although he was virtually alone in his portrayals of English low (and artifact-filled) life, there were others, such as Sir Godfrey Kneller (1646–1723) and John Zoffany (1733–1810), whose conversation pieces featured tableware and other artifacts with Netherlandish precision. In eighteenth-century France there were Antoine Watteau (1684–1721), Jean-Baptiste Chardin (1699–1779), and François Boucher (1703–70), all of whom could paint a candlestick or a cuff link with almost photographic fidelity. In America, however, competent painters were in short supply. The little-known John Greenwood of Philadelphia followed rather woodenly in the genre footsteps of Hogarth with his *Sea Captains Carousing in Surinam* (c. 1758); John Trumbull (1756–1843) specialized in retrospective scenes from the Revolution; and American-born portrait painters Benjamin West (1738–1820) and John Singleton Copley (1738–1815) did most of their work in London and made use of few helpful artifacts other than dress embellishments such as buttons, buckles, and swords.

As far as pictorial records of American daily life are concerned, it is not until the early nineteenth century that one begins to find a reasonable number of adequately observed paintings and drawings —and some of the best of them were the work of foreign travelers. The Russian Paul Svinin (1787–1839) explored the eastern seaboard from Maine to Virginia in the years 1811 to 1813 and produced a number of excellent watercolors of what he saw. In 1830–1 the French naturalist Charles Lesueur (1778–1846) did the same for the interior, on the Ohio. Fortunately, most expeditions into the West, from Lewis and Clark onward, were accompanied by at least one artist-cartographer, and the works of such men as the Kern brothers (Benjamin, d. 1846; Richard, d. 1853; Edward M., d. ?) in the 1840's did much to record the white man's first impressions of the unadulterated Indian. Some of the artists drew and painted their own companions in their frontier quarters, as did Charles Nahl in his *Sunday Morning in the Mines* (1850), wherein one finds excellent renderings of tools and cooking equipment. Most of the great artists of the western movement, such as George Catlin (1796–1872), Alfred Jacob Miller (d. 1874), and Albert Bierstadt

(1830–1902), were much more inspired, however, by the wonders of the great outdoors than they were with the things that were already familiar to them. Although painters continued to immortalize the American scene throughout the second half of the nineteenth century, from the artifact student's point of view the camera did a much better job, and, besides, the early photographers displayed a praiseworthy enthusiasm for the commonplace.

In addition to the well-known European, British, and American painters I have mentioned, there were many more who occasionally ventured from their normal fields to depict scenes of daily life. Photographs of such pictures frequently turn up in sale catalogs or in magazine advertisements; when they do, the student is well advised to cut them out and mount them in annotated scrapbooks. In this way it is possible to build up a sizable and invaluable library of source material. The same can usefully be done with magazine articles and antique dealers' advertisements illustrating any and every kind of artifact from apple scoops to zithers.

Particularly helpful are photographs of dated items. English silver candlesticks, for example, are each marked with a date letter. By collecting pictures of the sticks and mounting them chronologically in a single volume, it is possible to compile a fuller evolutionary series than is to be found in any published book. Because silver forms were copied in baser metals, the same compilation can provide a valuable general guide to the dating of brass and pewter candlesticks. Similarly, the assembling of photographic series of dated ceramics and glass can reveal evolutionary trends in shapes and decoration that can help determine the age of undated pieces. So absorbing can this cutting and pasting become that it can develop into an antiquarian hobby in its own right—one that is a deal cheaper than collecting the antiques themselves. My wife has been doing it for twenty years, and our library now sports close to a hundred volumes of these scrapbooks. Although there is nothing very difficult about developing such a project—other than finding the time and the back issues of the essential magazines, such as *The Connoisseur, Apollo, Country Life,* and America's only major contributor, *Antiques*—there is one important rule to remember. It is essential that each picture or article be accompanied by the name of the publication whence it came, plus the date and the volume and page numbers; otherwise the serious student has no way of citing the source of his information.

Just as useful as the assembling of artifact pictures into volumes is the collecting of copies of early newspaper advertisements, like that from the *Virginia Gazette* quoted on p. 33. Unfortunately, the Virginia newspapers have not been culled for this kind of material, but those of some of the other colonies have, and the results have been published. George F. Dow went through the Boston papers and reprinted the extracts as *The Arts & Crafts in New England, 1704–1775* (Topsfield, Mass., 1927); Alfred Coxe Prime did the same for *The Arts and Crafts in Philadelphia, Maryland and South Carolina 1721–1785* (The Walpole Society, Phila., 1929); while Rita Susswein Gottesman compiled two volumes of extracts from New York papers entitled *The Arts and Crafts in New York, 1726–1776* and *1777–1799* (The New-York Historical Society's *Collections*, Vol. 69, 1938 and Vol. 81, 1954). In the absence of similar compilations from early English newspapers, these publications must serve antiquaries on both sides of the Atlantic; I should add that they do so extremely well, because more than half the items listed were of British manufacture. Nevertheless, it is certainly a pity that no one has done a similar service for *Aris's Birmingham Gazette, The London Chronicle, The Morning Post, The Post-Man, The Public Register* (Dublin), *The Limerick Chronicle and General Advertiser,* or a dozen other English and Irish papers—and Scottish, too, for that matter.

We are fortunate that in the seventeenth and eighteenth centuries there were fewer ways of passing time than there are today; consequently, those who could write found pleasure in doing so. For this reason many more personal journals and diaries were written, and in such detail that it was not unusual for a gentleman to take two or three pages to describe the activities of a single day. In addition, such people seem to have been more observant and more inquiring. They were filled with curiosity and there was nothing derogatory in being described as *a very curious gentleman.* Some of these people took the trouble to both describe and draw new inventions and architectural details onto the margins of their journals; others simply doodled small sketches of the things they were discussing. Unfortunately, few—if any—of them were doing this as a conscious contribution to posterity, and, as the evolutions of most common objects happened slowly, hardly anyone noticed, and those who did saw no reason to keep records of them.

Since the industrial revolution, the waters of artifact evolution have been so muddied that only the most rugged landmarks remain visible. Machines eliminated the character of the craftsman and enabled a hundred companies in as many places to produce almost identical items. At the same time, the varieties of merchandise expanded to the point where no archaeologist could hope to absorb sufficient knowledge of them to be confident that there would be few items of his period to be found in the ground that he could not instantly identify. On the credit side one can point to the infallible *termini post quem* provided by registered patents and to the increasing ease with which companies can store their records. But companies come and go, and many manufactured objects were either not patented or not repatented when changes were made to them.

Take the Coca-Cola bottle, probably the most ubiquitous artifact of the twentieth century: how many of the changes that have been wrought in that bottle will still be documented and available to the archaeologists of the twenty-third century? How many users of those bottles are aware that changes have occurred, and how many have bothered to make a note of them in their diaries? The answer is undoubtedly circular. I venture to hope, therefore, that the following chronology will survive to provide collectors and archaeologists of the future with a beacon to light their way back into the darkness of the twentieth century:

1886   The original cola-nut syrup invented in Atlanta.

1894   First bottled, the bottle straight-sided, with a short, collar neck and a bulbous lip for the anchoring of a wired cork.

1900   With the introduction of the crown cap, the bottle was changed to give it the mouth and neck it still retains today. There was no standardization of inscription or color, and both pale green and "beer-bottle" brown were used.

1915   The fluted and waisted bottle shape inspired by the cola nut invented.

1916   The new, pale-green bottle first issued.

1918   The bottler's town name required to be embossed on the bottom.

1919   The manufacturer's mark and date digits embossed on

the bottle for the first time; e.g., CHATT 26 meaning "Chattanooga Glass Company, 1926."

1923–4   The embossed legend reading BOTTLE PAT'D NOV. 16, 1915 changed to . . . DEC. 25, 1923.

1933   Manufacturer's mark, year, and mold-cavity number moved from the lower wall to a point above the constriction.

1937   Bottle embossed BOTTLE PAT.D - 105529.

1951   Bottle embossed TRADE-MARK REGISTERED IN U.S. PATENT OFFICE. Manufacturer's mark moved to base.

1957   Contents notation changed from 6 ounces to read CONTENTS 6½ FL. OZS. Decal labeling was first used in that year and has since become general, eliminating the Coca-Cola name from the bottle molds.

This is precisely the kind of information one wishes survived from the seventeenth and eighteenth centuries, the kind that some of the more *curious* of us have spent a large part of our lives trying to piece together. The product of that piecing together provides the substance of this book. Much has still to be learned, and it may well be that in the years ahead some of these early and tentative conclusions will need to be modified, particularly those that relate to artifact types that have never been studied or written about before. None of these essays and notes is intended to be definitive; they are simply an attempt to provide signposts—and signposts, as every traveler knows, serve only to keep one on the right road. They do not shorten it nor do they substitute for one's destination. By the same token, my pointers direct the reader toward further research of his own or, if he hasn't the strength for that, they may at least encourage him to go on to read the books listed in the bioliography that follows each section. I should add that the cited books, papers, and articles are not an attempt to provide a full bibliography for each subject; they are merely points from which to begin.[5]

[5] A much more extensive bibliography, divided under similar headings, is to be found in the author's *Historical Archaeology* (New York, 1969) .

48

AN ALPHABETICAL
GUIDE TO
THE ARTIFACTS

§ ARMOR

Neither helmets nor plate armor are likely to be found on English colonial sites after the third quarter of the seventeenth century. Indeed, they are rare, even in fragments, on the earlier sites, for most armor was beaten out by the blacksmiths and the iron reused.

PETERSON, HAROLD L.: *Arms and Armor in Colonial America*. Harrisburg, Pa., 1956.

§ BAYONETS

Of the bladed weapons found on historical sites, the bayonet is probably the most common, and although the blades are likely to be broken and the sockets rusted through and encrusted with corrosion, there are a few simple pointers that will give some idea of their date. It may not be possible to identify the exact model, for there were many variants, some of which appear in none of the published literature, but it is generally a reasonably simple matter to answer the basic question: Is it Revolutionary, War of 1812, or Civil War? (Fig. 2)

49

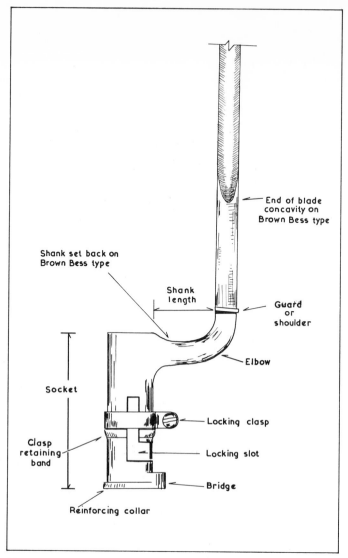

End of blade
concavity on
Brown Bess type

Shank set back on
Brown Bess type

Shank
length

Guard
or
shoulder

Elbow

Socket

Locking clasp

Locking slot

Clasp
retaining
band

Bridge

Reinforcing collar

Fig. 2. Bayonet-socket nomenclature.

The English Brown Bess and India Pattern muskets were fitted with a bayonet whose socket was a full 4″ in length, exceeding that of any subsequent type; furthermore, it was strengthened with a rear reinforcing collar that occurs on no nineteenth-century American-made bayonet with the exception of the rare Greene design of the Civil War period (socket only 3″ in length). The blade of the British bayonet was 1′ 4¾″ in length and triangular in section, the lower and shorter sides ending in a vestigial guard or block at the junction of blade and shank. This guard occurred on neither French nor American bayonets but was present on German examples of the Revolutionary period, a type readily distinguished from the British by the flattened hexagonal section of the blade and by the fact that the guard encircles the entire shoulder.

One of the most readily discernible characteristics of the Brown Bess bayonet was the shortness of the shank (1⅛") coupled with the fact that it was slightly set back from the end of the socket. American copies made in the Revolutionary period were longer in the shank (1½"), a feature springing directly from the fore edge of the socket. Another important detail, one common both to British bayonets and their American copies, was the flatness of the lower and shorter blade sides, which extended forward from the guard for a distance of 2" to 3". On all other bayonets used in America, the concavity of the under sides extended the full length of the blade.

Close dating for the Brown Bess bayonet is not possible as it continued without appreciable change throughout the eighteenth century and, as previously noted, was also used on the British India Pattern muskets that saw service during the War of 1812 and were used by Mexico in the 1846–8 Mexican War.

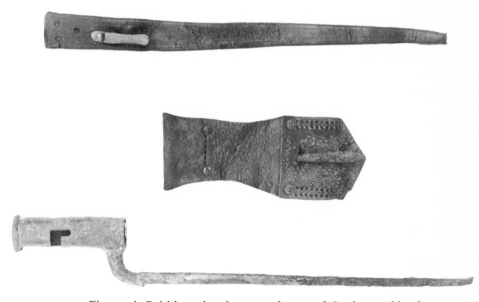

Fig. 3. A British socket bayonet, frog, and leather scabbard found in excavations at Fort Ligonier (built 1758) in Pennsylvania. Bayonet socket length 4".

Artifacts of Colonial America

Large numbers of French bayonets found their way into the British American colonies. The models of 1717 and 1746 are characterized by a short socket (2¾″) with no reinforcing collar, but while the 1717 type possessed a straight mounting slot with only a right-angled turn for locking, that of 1746 had a parallel mounting and locking slot connected by a right-angled channel. The next group, the 1763–74 models, were still short-socketed, but the former had both a reinforcing collar and a screw-gripped clasp that wrapped around the socket immediately below the collar. The 1774 style, on the other hand, did not use the clasp and was locked to the muzzle by a spring attached to the musket itself. The subsequent 1777 model returned to the clasp, but moved it down to the midsection of the socket, where it was prevented from sliding back by a retaining band that was forged as part of the socket. The socket also had a looped bridge spanning the mounting slot, thus holding the tube tightly at the rear.

American-made bayonets of the period 1795 to 1816 frequently possessed a T-shaped transverse and locking slot, usually in conjunction with the looped bridge, but without a reinforcing collar or locking clasp. The sockets varied from 2½″ to 3″ in length. In 1840 the United States adopted the 1777 French socket, differing only insofar that a stud on the side of it engaged in a recess in the locking clasp, limiting the latter to a quarter turn. Up to this time the blade shoulders on American bayonets had been square, but in 1842 they were sloped off (rounded on this model) so that the blade seemed to flow out from the shank. The upper face of the blade was now deeply dished. The weakened shoulders had occurred previously in 1816, but instead of being rounded off, the slope to the shank was straight; this form was revived in 1855 and was still used when the last American, socketed, angular bayonet type was issued in 1873. That remained in service until the introduction of the knife bayonet in the 1890's.

WEBSTER, DONALD B., JR.: *American Socket Bayonets 1717–1873*. Historical Arms Series, No. 3, Museum Restoration Service, Ottawa, Can., 1964.

§ *BEADS*

From the first years of colonization onward, beads played a major role in trade between settlers and Indians. It is worth noting, however, that Chambers' *Cyclopaedia* (Supplement, 1753) mentions only that they were used in the African trade. It has long been supposed that virtually all imported colored beads found on American sites were made on the island of Murano, the seat of Venetian glassmaking. It has now been determined that large quantities of beads similar to the Venetian were made at Amsterdam from the seventeenth to the nineteenth century. It has also been widely supposed that the glasshouse near Jamestown manufactured beads, but although there is documentary proof of the intention there is no archaeological evidence that so much as a single bead was actually made there. Until evidence to the contrary is forthcoming, it is reasonable to suppose that all beads found on American sites dating at least as late as the second quarter of the nineteenth century are likely to have been imported.

Most easily recognizable of the seventeenth-century types are those known as *millefiori* or chevron beads, which were made from layers of red, yellow, white, and blue glass, this last usually being on the outside. Sometimes such beads were left as square-sectioned rods with the various colors protruding only from the ends, but at other times they were ground and polished in spheres or lozenge shapes with the outer layers partially removed to expose those beneath. These beads were still being made as recently as the present century as African trade goods. However, they are rare on American sites after the mid-eighteenth century, while their period of greatest popularity seems to have been in the first half of the seventeenth century. Beads of this type were also known as "paternosters" because they were much used in strings used by Roman Catholics. In France, according to Chambers, the makers, stringers, and sellers of beads were known by the same name: patenostriers.

53

Opaque pale-blue glass beads are frequently found on seventeenth-century sites, many of them of extremely small size; also recovered in similar contexts are many dull-red examples usually in long or short cylinders which, when the ends are examined, are found to possess a green or white core. This type continued in use from the seventeenth at least into the beginning of the nineteenth century.

Glass beads, by and large, are extremely hard to date, and the vast majority possess no distinguishing features, being roughly globular in form with holes of varying sizes in glass ranging from bottle green, through straw and amber, to deep red, purple, and various hues of blue that end in black. In the journals of Lewis and Clark one discovers that among the Indians of the Columbia River "blue beads, which are called *tia commashuck*, or chief beads, hold the first rank in their ideas of relative value. The most inferior kind are esteemed beyond the finest wampum, and are temptations which can always seduce them to part with their most valuable effects."[6]

Wampum or beads of shell also included the so-called "porcelain" beads, which were in fact made from the money cowry shell, *C. moneta*, that was found in both the East and West Indies and which served as currency among the aboriginal peoples of both hemispheres. True porcelainous beads did not appear until the nineteenth century.

The most common beads of the first half of the nineteenth century were made from pieces of glass tube, generally shorter than their diameter and refined by careful faceting. These facets are restricted, on the smaller beads, to an average of seven facets cut around each end leaving the central sections untouched, but larger examples, usually in ultramarine blue, have many more. These faceted beads are known in the Northwest as "Russian" beads on the evidence of their having been found on Russian sites in Alaska. However, they are much more widely distributed and have been found in large quantities on a site on the Eastern Shore of Virginia, where they were associated with spoiled examples sometimes attached to sandever and waste glass of similar colors. The obvious explanation that the beads were made on the site has not yet been

---

[6] *History of the Expedition Under the Command of Captains Lewis and Clark* (New York, 1922; reprint of 1814 edn.) ; quoted in Arthur Woodward: *Indian Trade Goods*, Oregon Archaeological Society Publications, No. 2 (1956), p. 16.

substantiated by excavation or by the surface recovery of other essential glasshouse refuse. Also dating from the early nineteenth century, though going back into the second half of the eighteenth, are a broad class of beads loosely known as "fancy beads," which vary through tubular, lozenge, and globular shapes and which are made in a semblance of the ancient *millefiori* technique; but instead of the glass being laminated, colored threads are wrapped around a central core of white, black, blue, or red, in random patterns of swirls and dots.

GREGORY, HIRAM A., and CLARENCE H. WEBB: "European Trade Beads from Six Sites in the Natchitoches Parish, Louisiana," *The Florida Anthropologist*, Vol. 17, No. 3, Pt. 2 (September 1965), pp. 15–44. Covers the period 1714–1820.

PRATT, PETER P.: *Oneida Iroquois Glass Trade Bead Sequence, 1585–1745.* Fort Stanwix Museum publication (Rome, N.Y.). Syracuse, N.Y., 1961.

§ *BELLARMINES*

Bellarmines are a type of Rhenish stoneware bottle manufactured predominantly in factories in and around Frechen, are ornamented with a human or semihuman face sprig-molded onto the neck, and generally have one or more armorial or pseudo-armorial medallions on the body. The bottles varied in capacity from a pint to about five gallons and were made from a gray-bodied stoneware coated with an iron-oxide slip that broke into a brown mottle when fired in a saltglaze kiln—thus earning them the inaccurate descriptive term of "tigerware." Equally inaccurate is the *Bellarmine* association, allegedly based on the belief that the molded faces on the necks were caricatures of the hated Cardinal Roberto Bellarmino applied by Protestant potters. The body medallions, however, were frequently dated, and the earliest-known is marked 1550, when Bellarmino was only eight years old.

The earliest molded masks took the form of satyrs, from which the human face developed in the mid-sixteenth century. The latter

Fig. 4. Bellarmine or Bartmann bottles of the best period, when the masks were benign and fully human. Probably Cologne, c. 1580–1610. Ht. of left bottle 7½″.

Fig. 5. Three Bellarmines of the period c. 1650–70, with grotesque masks, meaningless medallions, and pear-shaped bodies. The corks are original. Frechen. Ht. 8½″.

Fig. 6. Bellarmine bearing the latest-recorded date, 1699. Ht. 10½". Another example of the same date in the collection of Colonial Williamsburg has a mask and proportions more akin to those in Fig. 5.

were then extremely well molded and generally wore a pleasingly paternal expression. (Fig. 4) By the second quarter of the seventeenth century, however, the masks were deteriorating and gradually became so stylized that the once-flowing beard had been reduced to a series of irregular strokes, while the features, too, became equally crude. (Fig. 5) At the same time the pleasing rotundity of the early bottles had been replaced by an elongated pear-shaped form with a disproportionately small base, heavy cordoning at the neck, and medallions that were no more than rosettes or meaningless pseudo-armorial devices. Earlier, they had carefully depicted the arms of monarchs, noblemen, patrons, towns, and merchants. The latest-dated example is marked 1699. (Fig. 6) The bottles, however, continued to be made in the Rhineland and exported through the first quarter of the eighteenth century, without either bearded masks or medallions, though sometimes adorned with incuse chevrons and rosettes.

HOLMES, M. R.: "The So-Called 'Bellarmine' Mask on Imported Rhenish Stoneware," *Antiquaries' Journal* (London), Vol. 31 (1951), pp. 173–9.
NOËL HUME, IVOR: "German Stoneware Bellarmines—An Introduction," *Antiques*, Vol. 74, No. 5 (November 1958), pp. 439–41.

See also STONEWARE, Rhenish.

§ *BELLS*

Little or nothing has been written on this subject, and although fragments of various types have been found in contexts from the early seventeenth century onward very little dating evidence is forthcoming. Nevertheless, the bell was one of the most common sights and sounds in colonial and nineteenth-century America. Examples some 10″ in height were used on plantations and farms to summon the hands in from the fields, and examples a third of that size hung on springs beside eighteenth- and nineteenth-century shop doors. Most of these bells, from church steeple to ship and down to the handled variety that called for the next course at an eighteenth-century dinner table, were of bell metal (though the last may have been tin-plated), an alloy made from twenty parts of pewter to a hundred of copper.

The most common type of bell found on colonial sites is the rumbler bell, often known as a sleigh bell: a ball-shaped object containing a loose iron ball, with a slot at one side and an ear for suspension opposite it. Such bells served many purposes depending on their size, which ranged from examples no bigger than a button to suspend from a baby's coral-and-bells or tie to a hawk's leg, to specimens the size of an orange to hang around the neck of a cow. The larger specimens are often found to bear the initials R and w, one on either side of the slot. (Fig. 7) These were probably the products of Robert Wells (1760–1826) of Aldbourne, Wiltshire, who operated his family's foundry from the late eighteenth century until his death. The business, however, had been established as

Fig. 7. An 18th-century brass rumbler bell from the factory of Robert Wells in Wiltshire, England; found in Williamsburg. The loop is conjectural. Diam. 2″.

early as 1694, and it is possible that previous members of the family had the same initials.

Mr. Hugh de S. Shortt, curator of the Salisbury Museum in England, has provided the following observations. Referring to the earliest versions, he noted that

> They are usually much smaller than the later bells, with a distinct ridge round the circumference; the bronze tends to be thicker, and I believe that the earliest of all have no design on them, but the loop is definitely angular, like a doorway. I cannot suggest a date for these, but probably this design lasted for a very long period in the Middle Ages. The next development is a design of petals round the dumbbell slot; there is often a cross, the central limb being cut in half by the slot. Occasionally a shield of arms takes the place of one-half of the cross. I suspect that this was at the end of the Middle Ages, perhaps towards 1500 or so. My guess is that it was in the seventeenth century that the bells tended to become larger; half of the cross was retained, but the other half gave place sometimes to a couple of initials, e.g. we have "w. g." in Wiltshire. These initials later became separated, one on each side of the slot, when of course the last traces of the cross vanished. Meanwhile the loop gradually became rounded at the top, losing its angular form, and in the case of the Aldbourne bells, for instance, it appears more like a plate of metal, rounded at the end, with a hole punched through it. It seems to me that it is with the initials on the bells that varying sizes, presumably intended to produce different notes, were introduced, though I doubt if they were used in sets until Robert Wells' time. He made them in at least thirty-two different sizes.

In addition to the initials already cited, the Salisbury Museum possesses a small seventeenth-century rumbler bell marked wk and another eighteenth-century example with ib on either side of the slot. The latter initials are thought to be those of James Burroughs of Devizes.

Bells of uncertain type were made by the gunsmithing and brassfounding Geddy family in Williamsburg in the mid-eighteenth century, and it is reasonable to assume that other colonial brassfounders also cast them.

Morris, Ernest: *Tintinnabula*. London, 1959.

§ *BOTTLES, Glass Liquor*

Glass bottles were in use in British America from the earliest years of colonization, though the first truly successful American manufacturing venture did not occur until 1739, when Caspar Wistar, an emigrant German buttonmaker, set up a glass factory in southern New Jersey. As virtually nothing is known about the products of American bottlemaking prior to the Revolution, it must be supposed that the majority found on colonial sites are of English manufacture. The admittedly biased Lord Sheffield, in his *Observations on the Commerce of the American States*, declared that "there is no article of glass in any part of Europe but the British, which will answer in the American market. There are glass works in Pennsylvania"; he added, "bad glass is made in New Jersey for windows; but there is not any quantity of glass ware made in America as yet, except bottles, and even of these the quantity is trifling."[7]

A great deal has been written about the evolution of the English glass wine bottle, and attempts have been made to provide a datable evolution of its shape. In broad terms these efforts have been fairly successful, and it is possible to tell the differences between bottles of, say, 1650, 1690, 1730, 1760, 1780, or 1820 without much trouble. The difficulties arise when we try to pin down the transitional forms that link these dates together.

Rather than republish evolutionary drawings which have been seen before, I have elected to show for the first time a series of bottles bearing dated (or closely datable) seals ranging from c. 1651 to 1834. (Figs. 8–13) In the interest of brevity I propose to let them speak for themselves. I would add, however, that there is some indication that the 1651 form may have been preceded by one with a neck half its length, perhaps in about 1645. At the other end of the series it should be noted that the first mold-made bottle (with

---

[7] John Lord Sheffield: *Observations on the Commerce of the American States*, 6th edn. (London, 1784), p. 24.

the exception of the string-rim) is thought to have been produced by the Bristol (England) firm of Henry Ricketts & Co. in about 1814, the process patented in 1822. Thus, bottles bearing mold marks and the word PATENT on their shoulders and molded inscriptions on their bases are unlikely to have been made any earlier than the latter date. Once the molding process was introduced, bottle-making entered an entirely new phase, with American manufacturers well to the fore.

The practice of affixing identifying glass seals to the bodies of wine bottles developed in the mid-seventeenth century. The earliest-dated seal known (now divorced from its bottle) was made for a certain John Jefferson, is marked 1652, and is in the collection of the London Museum. However, the earliest-intact and -dated sealed bottle was made for an unidentified King's Head Tavern in 1657 and is in the Northampton Museum in England. Undated, but unequivocally attributable to a year no later than 1652 are two bottles found in London with seals identical to another found at Jamestown, Virginia. (Fig. 8)

The earliest seals seem to have been made either for gentlemen or for taverns, but by the late seventeenth century all sorts of people had their own sealed bottles, and the practice continued into the early nineteenth century. In the second half of the seventeenth century, glassmakers provided single initial matrices for those customers who could not afford, or did not care to have, their own brass seals designed and cut. These single-letter stamps were mounted on a wooden handle in any combination that the purchaser desired. The majority of the resulting seals bear only two initials, but on rare occasions three were used to indicate family ownership. Thus the letters T^OA might be read as Thomas and Ann Osborne, the husband's Christian name always coming first, then that of his wife, and the surname initial capping both. It was a style in general use in the sixteenth and seventeenth centuries but which died out in the eighteenth.

Not all seals indicated ownership; a few related to the contents. The most common are those from bottles which had contained Piermont or Pyrmont Water and which came from the German province of Waldeck. They were common in the period c. 1720–70, those with the words PIERMONT WATER around a star belonging predominantly to the early years and those with the legend

PYRMONT WATER flanking a crowned shield of arms being later. Other English and European mineral waters were sold in seal-embossed bottles during the eighteenth century, such as those manufactured for H. EYRE PERVEYOR FOR MINERAL WATERS TO HER MAJESTY (probably Caroline of Anspach, d. 1737) and containing Holt Mineral Water. French bottles for both wines and olive oil continued to be sealed with the names of growers all through the nineteenth century; the latest example known to me is dated 1905. Yet another class of seal related neither to the contents nor the seller but to government ownership. English bottles of the late Georgian and Victorian periods made for the army and navy were often identified by a seal bearing the initials of the monarch (GR, WR, or VR, with a broad arrow or an anchor between the letters. Examples of all three have been found at Port Essington in Northern Australia, a site occupied between 1838 and 1849.

Prior to the appearance of the globular-bodied dark-green glass bottles of the mid-seventeenth century, the common large bottle was blown into a square-sided mold and had a nearly flat base and a short neck with an everted lip, the latter feature frequently concealed beneath a threaded pewter collar and cap. (Fig. 14) The bottles varied considerably in size, but because of their vulnerable flat surfaces they were sold, carried, and housed in cases or "cellars," each generally holding a dozen bottles. These case bottles have frequently been described as "Dutch gin bottles," probably because they were so used in the latter part of the eighteenth century. The Dutch bottles for "Hollands" or "Geneva," were certainly square-sectioned (though tapering toward the base), but that does not infer that all square-bodied bottles were of Dutch origin. On the contrary, they undoubtedly represented a very large part of the English bottle output of the first half of the seventeenth century.

Square-bodied bottles, 8″ to 10″ in height, with short, straight necks, and of a pale-blue metal, occur in contexts of the mid-eighteenth century and thereafter. (Fig. 15) It has been suggested that

Figs. 8–13. A series of English glass wine bottles, all bearing dated seals with the exception of those having a "P" prefix indicating that on other evidence those examples date prior to the given year.

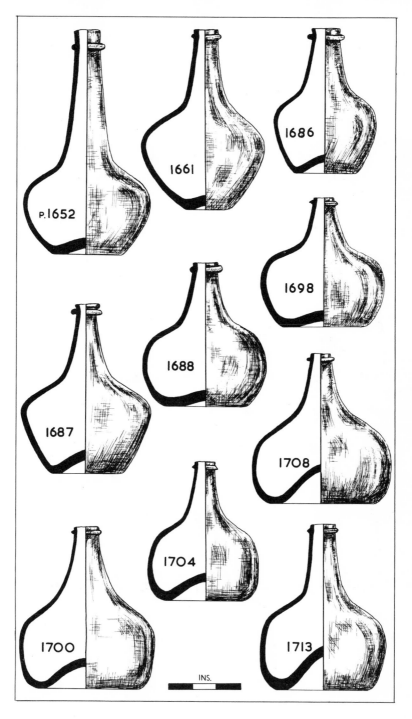

P.1652

1661

1686

1698

1687

1688

1708

1700

1704

INS.

1713

63

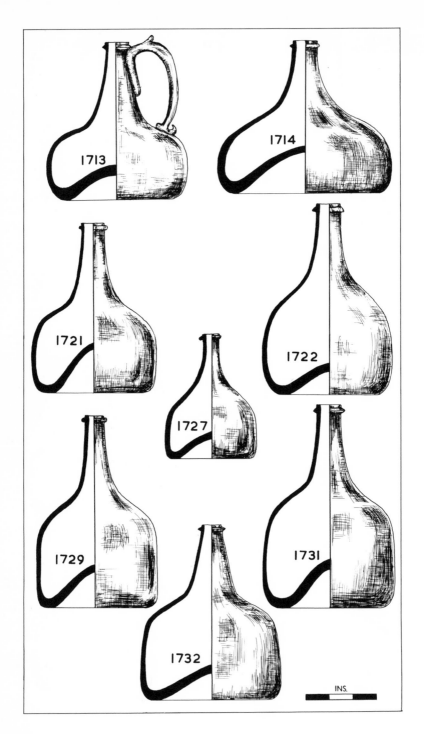

INS.

INS.

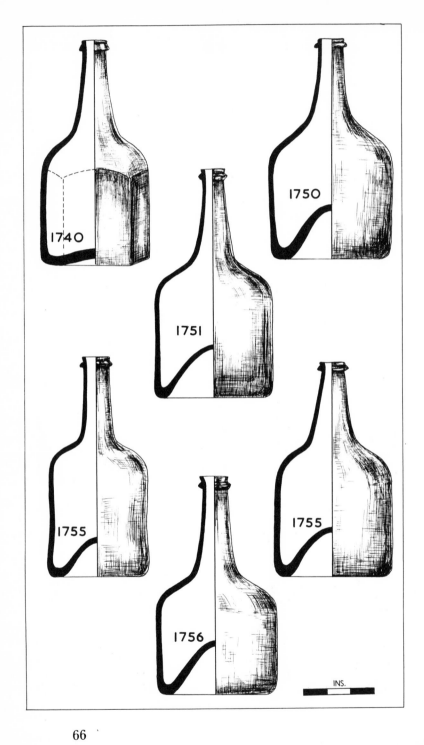

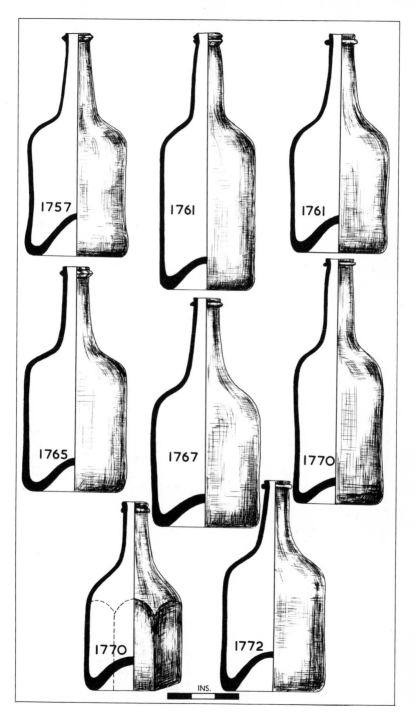

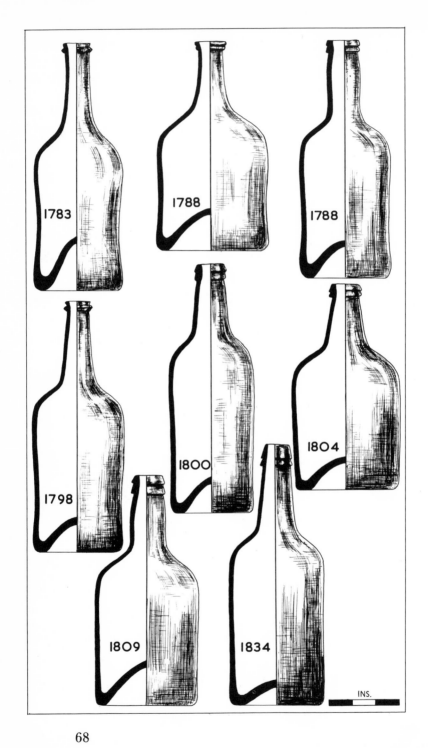

68

they may be of American manufacture, but the fact that they have been found in contexts of the same period in England makes this unlikely. However, the large numbers found on French colonial sites strongly point to France as their origin. I recently encountered a neck of such a bottle protruding from the mortar of a ruined French "great house" of the mid-eighteenth century near Gros-Islet on the island of St. Lucia in the West Indies. Others, in a variety of sizes, have been found in contexts of the 1740's on the site of the French fortress of Louisbourg in Nova Scotia.

A small number of irrefutably foreign bottles are found on English colonial sites, most of them French. (Fig. 16, right) Unlike the English wine bottles of the eighteenth century, these are generally broader at the shoulder than the base, with tall necks, a style that eventually developed into the typical weak-shouldered Champagne or Burgundy bottle of the late eighteenth and nineteenth centuries. Most French bottles of the eighteenth century had poorly applied string rims, round in section and pinched against the neck at only two or three points. This was in marked contrast to the

Fig. 14. Typical square bottle from a mid-17th-century context in Virginia. The form was common in the period c. 1625–75 and was made both in England and the Netherlands. This example retains part of a threaded pewter collar to house a cap of the same metal. Ht. 10⅛".

carefully tooled string rims on most English examples. More common throughout the colonial eighteenth century than the regular French wine bottle was the French wanded bottle, which was flat and oval in shape with a long, slightly writhen neck. The necks had no string rims and the bodies no feet, and they were cased in wicker or rushes rather in the manner of the modern Chianti bottle, though not always with a foot. The metal was generally brownish, turned black in the ground, and decayed rapidly into a sugarlike consistency.

Dutch bottles are rare on English colonial sites. Unlike the French, who seemed to have developed their own styles, the Dutch followed the English shapes, though they were rather slower to adopt them. Thus, long-necked types of c. 1660 were still being produced in the Netherlands at the end of the seventeenth century, while the squat forms of the early eighteenth century were being made there into the 1740's. Dutch bottles of the seventeenth century seem to have been a richer green than the English, but in the eighteenth century they tended more toward amber. The common Dutch variety of the first half of the eighteenth century had a squat body and a neck taller than on English examples and possessed a

Fig. 15. A pale blue and square-bodied bottle common in the mid-18th century. Probably French. Ht. 8⅝".

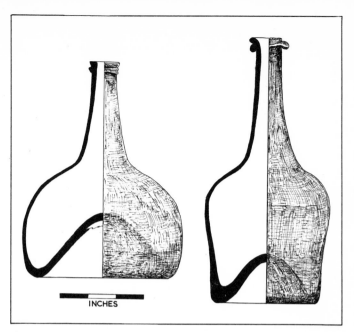

Fig. 16. Typical Dutch (left) and French (right) wine-bottle forms of the second quarter of the 18th century.

much more pronounced conical basal kick. (Fig. 16, left) The string rim was tooled flat or to a "V," but the ends of the trail were generally roughly overlapped, while the flat lip was everted above it making the mouth, rather than the string rim, the dominant neck feature. This did not occur on English bottles until the last quarter of the eighteenth century, at which time lip and string rim were tooled into a single entity.

In America the so-called black wine bottles seem to have been free-blown at least as late as 1820, and on the basis of slender evidence from New England and Philadelphia it would seem that they differed from comparable English bottles of the early nineteenth century in that their mouths were thick, broad, and gently rounded, either dwarfing the string rim below or eliminating it altogether.

CHAMBON, RAYMOND: L'Histoire de la Verrerie en Belgique du IIme Siècle à Nos Jours. Brussels, 1955.

KLEIN, W. H. A.: "Old Surinam Wine Bottles" in Antieke Gebruiksflessen in Suriname, Publications of the Surinam Museum, No. 7, Paramaribo, Surinam, 1966.

NOËL HUME, IVOR: "The Glass Wine Bottle in Colonial Virginia," Journal of Glass Studies (Corning, N.Y.), Vol. 3 (1961), pp. 90–117.

RUGGLES-BRISE, SHEELAH: Sealed Bottles. London, 1949.

SIMON, ANDRÉ L.: Catalogue of the Wine Trade Loan Exhibition of Drinking Vessels. Vintners' Hall, London, 1933.

§ *BOTTLES, Glass Pharmaceutical*

Pharmaceutical glassware was manufactured in England from the late sixteenth century onward, and small glass phials are commonly encountered on archaeological sites throughout the colonial centuries. In the period c. 1580–1640 there was much greater variety than at any time prior to the late eighteenth century. (Fig. 17) This was occasioned by the fact that in the years between, the glassmakers made smaller use of molds.

Common in the late sixteenth century was the Germanic "half-post" technique of inserting the first gather or "post" back into the crucible to be partially coated with a second layer of glass. The lower end, or combined posts, was then lowered into a vertically ribbed mold and twisted as it was withdrawn, creating a swirled or writhen effect. This technique, as used for small Tudor medicine bottles, was the same as that employed in making the famous Connecticut "Pitkin" flasks of the late eighteenth and early nineteenth centuries. Similar writhen ornament molded onto a single gather was used to decorate Tudor bottles of carafe type, and some of them survived into the seventeenth century. By and large, therefore, it is reasonable to conclude that when found on American sites, swirling-ribbed molding on thin bottle glass must date either early in the seventeenth century or later than about 1780. Direct-pattern molding, however, was employed by Henry William Stiegel at his factories at Manheim, Pennsylvania, between 1764 and 1774.

The early seventeenth-century English molds produced small

Fig. 17. Examples of pharmaceutical and related bottles from the 17th to the 19th centuries. 1. and 2. Very pale green. 3. and 4. Dark-green. 5. Olive-green. 6. Amber. 7. and 8. Medium-green. 9. Pale-green (occurs in pale blue). 10–13. Medium-green. 14. and 15. Clear. 16. Medium-green. 17. Clear (occurs in pale blue). 18. Olive-green. 19. Clear. 20. Pale-blue. Nos. 1–5 and 7–18 are English; 6, English or Dutch; 19, probably American; 20, American. Except in the case of No. 15, dating is approximate and based on archaeological evidences.

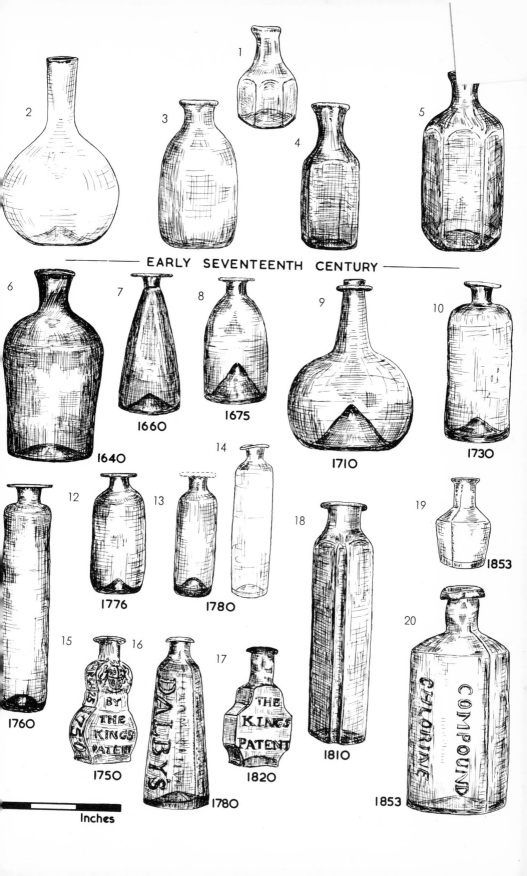

EARLY SEVENTEENTH CENTURY

1660

1675

1640

1710

1730

1776

1780

1853

1760

1750

1780

1820

1810

1853

green bottles with four, six, seven, and eight sides, generally with a short neck tooled out at the top to form a lip. From the same period one also encounters very thin globular bottles, pale green or straw in color, with straight necks struck straight from the blowing iron and with no attempt to create a lip. Cylindrical phials were also made in this early period and are characterized by being slightly broader at the shoulder than at the base. Colors range from pale green, through emerald, to a rich amber. The common deep- or blue-green phials so ubiquitous throughout the eighteenth century did not appear before the mid-seventeenth century. At the outset these were markedly weak in the shoulder, sometimes to the point of being conical and thus known to collectors as "steeple" bottles. Later they became more angular, and the broad, flattened lip of the early examples became smaller. The early specimens also possessed a conical basal kick, and this, too, became less pronounced as the form evolved. By the mid-eighteenth century the same types of phials were beginning to be made in clear glass, and these became increasingly common as the century drew to its close.

Molded phials were generally of clear metal, the earliest-recorded example being the cello-shaped bottles made for Robert Turlington's Balsam of Life and embossed with the date March 25, 1750. Turlington had been granted a patent for his twenty-six-ingredient "Remedy for Every Malady" in 1744, but it is not known whether a proprietory bottle was designed and issued at that time. The 1750 bottle is apparently known by only one intact example, that found in Williamsburg. (Fig. 17, No. 15) In 1754 a new and more angular bottle was substituted "to prevent the villainy of some persons, who buying up my empty bottles, have basely and wickedly put therein a vile spurious counterfeit sort."[8] Nevertheless, the pirating continued and was common practice in America in the second half of the eighteenth century and well on into the nineteenth century. American bottlemakers produced vast numbers of spurious Turlington's Balsam bottles, but invariably with longer necks and less pronouncedly everted lips. The later American versions were also often much lighter and thinner than the originals, and were frequently of a pale-blue metal. (Fig. 17, No. 17)

[8] Quoted in James Harvey Young and George B. Griffenhagen: "Old English Patent Medicines in America," *The Chemist and Druggist* (London), June 29, 1957, p. 718.

Square-sectioned bottles bearing molded inscriptions describing the contents became fairly common in the latter years of the eighteenth century. These, too, were of clear metal, and usually exhibited a diagonal mold mark across the bottom. When the contents were patented, the sides were often embossed in high relief with a crowned GR. Archaic in shape, but probably not dating before the last twenty years of the century were the steeple-shaped bottles for Dalby's Carminative. Although made in the usual eighteenth-century phial green, they were mold made, and the name of the contents was embossed vertically down the sides. Rather similar conical bottles were used for Godfrey's cordial, another long-established remedy dating back to at least 1721 and possibly much earlier. A version of this bottle shape was still being used for Godfrey's cordial in the early years of the present century. Other eighteenth-century patent medicines were dignified (but not much protected) by having their own bottles. In 1753, the account book (collection of Colonial Williamsburg, Inc.) of Dr. James Carter of Williamsburg shows that he ordered half a gross of empty "Stoughton Vials" for Stoughton's Elixir, along with "3 Quire Stoughton's Directions" undoubtedly with the intention of making and bottling his own. Unfortunately, I know of no surviving examples of this bottle.

Another anomalous class of bottle had appeared in the second half of the seventeenth century: miniature wine-bottle shapes in a thin, bluish metal. The earliest date from the 1660's, but the majority were made toward the end of the century and in the first years of the next. They were thin-walled, round-bodied, straight-necked, and had broad and flat string rims below the lips. (Fig. 17, No. 9) It would appear from the number that have been found on late-seventeenth-century archaeological sites that they were not uncommon in their period. It seems likely that they were used for oils or vinegar.

In conclusion, a word must be said about a class of phials resembling the typical angular-shouldered, cylindrical green medicine bottles of the eighteenth century (Fig. 17, No. 12) but missing their necks and everted mouths. These were ink bottles or wells. It has not been determined, however, whether they were stoppered and carried about, or whether they were seated in stands or set into the tops of desks as were the ceramic wells of the nineteenth century.

NOËL HUME, IVOR: "A Century of London Glass Bottles, 1580–1680," *The Connoisseur Year Book* (London), 1956, pp. 98–103.

————: "Neglected Glass," *Country Life*, Vol. 116, No. 3007 (September 2, 1954), pp. 716–17.

YOUNG, JAMES HARVEY, and GEORGE B. GRIFFENHAGEN: "Old English Patent Medicines in America," *The Chemist and Druggist* (London), June 29, 1957, pp. 714–22.

§ *BOTTLES, Pottery*

The principal pottery bottle of the seventeenth century was the Rhenish stoneware Bellarmine (*see* BELLARMINES), for it was strong and nonporous. Its shape was copied by the makers of English delftware, predominantly during the period 1640–60, these bottles being of a soft-yellow or pink earthenware coated with a thick lead glaze containing tin oxide that gave them a white (often slightly tinged with pink) porcelainlike surface, though without anything like its strength. The earliest were made in Southwark (London) and were decorated in blue in styles copied from Ming porcelain. Some are dated 1628 in cobalt below the base of the handle. The majority, however, were plain white and inscribed only with the name of the contents—Sack, Whit, Claret—plus the date, recorded examples ranging from 1642 to 1662; they were otherwise unadorned. There are a few exceptions, however, notably the latest-known example which is elaborately cobalt-painted with the arms of William Allen and is dated 1674. If these bottles were developed in the hope of capturing the Bellarmine market, their potters were disappointed, for the prize was quickly surrendered into the hands of the glass-bottle makers.

In addition to the bottles used on the table and in the tavern, there were those popularly known as costrels, some of which were carried when traveling. The most common of these was a completely circular ball, usually in a hard red ware—though examples range from buff to a purplish gray—with a slightly tapering neck protruding from one side. These vessels are thought to be French and were cased in wicker or rushes. They were manufactured in three parts, the body being fashioned as two slightly ribbed hemi-

Fig. 18. Spouted jug (handle missing) of a hard red ware, white slip coated and covered with a green lead glaze; found at Kecoughtan, Virginia. Iberian, second quarter of the 17th century. Ht. 11⅛".

spheres luted together; that done, a hole was pushed through the junction at one side and the neck attached. The handle of rope or rush was attached to the casing. Such bottles were common in the first half of the seventeenth century and go back into the late sixteenth century, while the latest example so far encountered came from a context of about 1670. Another, more elaborate costrel form was made in a red earthenware, coated with marbleized slip in white and green contrasting dramatically with the orange-brown surface produced in areas where the clear glaze lay directly on the red body. These costrels are tall, pear-shaped over a pedestal foot, and have long necks topped by a rounded mouth. There are generally two loop handles on either side, each molded in the form of lion masks through which a cord or leather thong was passed. The bottles are of French or Italian origin and seem to be confirmed to the period c. 1610–60. Equally distinctive are the strap-handled, small-necked, and bulbous-bodied bottles whose principal characteristic is a short conical spout at the shoulder. (Fig. 18) They are thought to be Spanish, are of a hard, thin red ware coated on the outside with a bright glossy-green glaze over a white slip and appear on sites dating as early as the first quarter of the seventeenth century. However, their full date range is not known. Also allegedly from Spain is a group of bulbous-bodied bottles flattened at back

77

Fig. 19. Typical 19th-century brown stoneware bottles used for: (rear, left to right) blacking, ink, and ginger beer, (front row) ink. These examples English, third quarter of the century.

and front, with narrow necks and pairs of long strap handles flanking them. The ware is usually thick and a very soft and poorly fired yellow, generally coated with the remnants of a lead glaze which seems semi-opaque but which chemical analysis shows to contain no tin. The flat body faces and shoulders may be decorated under the glaze with crude star, flower, or bird motifs in dull red or pale blue. These are found in contexts dating up to the mid-seventeenth century.

The need for pottery bottles quickly declined as the production of glass bottles increased, and in the eighteenth century the only common pottery bottles were of brown stoneware, the English descendant of the Bellarmine. The body was gray and covered to a point below the midsection with an iron-oxide slip that turned to either purple or a rich, brown stipple in the firing. The bodies resembled the late Bellarmines in shape, had a single strap handle, while the necks were generally cordoned below the lip. They came in various capacities from a pint to about five gallons, though the quart and gallon sizes are the most common survivers. No closely datable characteristics have so far been detected, and it is virtually impossible to tell the difference between those made in 1690 or 1770, though this would seem to be the span of their popularity.

Brown stoneware bottles came into their own again in the early nineteenth century, taking advantage of the 1812 doubling of duty on glassware imposed by the British Chancellor of the Exchequer. Although the incensed glassmen lobbied the Chancellor and caused a tax of five shillings to be levied on every hundredweight of stone bottles holding less than two quarts, the potters were undaunted. Cylindrical brown stoneware bottles were made in England in enormous quantities throughout the Victorian era, and many of them found their way to America. As Figure 19 shows, these bottles varied considerably in size, and not all of them were brown. Some omitted the iron-oxide slip and were buff or even white surfaced. The brown bottles were commonly used for ink, blacking, and mineral waters, each having a different neck and mouth shape. Those for ink invariably had a pouring lip, blacking bottles had wide collarlike necks and mouths, while those for ginger beer and comparable mineral waters were usually thickened and convex at the mouth so that string or wire could be tied below the rims to prevent the corks from escaping. Although the screw stopper was invented in 1872, the majority of mineral-water bottles continued to be made in the old way until the end of the century.

Small ink bottles or wells did not have the pouring spout as they were intended to be dipped into, and these came in two varieties— very squat cylinders or wide-based cones. The latter were also made in large quantities in America, and the best of them are virtually indistinguishable from the English.

Most of the English stoneware bottles of these types were made at Lambeth in London and are often stamped with the names and trademarks of such makers as James Stiff, Stephen Green and Co., and the still-in-business firm of Doulton, whose bottles, prior to 1858, were marked Doulton and Watts. Equally important was the firm of Joseph Bourne of the Denby Pottery near Derby, which was making cylindrical bottles throughout the Victorian era. Not all the stamped marks were those of the manufacturers; purchasers who bought in quantities often had their bottles made to order and stamped accordingly. Thus, bottles for Stephens' ink or Batey and Co.'s ginger beer proclaimed this fact on their sides.

The vast majority of the bottles discussed above were made in the period 1840–90, although some examples of the class were probably a little earlier. The brown bottles of the first decades of the century had been vastly more imaginative and were reminiscent of the early artistry of Fulham and Southwark. Cast in molds, the bottles were made in the shape of smiling and scowling faces, boots, hats, pistols, civic maces, and the like, while others had relief decoration sprigged on in the eighteenth-century manner. Most of the early examples were rather roughly finished and were boldly mottled, the slipped sections of the body often appearing reddish-brown. Such bottles have continued to be made in more recent years, but the glaze is usually darker and more uniform, while the molding and modeling is much cleaner and consequently lacking the rustic charm of the originals. I have yet to see any of the English decorative bottles on American archaeological sites.

The principal American stoneware bottles of the mid-nineteenth century and thereafter were shaped like a glass beer bottle and were made in a light-gray or buff body with a pale-yellow slip extending from the lip to the midsection. A few are stamped with makers' marks, but as far as can be determined no one has devoted any thorough study to them.

BLACKER, J. F.: *The A.B.C. of English Salt-Glaze Stoneware.* London, 1922.

HURST, J. G.: "Imported Flasks," *Publications of the Thoresby Society* (Leeds, Eng.), Vol. 51, No. 112 (1967), pp. 54–9. Limited to bulbous costrels.

NOËL HUME, AUDREY: "Stoneware Mineral Water Bottles of the Nineteenth Century," *Bottling* (London), No. 129 (July 1956), pp. 123 *ff.*

See also BELLARMINES.

§ *BRICKS and BRICKWORK*

While bricks are not the most collectible of artifacts, they are among the most common relics of early American domesticity. They have also served as a kind of Rosetta Stone for architects and archaeologists attempting to date old foundations and buildings. The sad truth of the matter is, however, that individual bricks are not nearly as informative as we are often led to believe, though when seen in their original coursing they can offer us a few general guidelines.

The supposed key to the dating of single bricks lies in their measurements, their color, and their hardness. To take the last two characteristics first, one has only to read what Richard Neve in his

Bricks and Brickwork

Builder's Dictionary (1736 edition) had to say about the burning of bricks to see that neither color nor hardness are consistent through one firing of a single clamp or kiln, let alone through the years in a multitude of different places and with as many different clays. Neve stated that there were three categories of brick to be obtained from each firing:

> The first and best sort for lasting are those which lie next the Fire, and have, as it were, a Gloss on them, which proceeds from the Salt-petre inherent in them, which by the Violence of the Fire, runs and glazes them; these are called *Clinkers*.
>
> The second and most general Sort for Building, are those which lie next in the Kiln, or Clamp, to those before mentioned.
>
> The third and worst sort, are those which lie on the Outsides of the Kilns and Clamps, where the Salt-petre is not digested for want of due Heat; and these, when they come to be exposed to the Weather for some Time, will moulder away like Dirt; and are called *Samel* or *Sandal-bricks*. 'Tis an Observation, that whilst Bricks are burning, those on the windy Side of a Clamp, are the worst of all.[9]

In theory the size of bricks were regulated by statute and for that reason the ordinary wall brick was known as a "Statute, small, or common brick" and according to Neve it "ought to be in Length within 9 n.; in Breadth 4½ n.; and in Thickness 2¼ n."—it ought to be, but it rarely was. A statute of Elizabeth I (1571) had ordained that bricks should measure 9" x 4¼" x 2¼"; while another, of George I (in 1725), identified two varieties, place bricks and stock bricks (though Neve said that stock bricks "differ not from Place-bricks in form") and stated that they should measure no less than 9" x 4¼" x 2½" and 9" x 4¼" x 2⅝", respectively. By Virginia standards, however, a nine-inch brick was large, and when it was that long it was often 3" in thickness; but, according to Neve, so thick a brick should have been 12" long and 6" broad and was known as a "Great Brick." By and large, eighteenth-century colonial American bricks were about 8¾" long, 4" wide, and about 2⅝" in thickness, give or take a little in every direction. It is true that bricks from seventeenth-century foundations tend to be larger than those from

---

[9] Richard Neve: *The City and Country Purchaser's and Builder's Dictionary*, 3rd edn. (London, 1736).

81

eighteenth-century sites, but when you have said this there is little more to be added.

The fallacy of trying to date a building by its brick sizes is exhibited time and again when one measures numerous examples from one foundation and finds half a dozen different sizes used in its construction. These variations may be all of the same date, but they may also be derived from the long-established practice of robbing abandoned buildings of their bricks and re-using them in later walls. Such loot can often be identified by the presence of more than one type of mortar on a single brick.

One hears a good deal about colonial houses being built of English brick, but while there is no doubt that some bricks were brought from England, the majority were made on the American sites where they were to be used. This is particularly true of the coastal clay areas such as that of Tidewater Virginia, to which bringing English bricks would have been like shipping coals to Newcastle. A historian specializing in the crafts of the eighteenth century has, however, recently disputed this conclusion, saying: ". . . we often hear that English bricks were rarely used in Virginia, but the import records show that 17,500 bricks and 70,000 tiles were imported into Virginia during 1750 alone."[1] He failed to mention the fact that 17,500 bricks would be far too few to line the shafts of even three forty-foot wells. The truth of the matter is that while a ship's captain might rather carry saleable bricks than useless ballast stone, he would much prefer to have carried a more profitable cargo. Besides, poor-quality bricks were liable to absorb water, and that could affect the stability of the ship. Be that as it may, bricks *were* shipped over, but which ones, and how many, remains in considerable doubt.

While the majority of bricks made from local clays exhibit the same range of colors, hardness, and general dimensions, there are a few that are obviously different and datably so. In the mid-eighteenth century in Virginia, for example, one sometimes finds small, cherry-red bricks that are tight-grained, highly fired (sometimes to a blue black), and extremely hard. They measure approximately

[1] Harold B. Gill: "Sources for Research in Virginia Local History," *Quarterly Bulletin* of the Virginia Archeological Society (Richmond), Vol. 22, No. 3 (March 1968), p. 90.

7½" x 3½" x 2", and they are sometimes described as English, though on what evidence I have not been able to determine. One's first reaction is that they were made for some special purpose, but I have only seen them in use in foundation walls—just as one does the normal statute, place, or stock bricks.

The second anomalous variety is yellow or buff in color and is generally confined to seventeenth-century sites, though Neve writes of their continuing use in England somewhat later. They are known as Dutch or Flemish bricks, and those that I have measured in Virginia average around 7⅛" x 3¼" x 1⅜". Neve reported that they were smaller, saying: "I am informed that they are 6¼ n. long, 2½ n. broad, and 1¼ n. thick"; to which he added, "for my part, I never measured any of them." He went on to state that such bricks were often used in paving laid in herring bone patterns and also for building cisterns and soap boilers' vats. At Jamestown they were used in laying cellar steps at the structure tentatively identified as the First State House. It should be noted that there are considerable size variations among examples from Jamestown, as there are among specimens found in Dutch Surinam, though all are small by comparison with the normal, red building bricks of the seventeenth and eighteenth centuries.

Neve and other writers list numerous varieties of English-type bricks some of which can no longer be identified. The most common variants are half-round copying bricks used to cap garden and churchyard walls, truncated wedge-shaped bricks used in lining colonial wells, and slightly bent regular bricks sometimes used for lining cisterns and drains. Other variations are generally simply doctored statute bricks, such as those that are rounded at one end and which were used to create the beveled upper course of water tables. Others were ground out into concave ends or sides to be used in conjunction with copying bricks. Then again, others were simply filed or rubbed so that the surface was smooth and tight-grained, and these were used, along with very fine mortar, to create dominant architectural details such as bibs beneath windows and architraves around doorways. In Virginia, at least, such details tended to be most common in the eighteenth century.

The way in which bricks were laid is generally a better guide to period than are the bricks themselves, though even here the hallowed criteria must not be slavishly followed. There were two principal bonds in use in colonial America (and, of course, in seventeenth- and eighteenth-century England): English bond, and Flemish bond. The former comprised alternate courses of headers (ends) and stretchers (sides), while the latter was laid with alternating headers and stretchers in each course. English bond was the popular type of the seventeenth century, while Flemish was most widely used in the eighteenth century. It has been contended that English bond was then used only for basements and exterior walls below the water table. I have seen many eighteenth-century buildings, however, whose entire foundations are laid in Flemish bond. On the other hand, footings were frequently built in a mixed or haphazard bond. In addition, there were other less well-known forms such as Yorkshire bond, which used two stretchers to every header in one course, while the next was laid entirely in stretchers. In the early nineteenth century a new style known as American bond began to appear; this at first employed four courses of stretchers to every one of headers, but by 1850 up to seven courses of stretchers were used.

LLOYD, NATHANIEL: *A History of English Brickwork.* London, 1928.
NEVE, RICHARD: *The City and Country Purchaser's and Builder's Dictionary: or, The Complete Builder's Guide.* London, 1736 (1st edn. 1703).

§ *BUCKLES*

These fall into two broad categories, dress and harness, and neither is closely datable. Under the former heading buckles may be divided again into shoe, spur, belt, baldric, stock, knee, and hat, and of these the shoe buckle is by far the most common. (Fig. 20) Throughout most of the seventeenth century shoes were fastened with rosettes, thongs, or bows, and although the famous portrait of Charles II by John Wright (c. 1662) showed the monarch in his coronation robes with diamond buckles on his shoes, it would seem that this innovation did not become commonplace until the last years of the century. According to William Hone's *Every-Day Book*

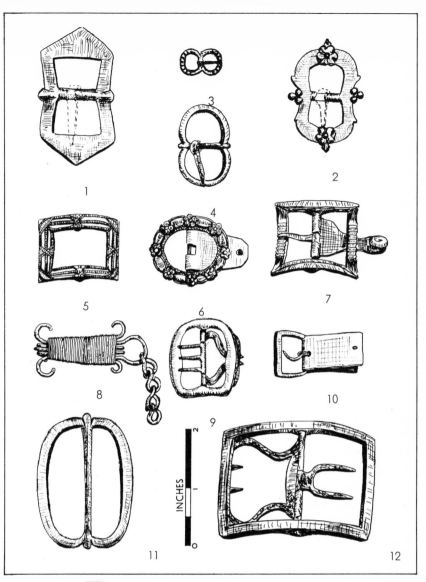

Fig. 20. Apparel buckles and other fastenings. 1–4. Figure-8 types for belts (Nos. 1, 2, and 4) and spurs (No. 3), all brass with iron tangs—Nos. 1 and 2, second half of the 17th century; No. 3, late 16th–17th century; No. 4, 18th century. 5. Woman's shoe buckle frame, brass, discarded after c. 1755. 6. Belt buckle, silver, with folded plate and rivet; second half of 17th century. 7. Belt or harness buckle, brass, anchored to leather strap by means of a stud; 17th–18th century. 8. Cloak fastening made from brass wire; probably mid-17th century. 9. Knee buckle, tin-plated brass, discarded c. 1760. 10. Strap-end buckle, brass, with folded plate and rivet; 17th century. 11. Wide belt or baldric buckle, brass, discarded c. 1775. 12. Shoe buckle, pewter frame and steel tines; late 18th century.

(London, 1827), Vol. 2, pp. 677–8, shoe buckles had been common in the first half of the sixteenth century and "revived before the revolution of 1689, remained fashionable till after the French revolution in 1789; and finally became extinct before the close of the eighteenth century." It is reasonable to contend that they do not occur on American sites prior to c. 1700 and that they will be rare after c. 1815. The most elaborate varieties of shoe buckles were of silver set with jewels, but plain cast silver was used by most of the gentry, while feet planted on the next rung down the ladder were adorned with brass or copper buckles often plated with tin to resemble silver. Cheap though they were, many of these buckles were extremely elaborately cast. Next to the bottom rung were those of pewter, and those two could be molded into delicate and elaborate forms, while at the foot one came to the buckles of iron with which little could be done but shape them into a simple rectangle. Little or no study has yet been devoted to these ubiquitous objects, and it is therefore impossible to date the various styles with any accuracy. There seems little doubt, however, that something useful can be done with them; in the meantime I can only note that the more elaborate rococo forms in brass seem to be confined to contexts dating after c. 1730, and that they were being made in Williamsburg, Virginia, prior to 1760. (Fig. 21)

It should be noted that the moving parts of all buckles were of brass or steel and comprised a toothed loop and a two-tined fork, each independently attached to a central pivot spanning the width of the buckle.

Stock, knee, and hat buckles were made in the same manner as shoe buckles but were generally less than half the size. They were rarely elaborately molded but were either set with gems or were engraved with simple ornamental devices. In addition, they differed from most shoe buckles in that the pivot frequently spanned the length rather than the width of the frame.

Belt (generally sword-belt) buckles are often indistinguishable from those used for light ornamental horse harness and are as yet virtually undatable. The most common variety was the double buckle, i.e., cast with a central bar dividing the frame into two parts. These were usually of brass and had an iron or occasionally brass tang looped over the bar. Figure-8 and rectangular shapes were common in the first half of the seventeenth century. Some were circular, but it is generally supposed that these belong to the fifteenth and sixteenth centuries. The early figure-8 types are rarely decorated, but the rectangular forms which are flat surfaced are often crudely incised with hatched lines or circles. Figure 8's of the late seventeenth to early eighteenth century, however, were mold ornamented in the manner of the brass shoe buckles. It should be noted that figure-8 buckles of less than 1″ in length are almost certainly from spurs. (Fig. 20, No. 3)

The leather straps to which the above varieties were attached were generally wrapped around the central bar. They could also be anchored by means of a strip of brass or silver that was folded around both bar and strap and then riveted to the latter. I have seen examples of this technique in fifteenth-to-eighteenth-century contexts. (Fig. 20, Nos. 6 and 10) Another variation found in contexts of the late seventeenth century occurred in brass or pewter and comprised a rectangular frame, single tang, and a flat plate with a stud at the end of it—all made from the same materials. (Fig. 20, No. 5) The tang and plate were anchored to the frame by an iron

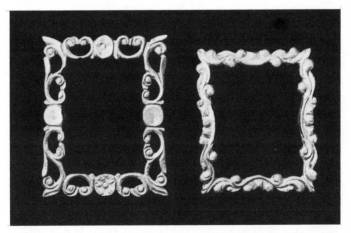

Fig. 21. Copper-alloy shoe buckles made in Williamsburg, Virginia, in the mid-18th century. Note that the intact frame at left was partly decorated in the mold but that the rosettes were to be added afterward, though only one was completed. Neither this nor the complete frame at right has been drilled to house the central pivot. Length of left example 2⅛″.

pin, while the leather strap was attached by means of a hole through which the stud projected.

Military buckles, particularly the large double, rectangular, baldric varieties, are sometimes indistinguishable from those used on horse harness. The majority, however, were slightly curved, and some were cast with ornaments incorporating regimental emblems. The latter's dates can therefore be discovered by pursuing the particular regiment's history and determining the length of its tour of duty in the area where the buckle was found.

Harness buckles appear to be undatable. They were generally of brass or iron and double or single framed; I have yet to see an example with an independent pivot. I would add (though it may not mean anything) that I have never encountered a brass single-frame harness buckle in a seventeenth-century context. Sizes in double buckles for harness extend all the way up from 2″ in length to as much as 9″, though very large brass examples were used to hold leather coach springs and so are not strictly harness items.

§ *BUTTONS and SLEEVE BUTTONS*

Considerable research has been done into the evolution of the button in England, but unfortunately very little of it has been published. It is, however, generally accepted that doublet and jerkin fashions of the late sixteenth and early seventeenth centuries called for small, round, ball-shaped buttons, and the majority of excavated examples have been found to have been of brass or white metal cast in two pieces and braised together. The shanks were normally of brass wire and were flanked by two holes which served to let gases escape when the parts were being joined together. The same technique of manufacture continued into the eighteenth century, though the buttons became larger and ovoid in section. The presence of a central nipple, however, on the faces of a few of these specimens has caused some collectors to attribute them to the late sixteenth rather than the early eighteenth century. There are, unhappily, few easy rules of thumb that can be followed in the dating

Fig. 22. Small buttons and sleeve buttons, c. 1660–1720. *Top row*: portrait of Charles II; two examples of crowned hearts possibly commemorating the marriage of Charles to Catherine of Braganza; simple decorative, late 17th century; all four are solid cast. *Bottom row*: two hollow-cast examples with characteristic decoration, late 17th or early 18th century; Queen Anne portrait, solid cast; fire insurance company solid cast, 18th century. All are of copper alloys except Nos. 1, 2, and 8, which are of pewter. Diam. of No. 1: 5/8".

of buttons. Sleeve buttons (cuff links) followed much the same trends, but because these are sometimes decorated with attributable devices it is possible to draw tentative dating conclusions from them. Thus, a sleeve button in white metal commemorating the Restoration of Charles II (1660), round, flat-faced, and molded with a portrait of the king, and with the shank cast out of the molding seam at the back, clearly demonstrates that the hollow button was not the only variety manufactured in the third quarter of the seventeenth century. (Fig. 22, top left) Similar buttons bear the portrait of Queen Anne (1702–14), but these are more often octagonal than round, a style that seems to have been plentiful through the first half of the eighteenth century. Oval sleeve buttons, on the other hand, do not seem to have become popular until the second half of the century and are most common in the 1770's and thereafter.

In the evolution of the ordinary coat button, certain basic steps can usefully be remembered. Hollow-cast examples, usually in white metal or brass, and often with embossed decoration, plain or gilded, were the rule in the first half of the eighteenth century, while flat copper-alloy disks predominated in the second, getting larger and larger toward the end of the century. These later flat expanses required to be decorated, sometimes with engine-turned engraving but more often with gilding or plating. William Hutton's *History of Birmingham* stated that by 1818, "the art of gilding buttons was arrived at such a degree of refinement . . . that three pennyworth of gold was made to cover a gross of buttons."[2] In 1742 silver-plating had been invented in Sheffield (hence Sheffield plate) by Thomas Bolsover, who first used the process for decorating buttons. It was not until the process was further refined during the late 1750's that it began to be used for more complicated products, such as coffeepots and candlesticks. Electroplating was not invented until 1840, and consequently silver-plating remained too big a problem, and the result too costly, for the small buttonmaker to attempt it. Instead he did the next best thing; he tinned them. A great many of the buttons found on archaeological sites of the mid- or later eighteenth century bear a gray, slightly silvery coating on both sides. This is tin, not silver. Silver-plating was applied to the front only, was much thicker than the tin, and has generally turned black (silver sulphide) in the ground.

Mr. Stanley South, director of excavations for the North Carolina Department of Archives and History, has made a study of the large number of buttons found at the site of Brunswick Town (1726–76, 1800–30) and at Fort Fisher (1837–65). His typology, in Figure 23, illustrates most of the forms common in the eighteenth and nineteenth centuries: types 1–16 (Type 3 overwhelmingly predominant) belong to the period 1726–76; 17–23 to the period 1800–30; and 1, 7, 11, 15, 16, and 18–32 occur between 1837 and 1865, with Types 20, 22, and 23 the most plentiful.

In using the South typology it should be noted that 78 per cent of the buttons from Brunswick Town come from the site of a single tailor's shop, and they may therefore represent unsold (and unpop-

---

[2] Quoted in William Hone: *The Table Book* (London, 1827), p. 713.

Fig. 23. A typology of button characteristics derived from 18th-century examples found at Brunswick Town and 19th-century specimens from Fort Fisher, both in North Carolina.

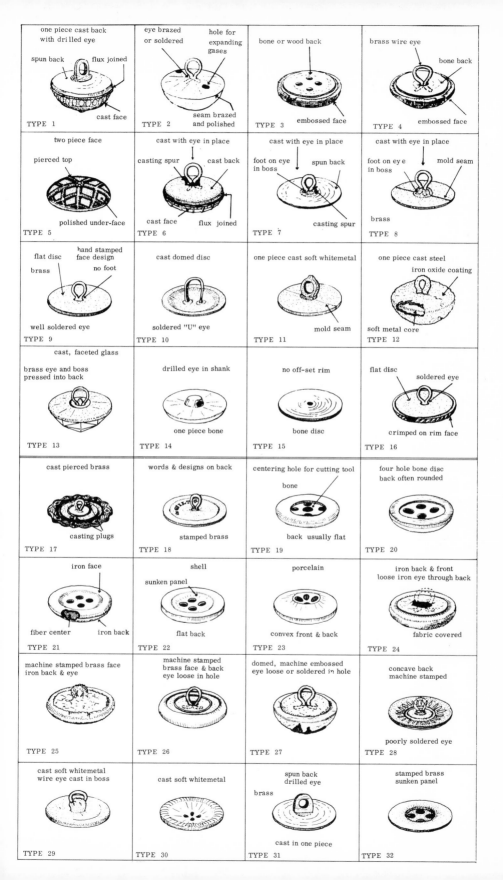

TYPE 1 — one piece cast back with drilled eye; spun back; flux joined; cast face

TYPE 2 — eye brazed or soldered; hole for expanding gases; seam brazed and polished

TYPE 3 — bone or wood back; embossed face

TYPE 4 — brass wire eye; bone back; embossed face

TYPE 5 — two piece face; pierced top; polished under-face

TYPE 6 — cast with eye in place; casting spur; cast back; cast face; flux joined

TYPE 7 — cast with eye in place; foot on eye in boss; spun back; casting spur

TYPE 8 — cast with eye in place; foot on eye in boss; mold seam; brass

TYPE 9 — flat disc; brass; hand stamped face design; no foot; well soldered eye

TYPE 10 — cast domed disc; soldered "U" eye

TYPE 11 — one piece cast soft whitemetal; mold seam

TYPE 12 — one piece cast steel; iron oxide coating; soft metal core

TYPE 13 — cast, faceted glass; brass eye and boss pressed into back

TYPE 14 — drilled eye in shank; one piece bone

TYPE 15 — no off-set rim; bone disc

TYPE 16 — flat disc; soldered eye; crimped on rim face

TYPE 17 — cast pierced brass; casting plugs

TYPE 18 — words & designs on back; stamped brass

TYPE 19 — centering hole for cutting tool; bone; back usually flat

TYPE 20 — four hole bone disc; back often rounded

TYPE 21 — iron face; fiber center; iron back

TYPE 22 — shell; sunken panel; flat back

TYPE 23 — porcelain; convex front & back

TYPE 24 — iron back & front; loose iron eye through back; fabric covered

TYPE 25 — machine stamped brass face; iron back & eye

TYPE 26 — machine stamped brass face & back; eye loose in hole

TYPE 27 — domed, machine embossed; eye loose or soldered in hole

TYPE 28 — concave back; machine stamped; poorly soldered eye

TYPE 29 — cast soft whitemetal; wire eye cast in boss

TYPE 30 — cast soft whitemetal

TYPE 31 — spun back; drilled eye; brass; cast in one piece

TYPE 32 — stamped brass; sunken panel

ular?) stock and so may not be entirely typical of the taste of the period. Furthermore, the inability to date any of the specimens within archaeological brackets narrower than that of the town's life span should not be taken to mean that stylistic or technical changes did not occur during that period. It is certainly true, for example, that Types 7–9 became both larger and more common as the eighteenth century progressed and that they continued into the early nineteenth century. It may also be added that the regulation white-metal buttons worn by "other ranks" of the British Army in the Revolutionary period were flat-faced with a very pronounced boss on the backs, into which an iron-wire eye was anchored. The Continental Army buttons, on the other hand, were of similar construction to Stanley South's Type 11. These buttons bore the molded letters USA—the dropping of the A did not occur until the War of 1812.

In the absence of evidence to the contrary, it must be assumed that the vast majority of buttons used in America prior to the nineteenth century were imported. In 1784, Lord Sheffield in his *Observations on the Commerce of the United States* stated that "Whilst Great Britain supplies a great part of Europe with this article, it cannot be questioned from whence the Americans will import it; and this will be one of the last manufactures which it will be worth the while of the Americans to attempt."[3] Nevertheless, Caspar Wistar, who, in 1739, established one of the first American glass manufactures, was also a prosperous Philadelphia buttonmaker. He continued with both endeavors until his death in 1752; thereafter they were carried on by his son Richard. In 1750, one of Caspar Wistar's apprentices, Henry Witeman, set up his own brass-button business in Maiden Lane, New York City. Ten years later, Witeman moved to a new shop "At the Sign of the Buttons and Buckles" near the city's Oswego Market and there announced that, as "Philadelphia Buttons" were being counterfeited, he would thenceforth call his own "New-York Buttons."[4] By 1793 the firm of Cornwall and Martin from Birmingham (England's principal buttonmaking center) had set up in business at Corlear's Hook,

---

[3] Sheffield, op. cit., p. 26.
[4] Geoffrey Wills: *Collecting Copper & Brass* (New York, 1963), pp. 71–2.

New York City, making both gilt and plated buttons. Theirs was almost certainly a large-scale, machine-operated venture. It is reasonable to assume, regardless of Lord Sheffield's comment, that flat or solid white-metal buttons had been cast in sand or in two- or three-piece hand molds (somewhat akin to those used in making bullets) by colonial metal workers throughout most of the eighteenth century.

CALVER, WILLIAM LEWIS, and REGINALD PELHAM BOLTON: *History Written with Pick and Shovel*. New York, New-York Historical Society, 1950.

NOËL HUME, IVOR: "Sleeve buttons: diminutive relics of the seventeenth and eighteenth centuries," *Antiques*, Vol. 79, No. 4 (April 1961), pp. 380–3.

SOUTH, STANLEY: "Analysis of the Buttons from Brunswick Town and Fort Fisher," *Florida Anthropologist*, Vol. 17, No. 2 (June 1964), pp. 113–33. Covers the periods 1726–1830 and 1837–65.

WILLS, GEOFFREY: *Collecting Copper & Brass*. New York, 1963.

§ *CANDLESTICKS and LIGHTING ACCESSORIES*

The evolution of the candlestick is best traced through the study of silver examples, for those of English manufacture were required to be stamped with a date letter as well as with the assay office and maker's marks. Candlesticks with shaped cups to hold the candle were uncommon until the second half of the seventeenth century, though examples do occur at least a century earlier. In the early seventeenth century tripod-footed holders of iron with pricket attachments were plentiful, as also were the open-flamed oil lamps, or cressets, generally known as "crusies." By the 1650's candlesticks of silver, pewter, or sheet brass were made with broad trumpetlike feet sweeping up into straight stems encircled by a drip tray at the midsection almost as wide as the foot. By 1666 a more architectural form had developed comprising a hexagonal foot beneath a straight, clustered column. This form developed into a more elaborate fluted column with ribs ascending between the flutes to a third of its

Fig. 24. Brass candlesticks of types common in 18th-century homes. The left and right examples are typical of the mid-century. Note the poorly concealed vertical join up the shaft and socket of the right example. This stick originally had a detachable *bobêche* (socket lining and drip tray), a detail common in the second half of the century. The smaller central stick with its pillarlike stem is typical of the last quarter of the 18th century.

height. A small drip tray survived at the base of the flutes, and the feet were generally octagonal, or square with clipped corners. On rare occasions the tops of the columns were embellished into a rudimentary Corinthian capital. Such sticks were popular between 1680 and about 1706. Starting slightly earlier, in about 1670, there developed the baluster candlestick, whose principal stem feature was an inverted, acorn-shaped knop, which detail, in the late years of the century, was sometimes gadrooned. The form had developed into other more elongated balustroid shapes by 1710.

An important innovation of the late seventeenth century was the development of the two-piece mold, which enabled stems to be cast in two vertical halves and then joined together. It was a technique that continued until the close of the following century, at which time single-mold castings became the rule. Thus, most English candlesticks with vertical seams can be attributed to the eighteenth century. (Fig. 24) It is often difficult to distinguish between English and European sticks of the late seventeenth and eighteenth centuries, for the styles, though not necessarily of comparable date, were often very similar in shape. It is therefore worth remembering that Dutch and Flemish candlesticks generally had a small hole drilled through one side of the holder—usually in the midsection—to enable a pointed tool to be pushed through to pry up the butts of spent candles. This convenient feature is not found on English specimens.

A high-domed foot was a characteristic of many later seventeenth-century sticks, having evolved from the bell-shaped stand that had been common in the first half of the century. The flattened domed foot continued into the early eighteenth century and is found in conjunction with true baluster stems. By 1710 the inverted baluster had developed from the acorn knop into a tall

94

trumpet form which persisted along with ever-increasing embellishment through most of the century. The early 1740's saw the introduction of rococo molding on both stems and feet, a step forward from the scalloped foot that had appeared in the mid-1730's. By about 1750 the sense of unity that characterized the candlesticks of the first half of the eighteenth century was disappearing and the balusters and knops now seemed almost separated from each other, so slender were the collars that connected them. Around 1755 the square foot (without clipped corners) reappeared and continued as the most popular foot form until about 1790, when circular feet, round stems, and vase-shaped holders were the vogue. Previously, in about 1760, the architectural column had regained popularity, but although the shaft itself remained almost identical to that of the late seventeenth century, the vestigial drip tray was missing and elaborate Corinthian and Ionic capitals became the rule rather than the exception. These silver elaborations were rarely transferred to brass; nevertheless the straight, unfluted and uncapped column with a square foot became common among brass candlesticks in the period c. 1760–90. (Fig. 24, center)

Glass candlesticks were made from the late seventeenth century onward, but their rarity is such that they need not be discussed here. Ceramic examples, on the other hand, were comparatively common, and they occur from at least 1630 on through the nineteenth century. The shapes were closely akin to those of the metal sticks, beginning with London delftware versions of the silver forms with straight stems, trumpet feet, and wide drip trays. These were generally undecorated, but later delft potters took the metal shapes and adorned them in the styles then popular for other delftware products. As far as I can tell, decoration was confined to blue, and the earliest example, with bell foot and wide drip tray, is painted with the "Chinaman and rocks" motif popular in the 1680's.

In the mid-eighteenth century, candlesticks in the current metal forms were made in white salt-glazed stoneware with the feet decorated in the "dot, diaper and basket" or "barley" motifs used

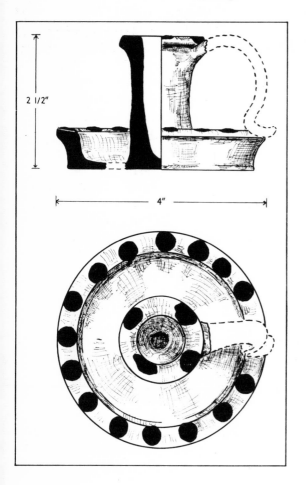

Fig. 25. A Staffordshire slipware candleholder, yellow with dark-brown dots; found in Williamsburg, Virginia. Mid-18th century.

for the rims of saltglaze plates. They were subsequently produced in creamware and are illustrated in the 1783 design catalog of Hartley, Greens, and Co., of Leeds. The creamware shapes are those of the fluted and plain columns with stepped square feet, common to metal sticks of the late eighteenth century influenced by the classical revival in Europe. The Wedgwood shape and pattern book of c. 1810 shows three creamware sticks of the same types, one of them comparable to that shown in Figure 24, center, and another having a similar shaft but with a circular foot.

Little attention has been devoted to candlesticks made by coarse earthenware potters, and it is generally assumed that their contributions to this field were largely confined to short-stemmed chambersticks with which the less wealthy lighted their way to bed. These had wide trays or saucers with a loop handle at one edge and were commonly made in a cheap, lead-glazed red earthenware. They were also made in Staffordshire slipware having a yellow body under a transparent glaze and decorated around the lip and tray rim with brown dots. (Fig. 25) By the last quarter of the eighteenth century, coarse earthenware chambersticks had shallower trays to which a cone-shaped projection was attached. This was capped by a snuffer of the same ware. The previously cited Wedgwood shape book shows two chambersticks (calling them "candlesticks"), one with the snuffer and one without.

Although the short stick was easier to make from a coarse clay and was less inclined to warp in the kiln, there is evidence that the less sophisticated factories sometimes produced sticks comparable to those of the metalworkers. Although I have yet to see an intact example, there is an unglazed candlestick cup of excellent quality from the late-seventeenth-century kiln site at Green Spring plantation in Virginia.

The cheapest seventeenth- and eighteenth-century candles were of tallow (usually of fifty-fifty blend of sheeps' and bullocks' fat) and the best of wax. Wicks for both varieties were of twisted cotton, which failed to bend outward into the oxidizing area of the flame as it burned and so were left to accumulate. To prevent the resulting char from dimming the flame, it was necessary to trim it off at frequent intervals. Consequently candle snuffers were essential lighting accessories. They remained so until 1825, when a Frenchman named Cambacères invented a braided wick impregnated with a mineral material that helped to make it self-consuming.

Snuffers were manufactured in silver, brass, and iron, from at least as early as the beginning of the seventeenth century. They resembled a pair of scissors with a rectangular box attached to one blade and a vertical pad to the other that fitted snugly inside the box when the scissors were closed. The pad was attached to the end of its blade, but the box was not, there being a tapering projection beyond it. The handles of seventeenth-century examples were often looped around like rather tight shepherds' crooks, while those that came later had the loops or bows welded or braised into a closed ring. The same evolutionary step occurred with the loops of ordinary scissors. (Fig. 87) Handle fragments are often found in excavations divorced from their blades, and sometimes it is hard to distinguish between those from snuffers and those from early sugar tongs, though as a rule the latter were smaller.

Finally, a word should be said about candle molds; being made of tin or sheet iron, they rarely survive intact in the ground but are often represented by clusters of six or a dozen rusted cylinders too fragile to be salvaged. These multiple molds usually terminated in a rectangular, spread-collar foot matching a comparable lip at the top, and often had a strap handle attached to one side. Single molds were usually without feet but had small circular lips. Close dating for either type is impossible.

GROVE, JOHN R.: *Antique Brass Candlesticks 1450–1750.* Queen Anne, Md., 1967.

LINDSAY, SEYMOUR, JR.: *Iron and Brass Implements of the English and American Home.* London, 1964 (first pub. 1927).

§ CERAMICS, American

Potterymaking in the British American colonies had begun by 1625 and by the mid-century much of the colonists' ceramic need was filled by local craftsmen. The word *local*, however, remained the key to American potting well into the eighteenth century, for most of the products were vastly inferior to imported wares and so did not find markets beyond their area of manufacture, where they had the advantages of cheapness and availability. In the lowly field of coarse, lead-glazed earthenwares the colonial potters were the match of their English cousins. In New England, slipware potters of the second half of the seventeenth century were turning out products similar to the "Metropolitan" wares of Essex, while from the mid-eighteenth century onward German immigrants in Pennsylvania manufactured traditional slipwares of excellent quality, sometimes sgraffito-decorated through a white slip onto a red body, or marbleized in the manner of Staffordshire but with the addition of splashes of copper green. The latter wares were widely distributed in the late eighteenth and early nineteenth centuries. At Green Spring plantation in Virginia in the 1680's a potter was throwing coarseware dishes of shapes comparable to the delftware chargers produced at Southwark (London) in the same period. In the second half of the eighteenth century, Moravian potters at Bethabara and Salem in North Carolina were producing teacups, saucers, and plates of a thinness that would have done justice to Whieldon of Staffordshire. Unfortunately, the clays and glazes were as important to the final product as was the skill of the thrower, and none of the early American earthenware products matched their English counterparts. The Salem potters received instruction from an English Staffordshire potter in the art of making creamware in 1773, but as far as can yet be determined, the products resembled it only in shape. Ellis, the English potter, had worked for another Staffordshireman, John Bartlem, who three years earlier advertised that he was making cream-colored earthenwares in Charleston, South Carolina. Unfortunately, not one of the Bartlem products has yet been identified.

Another effort to make creamware was launched at Red Hook Landing on New York's North River in 1798. None of its products appear to have survived, and our knowledge of it is confined to an advertisement of intent published in *Argus, Greenleaf's New Daily Advertiser* for May 12th of that year. Mr. J. Mouchet then informed the public that he had established "A new Manufactory of yellow or cream Ware, such as never was made in this country before . . . under the name of Tivoli Ware, where any command for all sorts and shapes of ware, with different colored edges" would be met. The notice ended by offering apprenticeships and adding that the lucky lads would be "taught by the most skillful European hands."[5]

The first American attempt to make porcelain that enjoyed any measure of success was launched in the fall of 1769 by the Philadelphia firm of Gouse Bonnin and George Anthony Morris. Production, however, was slow to start, and their "first Emission of Porcelain"[6] was being advertised in January 1771. Very few examples of their ware survive. Those that are known are not sufficiently hard to be called porcelain and are decorated in underglaze blue with floral motifs reminiscent of Derby but tending to run in the manner of Bow. Fruit baskets and trinket boxes were decorated at the rim with a wide lattice pattern of intersecting arcs, with applied flowers at the junctions. The Bonnin and Morris advertisement in the *Pennsylvania Journal* for January 10, 1771, stated that "all future emissions from this factory will be marked s."[7] The known examples are, however, clearly marked P. Recent excavations on the kiln site by John L. Cotter, an archaeologist for the United States National Park Service, yielded extremely important wasters, including pieces of the flower-decorated lattice rims as well as fragments of bowls and saucers in both biscuit and glazed states. Unfortunately, like so many early American quality potting ventures, Bonnin and Morris did not prosper, and the factory and its contents were for sale in November 1772.

In the field of stonewares the colonial potters were much more successful, and in the second quarter of the eighteenth century William Rogers of Yorktown, Virginia, was producing brown-stoneware tavern mugs, bottles, and pitchers every bit as good as those manufactured in English kilns at the same date. In addition he made a series of excellent hemispherical bowls with a brown band at the rim, a type unknown elsewhere. In Philadelphia, in the 1730's, Anthony Duché was making the first American cobalt-

---

[5] Quoted in Rita Susswein Gottesmann, comp.: *The Arts and Crafts in New York, 1777–1799* (New York, 1954), pp. 95–6.
[6] Alfred Cox Prime, comp.: *The Arts and Crafts in Philadelphia, Maryland and South Carolina, 1721–1785* (Philadelphia, 1929), p. 117.
[7] Ibid.

decorated gray stoneware in the manner of Westerwald. The ware was good but different from the German in that Duché's products were produced largely by hand, while the Germans mass-produced their chamber pots and tavern mugs making much use of templates and jigs. The Duché achievement does not seem to have been sustained, but by the end of the eighteenth century and well through the nineteenth century American-made "blue and gray" stoneware was produced in many kilns and was to be found in most homesteads, kitchens, dairies, and taverns. A successful gray stoneware kiln was in operation at Cheesequake near Madison, New Jersey, by 1775 and was operated by General James Morgan. Fragments from the waster dumps are now in the Brooklyn Museum and included jug sherds dated 1775 and 1776. Some poorly fired mug fragments found on domestic sites in the Hudson Valley suggest that there was a stoneware potter there who copied German forms, probably in the second half of the eighteenth century, but the majority of the American "blue and gray" products were larger items such as harvest bottles, creampans, storage crocks, pinched-neck pitchers, and cuspidors. They are generally much thicker than the German stonewares, and, whereas the latter are decorated with incised and molded ornament and made use of cobalt and manganese to block in the devices thus created, the later American wares were generally adorned with the cobalt alone, either painted in freehand or applied through a stencil. Size numbers and factory labels are often stamped on examples of the early to mid-nineteenth century. Some of the later jugs and pans are coated on the inside with a dark brown, high-gloss surface known as an Albany slip.

Almost as common as the "blue and gray" stonewares in the mid-nineteenth century were pitchers and large teapots thrown or cast in a hard yellow body and coated with a thick, molasseslike lead glaze creating a somewhat uneven, blotched brown surface in the manner of the English Rockingham ware developed at Swinton, Yorkshire, in about 1788. The American versions were made in a number of factories, notably at Bennington, Vermont, and in Baltimore, Maryland, where jugs molded in relief depicting "Rebecca at the Well" were particularly popular.

RAMSEY, JOHN: *American Potters and Pottery*. Clinton, Mass., 1939.
WATKINS, LURA: *Early New England Potters and Their Wares*. Cambridge, Mass., 1950 (reprinted 1968).

§ *CERAMICS, British*

English pottery of the seventeenth century can be divided into three sections, lead-glazed earthenwares, delftware, and stoneware. As in America, the earthenwares were the easiest to make, also the cheapest, and so the most widely used. Those reaching America came predominantly either from southeastern England or from the West Country, largely from Devonshire and perhaps from Somerset. Bulbous drinking mugs with padlike feet in a buff ware, decorated on the outside with a mottled tortoise-shell glaze and on the inside with the same, or alternatively with a yellow or apple-green glaze, were produced in the southeast and were common from about 1590 to 1640. Mugs with straight necks and bulbous bodies of a similar ware with a bright apple-green glaze appeared in the mid-sixteenth century and continued into the seventeenth century, and these, too, came from southeastern England, possibly from Surrey. Tall, black-glazed, red-bodied mugs, generally with two or more handles, are known as "tygs" and were produced in various parts of England from the fifteenth century into the first half of the seventeenth century. Examples are often found on early colonial sites, and many of these probably come from kilns near Harlow in Essex. They usually date prior to 1640, though they are sometimes found in contexts dating twenty years later. Also common in the southeast of England were yellow-bodied tripod-legged pipkins with ribbed walls, hollow tubular handles projecting from one side, and decorated on the inside only with a yellow or pale-green glaze. These occur on American sites of the first half of the seventeenth century and were long thought to be of Flemish origin, but recent researches have revealed their English manufacture.

Readily identifiable slipwares were made in the Harlow area (1625–80) and at Wrotham in Kent (c. 1610–1715), and examples of the former occur on American sites of the mid-seventeenth century. Their export, however, does not seem to have continued as long as the wares were produced. The so-called "Metropolitan"

Fig. 26. A late "Metropolitan" slipware dish, lead glaze over a red body decorated with white slip, the latter appearing yellow under the glaze. Discarded c. 1680. Diam. 10¾".

slipwares of Essex are red-bodied and are coated with a clear glaze which gave them a bright ginger-brown surface. (Fig. 26) They were ornamented beneath the glaze with white pipeclay which, when applied to pitchers, small mugs, and chamber pots, often took the form of pious or secular exhortations such as PRAISE GOD AND HONOUR THE KING (Fig. 57) or BE QUICK AND PIFF, and sometimes THE GIFT IS SMALL GOOD WILL IS ALL. Such inscriptions were sometimes followed by the date, which ranged from c. 1630 to at least 1656.

The Wrotham slipwares were also red-bodied, but their glaze was generally deliberately darkened and the white slip was applied in sprig-molded pads containing initials and dates, the latter ranging from c. 1612 to the early eighteenth century. Floral and other devices were also applied in sprig molds, and additional pipeclay was applied in spots and runs to give the majority of Wrotham pieces a "busyness" that is often excessive. Large "tyg"-like drinking vessels, sometimes with as many as nine double-looped handles capped with pipeclay finials are the best known of the Wrotham slipwares (Fig. 27), though it is probable that many other shapes less characteristically ornamented were also produced and are not now recognized.

In the West of England, principally in the Barnstaple-Bideford section of North Devon, an entirely different type of slipware was being produced throughout the second half of the seventeenth century, and much of it was exported to the colonies. The ware was red, coated with a white slip through which geometric and floral patterns were incised; the result was then covered with a clear (really a pale-yellow) glaze that produced a rich yellow surface and light-brown ornament where the body color showed through. (Fig. 28) This sgraffito technique continued to be used in the West Country as recently as the early twentieth century. The principal seventeenth-century shapes were dishes, single-handled mugs with bulbous bodies and straight collar necks, and pitchers with heavily ribbed necks. The earliest examples yet found occur in Virginia in contexts of about 1650, and they seem to have continued through to the end of the century. Unfortunately, none of the excavated examples is dated. There is in existence, however, a harvest jug dated

Fig. 27. Posset cup of Wrotham slipware, dark-brown lead-glazed body with thick white pipeclay slip appearing yellow under the glaze. Dated 1695. Ht. 6¾".

Fig. 28. Examples of North Devon sgraffito slipware, pink body beneath a white slip turned yellow under the lead glaze; all found at Jamestown, Virginia. C. 1670–90. Diam. of foreground dish 12".

1698 that is reputed to have a long Delaware history. These jugs stand as much as 18" in height, have bulbous bodies decorated with sgraffito birds, animals, portraits, ships, and doggerel; dated examples occur at least into the early nineteenth century. I have yet to hear, however, of any of this West of England sgraffito ware being found in American archaeological contexts dating later than c. 1740. Rather similar sgraffito wares were produced at Crock Street and at the nearby village of Donyat in Somersetshire, but they differ in that they were splotched with copper green under the glaze. Dated examples occur from the eighteenth to the present century, though the only example from an American context that I have seen was discarded in about 1765. (Fig. 29, bottom right)

The most important ceramic development in England in the seventeenth century was the successful growth of the so-called delftware industry which had been started by immigrant potters from Antwerp in Norwich in about 1567; at least one of these potters moved to London some three years later. The ware is pale-yellow or sometimes pink, coated with a lead glaze containing oxide of tin that turns it opaque-white, the result generally being known as a tin enamel. This enamel could be painted before firing with cobalt blue, manganese purple, copper green, antimony yellow, and an orange derived from iron rust. It was not a new technique, for it had been used in Spain and Italy from the fourteenth century onward and was there known as maiolica. The same term described the products of Italian craftsmen who moved to Antwerp in the sixteenth century and thence to England. In France similar tin-enameled wares were known as faïence, but in England the term *delftware* (which was actually not used there before the eighteenth century) became the generic term for the ware, just as it did in Holland where the town of Delft (previously renowned as a brewing center) did not develop its tin-enameled earthenware industry until the mid-seventeenth century. Thus, when writing of the English counterparts, *delftware* should always be written with a small *d* to avoid confusion with the products of Delft itself. In England, through most of the seventeenth century, the pottery was known as "galley ware," a term dating back to at least 1465, when it probably referred to maiolica brought from the Mediterranean aboard galleys.

Just as "delftware" is a misnomer, so also is the much-used word *Lambeth* to mean London delftware of the seventeenth century. The original center of the industry was in the Borough of Southwark further east on the south bank of the Thames, principally in the vicinity of Tooley Street near London Bridge in what is now the Borough of Bermondsey. One or more factories were in production there as early as 1618 and for at least a century thereafter. Other potters were working further west near Southwark Cathedral and beyond it on the Bankside. It was not until 1671 that a Dutchman took out a patent to make delftware tiles at Lambeth, while the first-known record of an Englishman making "Holland China" in Lambeth occurred two years later. These enterprises would appear to have launched the Lambeth-Vauxhall industry, which continued until the early nineteenth century. The first centers to be established outside the London area were at Bristol and Brislington, where delftware production seems to have begun in the 1660's or perhaps a decade earlier. Later, in the first years of the eighteenth century, production began at Liverpool, and both Bristol

Fig. 29. Fragments of lead-glazed slipware dishes. *Top row*: both combed with iron-oxide stripes through a white slip on a buff body; left, probably third quarter of the 18th century; right, second quarter. *Bottom row*: left, bat-molded decoration with thick iron-oxide coloring over white slip on a buff to pink body, Staffordshire, second quarter of the 18th century; right, sgraffito decoration cutting through white slip splashed with copper green over a red body, probably from Donyat, Somersetshire, third quarter of 18th century. Length of the sgraffito sherd 7".

and Liverpool delftware manufacturing declined together as the ware was superseded by other, better products in the third quarter of the eighteenth century. The same was true of Glasgow in Scotland, whose Delftfield pottery began production in 1749 and continued until about 1800. Much of its output was shipped to America in the third quarter of the eighteenth century, and it continued to be exported as late as 1791. In the late 1760's and 70's, however, Delftfield followed Bristol and Liverpool in the march of fashion and technology, adapting part of its operation to the manufacture of white salt-glazed stoneware and creamware. To be strictly accurate, therefore, delftware made in Great Britain after 1749 but whose factory cannot be positively identified should be described as *British* rather than *English* delftware. The same should be said of

Fig. 30. *Left*: English tin-glazed earthenware (delftware) "blue dash charger" or dish decorated in blue, yellow, orange, and green, depicting Adam and Eve reviewing the merits of a piece of fruit; c. 1640; diam. 14″. *Right*: dish of similar ware and type decorated with a tulip design in blue, yellow, and red; c. 1680; diam. 13½″. Both lead-glazed on the backs and both probably from London kilns.

imperfectly provenanced salt-glazed stoneware and creamware after the early 1760's.

The earliest English delftware was generally elaborately ornamented with Italianate or chinoiserie designs, and it was not until the 1640's that potters in need of mass production methods began to produce plain white vessels entirely without decoration. This simplicity may, to some extent, have been influenced by the sobering effect of the Civil War and the subsequent era of the Commonwealth, for London was the principal center of Parliamentary influence, and the delftware industry was still confined there.

After the restoration of the monarchy in 1660, colorfully painted delftwares became popular again, particularly the large dishes with blue dashes round their rims (known to collectors as "blue dash chargers") and with the centers adorned with floral and fruit patterns (Fig. 30, right) or Adam and Eve cartoons or royal portraits, sometimes standing but more often on horseback. In addition to sketches of all the monarchs from Charles II to George I, these dishes are sometimes ornamented with portraits of other national figures who are identified only by their initials. Such dishes were intended to be decorative as well as useful and were frequently used as wall or dresser ornaments. Fragments occur on colonial sites of the second half of the seventeenth century, but they are not nearly as common as they are in England.

Plain white plates, both round and octagonal, and with wide rims, were manufactured in London in the third quarter of the seventeenth century. Most of those that have survived in museum and private collections are decorated in the centers with dates and convivial inscriptions in blue. In the last quarter of the century the rims became narrower and the bases proportionately broader. Inscriptions (often only initials and dates) were contained in a cartouche having a crown above and a faintly angelic face below and flanked by griffins or winged horses' heads. A group of plates and other items decorated with the griffin cartouches (painted on the rim and to one side of the plates) was long thought to be the work of Dutch painters employed at Lambeth, a conclusion based on the evidence of their garbled English inscriptions. More recently, this class has been reclassified as having been made in Holland for English customers. To the same general class belong the plain-rimmed English plates of the eighteenth century which are decorated in the centers with blue-painted wreaths containing initials, dates, and inscriptions. Many of these last are numbered from one to six and carry such cheerful observations as the following: (1) "What is a merry Man"; (2) "Let him doe what he Cann"; (3) "To Entertain his Guests"; 4) "With Wine & Merry Jest"; (5) "But if his Wife does frown"; (6) All merriment Goes Down." Dated examples are recorded between 1710 and 1742. Although it will hardly concern the archaeologist, collectors would do well to note that these inscribed plates are among delftware's more common fakes.

The later seventeenth-century delftware potters produced mugs, jugs, candlesticks, flower vases with pedestal bases, and, of course, common chamber pots and washbasins, as well as apothecaries' drug pots. (Figs. 56 and 67) Pseudo-Chinese motifs, human figures, birds, and perforated rocks in Ming style, reappeared in the 1670's (Fig. 31, No. 2) and continued into the early eighteenth century, when even more elaborate Chinese designs were copied.

Most alleged "experts" seem to believe that they are liable to

Fig. 31. English delftware plates exhibiting design features encountered on American colonial sites. *Top left to bottom right:* 1. mimosa pattern painted in underglaze blue and overglaze red, perhaps Bristol, c. 1720–35; 2. chinoiserie motif in a style typical of the second half of the 17th century, painted in shades of blue, London, c. 1680; 3. chinoiserie motif painted in a rich blue, Bristol or London, c. 1730; 4. peacock design in polychrome, the trees in sponged manganese, probably Bristol, c. 1725–40; 5. squirrel motif with other features attributed both to London and Bristol, painted in blue, c. 1750, rather later than is often supposed (the squirrel, foliate, and ground features have all been found in Williamsburg, but on separate items—the squirrel on plates, a bowl, and a tankard, the leaves on plates, and the ground "wheels" on a bowl); 6. geometric design in pale blue, red, green, yellow, and purple, the style sometimes attributed to Liverpool, c. 1750. Nos. 4 and 5 were found in Williamsburg. Diam. of No. 5: 11½".

lose face if they are unable to distinguish between the products of London and Bristol. I venture to suggest, however, that such distinctions, at least in the seventeenth century, must be treated with caution, as painters moved from factory to factory and everyone produced the designs most popular at the moment. It has been claimed that Bristol wares can be identified by the use of a deep red that had to be added in a second, low-temperature firing and which is therefore raised and rough to the touch. I have, however, found similar fragments on the Tooley Street kiln sites in very early eighteenth-century contexts. The design known as the "mimosa" pattern and the distinctive square brush strokes associated with it (Fig. 31, No. 1) are both features that have been attributed to Bristol (Brislington), yet comparable sherds have been found at Lambeth. The large dish with the squirrel design in the center (Fig. 31, No. 5) is usually classified as Lambeth, though I have seen another plate decorated with identical foliate brushwork that is said to be Bristol and a bowl with the same two-tone wheel-like flowers with a like attribution. All three motifs—squirrel, leaves, and flowers—have been found on separate examples from Williamsburg excavations, none of them in contexts datable prior to about 1750; yet the most recently published example of the combined designs—as Figure 31, Number 5—is claimed to date as early as c. 1720. The novice should be warned that he is entering dangerous and poorly charted waters,

and he would do well to avoid committing himself. Instead, he should seek published parallels by reputable authors and cite their attributions—with acknowledgments.

Delftware tried to compete with the Englishman's desire for Chinese porcelain, but such small vessels as teacups were prone to lose their glaze at the lips and so were never very popular. As a rule it is fair to contend that they are rarely found in colonial use after about 1750. Larger tablewares such as plates, mugs, and punch bowls held their glaze better, and as they did not come in contact with the mouth they were accepted by the public much longer; and we know that plates were being made as late as 1802 and decorated mugs until at least 1793. Pharmaceutical pots were produced considerably later, and London directories of the early nineteenth century still listed makers of "delph," though generally in conjunction with other wares. The firm of Alfred Singer Sr. Co., of Vauxhall, was thus identified as late as 1852.

The manufacture of salt-glazed stoneware had been a virtual Rhenish monopoly through most of the seventeenth century until

111

Fig. 32. English brown stoneware mugs of half-gallon and pint capacities, a type made in London, Bristol, and elsewhere through most of the 18th century. The pint mug exhibits the usual WR excise stamp below the rim. The large example at left is rare in this undecorated form. It was found at Lightfoot, Virginia, and stands 8" in ht.

John Dwight of Fulham perfected an English version in 1671. Dwight's stoneware is thought to have copied the so-called Bellarmine bottles, and a number of not very well-made examples are attributed to his factory. At the other end of the scale he produced some magnificently sculptured busts of Charles II, James II, and Prince Rupert, and a recumbent figure of his daughter Lydia, who died in 1673. Between these extremes were numerous small drinking mugs with reeded necks in gray to white stoneware, as well as a marbelized version of the same form. At least one fragment likely to belong to this class has been found on a late seventeenth- to early eighteenth-century site in Virginia.

Just as Lambeth became synonymous with London delftware, so

112

Fig. 33. A fine-textured brown stoneware loving cup, dated 1759; the ware was developed at Nottingham but was closely paralleled by others produced in Staffordshire, Derbyshire, and Yorkshire through much of the 18th century. Possibly Swinton. Ht. 9⅞".

Fulham became the popular attribution for a wide range of tavern tankards and bottles made in the London area throughout the eighteenth century. (Fig. 32) Excavations in Southwark have demonstrated that they were also made there, while digging in Bristol has yielded almost identical wasters. The mugs of pint and quart size are normally stamped below the rim with an impressed, crowned WR (William III Rex) indicating that they are made to conform to government-prescribed standards of capacity. It should be noted, however, that the WR stamps continued to be used as late as 1792, although occasional AR (Anna Regina) and GR (Georgius Rex) stamps are known. Many of the mugs were incised with the name of the tavern keeper and the date, as well as being adorned with sprig-molded panels depicting the sign of the tavern to which they belonged. By the 1760's the names and dates were frequently stamped into the body with printer's type, robbing the mugs of much of the character provided by the earlier free-hand inscriptions. These mottled brown saltglaze mugs also came in much larger sizes, some holding two and a half quarts, and many of those were decorated with sprig-molded hunting scenes, trees, houses, and sometimes with a relief rendering of Hogarth's famous painting *The Midnight Modern Conversation* (1733). It is safe to say that all English mottled brown stoneware mugs found on American domestic sites date between 1690 and 1775. Exceptions are likely to be found in New York, which continued to receive British exports during the Revolutionary War years, and on British military sites to which the troops brought their own supplies undeterred by American boycotts.

In 1684, Dwight sued James Morley of Nottingham for infringing his patent. The latter (and his family after him) produced a smooth brown stoneware with a glossy surface over a drab body, the principal products being tavern mugs, bowls, pitchers, and double-handled loving cups. These vessels were often inscribed in incised freehand with names and dates, the latter ranging from 1700 to 1799. As a rule all of these shiny-surfaced brown stonewares are attributed to Nottingham, but it is now known that similar products were made at Burslem and probably at other locations in Staffordshire and Derbyshire as well as at Swinton in Yorkshire. (Fig. 33) It is generally possible to tell the difference when the examples are in fragments, for the Nottingham pieces have a thin white line separating the glaze from the body. Insufficient evidence is yet forthcoming to determine the full date range of the Burslem ware, though it is frequently found in contexts of the mid-eighteenth century.

By far the most important stoneware development was the production of an entirely white ware, the earliest-known documented example of which, a two-handled loving cup, is incised with the date 1720. Small, waisted cups with flaring rims comparable to those made by Morley were in use in colonial America by the mid-1720's. So, also were cups, mugs, and jugs of a drab, gray ware coated with a white salt-glazed slip. Because the slip tended to fall away in the firing from rims, spouts, and the tops of handles expos-

Fig. 34. *Left*: dipped saltglaze mug, white-slipped over a gray core and the rim and handle topped with an iron-oxide slip to prevent the body from showing through. *Right*: a regular white saltglaze mug illustrating the finer and more elegant treatment of the foot and handle not possible in the heavier, dipped ware. Both mugs found together in a context of c. 1755. Ht. of left 5½".

ing the gray body beneath, these extremities were coated with a band of brown iron-oxide slip. It was generally supposed that this represented the earliest of the widely produced white saltglaze wares, but since fragments of this type have been found in contexts on through the eighteenth century up to the Revolutionary period, it must be deduced that it continued to be made alongside the solid white. (Fig. 34) Nevertheless, it has been found in the ruins of a plantation house that burned in 1729, and another is dated 1723.

The true white saltglaze that became the typical English tableware of the mid-eighteenth century severely damaged the delftware potters' business. By the late 1730's block molds had been introduced to enable saltglaze plates, teapots, tankards, caddies, etc., to be cast in elaborate relief. Thus, it is reasonable to contend that the well-known series of plates with their rims ornamented in "dot, diaper and basket" or "barley" patterns (Fig. 35) date no earlier than about 1740. Popular in the 1750's were plates with rims decorated with elaborate floral patterns in relief. To the same period belong a group of saltglaze plates lauding Britain's alliance with Prussia during the Seven Years War. The rims bear a portrait

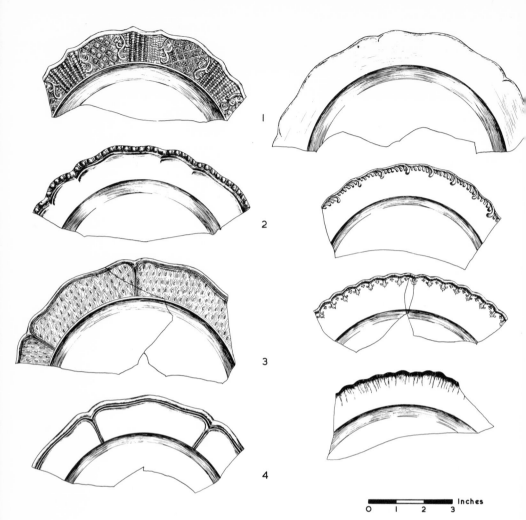

Fig. 35. The evolution of English plate rims from white salt-glaze to pearlware, c. 1740–85. **1.** Dot, diaper and basket pattern, saltglaze. **2.** "Bead and reel," saltglaze. **3.** "Barley" pattern, saltglaze. **4.** Queen's shape, creamware. **5.** Royal pattern, creamware. **6.** Feather-edged creamware. **7.** Spearhead, creamware. **8.** Shell-edged pearlware. Nos. 1–3 also occur in Whieldon-Wedgwood clouded ware, Nos. 4–6 in saltglaze, and No. 8 in creamware. Nos. 4–6 and 8 are original rim names.

bust (or very occasionally an equestrian figure) of Frederick the Great, as well as an eagle, a military trophy, and the molded inscription: SUCCESS TO THE / KING OF PRUSSIA / AND HIS FORCES. As far as I can determine, all the known surviving examples are nine-inch plates, as are all the fragments I have seen from American excavations. However, an advertisement in the *Boston Gazette* for November 13, 1758, offered "White Stone, Prussian & Basket work'd

Plates and Dishes," and a rim sherd from one such dish has been found at Port Royal, Jamaica. Other, rather later border designs were confined to edges rather than the entire rim and occur in what is known as "rope" and "bead and reel" designs. These continued to be made into the 1770's, though it is uncertain whether the more elaborate patterns went quite as late.

In the mid-eighteenth century white saltglaze began to be decorated with incised ornament that was filled with cobalt before firing, great care being taken to brush off all excess color so that the result would be patterns of thin blue lines. This technique has come to be known as "scratch blue," and the bulk of it was confined to the third quarter of the century. (Fig. 36) It was much used to ornament cups and saucers, usually with simple floral motifs, and also to decorate and inscribe pitchers, punch pots and loving cups. The ware is fairly common on late colonial sites and is a valuable dating guide. Occasionally one encounters pieces whose scratched lines are filled with brown iron oxide instead of the cobalt-blue. Such examples are invariably early, predating "scratch blue," and are attributable to the 1720's and 1730's. The earliest recorded specimen is a pocket flask inscribed in brown slip Ƚ M 1724.

Although common utility wares such as washbasins and chamber pots were produced in white saltglaze in large quantities up to the 1760's, the imported German blue and gray stonewares of the Rhineland commanded a considerable part of the British market. (Fig. 93) At that time the English saltglaze potters made a strong

Fig. 36. English white saltglaze tea bowl with "scratch blue" decoration. C. 1760–75. Diam. 3".

and successful bid to oust the German imports by producing chamber pots, mugs, and pitchers in "scratch blue" but allowing the
excess cobalt to remain roughly within the areas of the incised design in the German manner. They also adorned all three items with
sprig-molded medallions bearing the cypher of George III and
sometimes a profile portrait of the monarch. (Fig. 37) This debased
"scratch blue" was at its best in the period 1765–75, but it continued much later and was exported to America after the Revolution, the royal medallion being replaced by a poor rendering of the
Great Seal of the United States. It seems unlikely, however, that the
ware was made after about 1790. (For additional details, *see*
CHAMBER POTS.)

There were a number of variations on the white saltglaze theme,
the most distinctive being the black-bodied stoneware with a white
slip on the inside and thin trails of white pipeclay in bands around
the exterior. This black-and-white ware was fired in a regular saltglaze kiln which gave the white slip its characteristic pitted surface.
The ware was patented by Ralph Shaw of Burslem in 1733, at
which time it was described as "a curious ware . . . whose outside
will be of a true chocolate colour, striped with white, and the inside

Fig. 37. Chamber pot of debased "scratch blue" stoneware with
crowned cipher medallion of George III. Probably Staffordshire,
c. 1770. Ht. 4¾".

118

Fig. 38. Dark-brown to black stoneware jug and can decorated with a white slip on the inside and similar bands and ornament on the outside, fired in a saltglaze kiln. This distinctive combination conforms to the description of a ware that Ralph Shaw of Cobridge tried to patent in 1732 but which was subsequently widely copied. Staffordshire, c. 1740. Ht. of jug 4⅜".

white, much resembling the brown chinaware, and glazed with salt."[8] Shaw's patent, however, was withdrawn as invalid in 1736 and the ware was produced by other potters up to about 1750. (Fig. 38) Another, rather later technique was the coating of white saltglaze with cobalt blue mixed with clay and frit to produce a lustrous blue surface known as "Littler's blue," being named after William Littler of the porcelain factory at Longton Hall, who, with his brother-in-law Aaron Wedgwood, developed it. Contrary to popular belief the blue coating could be applied before firing and did not require a second trip through the kiln. The principal items treated in this way were teapots (often with tripod zoömorphic feet and collar necks), pitchers, and bowls. (Fig. 39) They were fre-

[8] Quoted in Simeon Shaw: *History of the Staffordshire Potteries* (London, 1900), pp. 146–7; first pub. Hanley, Staffordshire, 1829.

Fig. 39. White saltglaze teapot coated with a cobalt-colored leadglaze known as "Littler's blue," with additional overglaze oil-gilding. Staffordshire, c. 1760. Over-all ht. 3¾".

quently decorated after firing with white enamel or oil-gilding. Exact dates for the production of "Littler's blue" saltglaze have not been established, but a bracket of c. 1750–65 seems probable.

The stoneware revolution launched by Dwight in the late seventeenth century was not his only achievement, for he also produced a hard dry-bodied redware that was described as "red porcelain" and which had been developed in the Netherlands in imitation of a similar product, a dry-bodied red stoneware, imported from Yi-hsing in China. Dwight sued the brothers Elers (two Dutch silversmiths turned potters) for stealing his secrets and his workmen, but that did not prevent them from setting up shop in Staffordshire and producing a comparable, finely turned redware that now bears their name. Many students have erroneously attributed all dry-bodied redwares to Elers, but the truth of the matter is that they were produced by many Staffordshire potters well through the eighteenth century; Josiah Wedgwood called his version "rosso antico." Teapots are the most common form, usually copying silver shapes and adorned with very thin and cleanly molded sprigged ornament in rococo motifs. (Fig. 40) Some pieces are marked on the base with pseudo-Chinese marks, and some bear the figure 45 in their design, a political jibe referring to the forty-fifth edition of John Wilkes's radical newspaper *North Briton*, which was published in 1763 and brought down the wrath of injured majesty upon his head. Other teapots in this ware were engine-turned (a technique that Wedgwood claimed to have introduced into the potteries in 1763) and some were lead-glazed, obscuring the characteristic red body. Both varieties are found in American contexts of the third quarter of the eighteenth century, but as far as is known, not one truly Elers piece has yet been recovered from a colonial site.

A comparable dry-bodied stoneware in black (fired in a reducing atmosphere) began to be made after 1750, and this was brought to prominence by Josiah Wedgwood, who used it for his famous Etruscan vases and called it "black Basaltes." It continued to be used, however, at a more mundane level by the makers of thrown, cast, and engine-turned tea wares, and in 1787 there was at least one

Fig. 40. Dry-bodied redware teapot decorated with sprigged ornament comprising a crowned griffin within a rococo cartouche flanked by floral scrolls and topped by a figure of Britannia. The 45 on the latter's shield refers to the 45th edition of John Wilkes's radical newspaper, the *North Briton,* which was issued on April 23, 1763. Staffordshire or Leeds. Ht. 3″.

Fig. 41. Bowl of rich, lead-glazed redware with sprigged decoration in white pipeclay commemorating the capture of Portobello by Admiral Vernon in 1739. Probably from the factory of John Astbury. Staffordshire. Ht. 3".

Burslem potter who made nothing but "black and red china ware."[9] The unglazed black ware retained its popularity after that of the red declined, in part because it had become the fashion to use it in times of mourning.

The new techniques developed by Dwight, Morley, and the Elers brothers marked the beginning of the English conquest of the world-wide ceramic market, which it enjoyed well through the nineteenth century. The finely turned redwares were quickly copied and adapted by other potters, notably by John Astbury, who

[9] "Survey of the Counties of Stafford, Chester and Lancaster, compiled and published at Namptwich in 1787 by Wm. Tunnicliffe, land surveyor, of Yarlet near Stone; and a Directory of the principal merchants and manufacturers"; quoted in Josiah Wedgwood and Thomas H. Ormsbee: *Staffordshire Pottery* (New York, 1947), pp. 65–6.

is reputed to have stolen secrets from the Elers brothers. The products known as "Astbury ware" are hard, red-bodied, and lead-glazed to give them a ginger or light-chocolate-brown surface generally decorated with sprig-molded birds, squirrels, flowers, and royal arms, in white pipeclay. (Fig. 41) Such pieces usually belong to the second quarter of the eighteenth century and were actually made by numerous factories. A similar product, though with pipeclay ornament usually confined to bands at rims, feet, and spots on the tops of handles, was made at Newcastle-under-Lyme by Samuel Bell in the period 1724–44. However, almost identical wasters from an unidentified kiln have been found at Bristol.

Another easily recognized class of thinly turned wares is loosely known as "Jackfield" and was produced in quantity from about 1745 to 1790. The body is usually fired to purple or gray and is coated with a deep-black glaze, which in turn was often oil gilded in floral and foliate designs. The Jackfield Pottery in Shropshire was founded by Maurice Thursfield in about 1750, but a very similar ware was made in the same period by Thomas Whieldon and others in Staffordshire, Whieldon's having a red body and a slightly more brilliant black glaze. Both produced tea wares and pitchers, and examples are common on American sites in contexts of the 1760's. (Fig. 42)

The most important development of the eighteenth century was the gradual perfection of a thin, hard-firing, pale-yellow or cream-colored earthenware which, after a preliminary firing, could be dipped in a clear glaze. Pioneer efforts in this direction were made by Thomas Astbury and Thomas Whieldon, who mixed ground flints into the clay that yielded white saltglaze when high-fired and produced a cream-colored body at lower temperatures. The combination of the cream body and the dip glaze resulted in the production, in about 1750, of tea wares colored under the glaze in purple, blue, brown, yellow, green, and gray, which are generally known as "clouded" wares. (Fig. 43) The new cream body was used in virtually every manner that the current state of ceramic technology permitted. Excavations in Williamsburg, Virginia, in 1966 have revealed fragments of a cream-bodied teapot coated with "Littler's blue" and of the same shape as the blue saltglaze pots. Such a piece was hitherto unknown. The 1750's also saw the emergence of tea

Fig. 42. Teapot and jug having a hard, purplish body coated with a lustrous, black leadglaze often known as Jackfield ware. The teapot has a crabstock handle and is oil-gilded, while the jug is undecorated and has a handle typical of white salt-glazed stoneware. Shropshire and Staffordshire (?), c. 1755. Jug ht. 6⅝".

wares cast in relief in naturalistic designs derived from pineapples and cauliflowers. All these colorful styles are loosely classed as "Whieldon ware," though here again Whieldon was not the only manufacturer. Their date range covers the period 1750–75.

In the late 1750's Josiah Wedgwood was in partnership with Whieldon, and together they worked to refine the cream-colored body and also to produce an even-firing, rich green glaze. The latter was achieved in 1759, and therefore the presence of wholly green-glazed cream-bodied wares on archaeological sites provides a valuable *terminus post quem*. In that year Wedgwood went into business on his own at Burslem, initially to produce the new green ware. It was not particularly popular, however, and he quickly turned his attention to the further refinement of the plain cream-colored ware, later dubbed "Queen's ware" and now universally known as creamware or (most misleadingly) "Leeds ware." It is impossible here to pursue the history of Wedgwood or to discuss the many elaborate innovations that were his. It is the creamware that is of archaeological importance, for it turns up on most American sites of the late eighteenth and early nineteenth centuries. Indeed, so ubiquitous was it that I have found fragments on the now-uninhabited edge of a steaming volcano on the West Indian island of Nevis and high on Admiral Rodney's lookout point on tiny Pigeon Island off St. Lucia.

Wedgwood may have perfected creamware by 1762, at which date he is said to have presented a caudle and breakfast set to Queen Charlotte, the plates' rim design being taken from "barley" pattern molds used on saltglaze but omitting the barley. (Fig. 35) Shortly afterward, according to some authorities, the raised ridges that extended across the marly, dividing it into panels, were omitted, creating a style known as the "Royal" pattern—traditionally created at the request of George III. Somewhat later, perhaps around 1765, an entirely new rim design using relief-molded fronds was produced and called "feather-edged." (Fig. 45) The ornament was simultaneously cast in white saltglaze, perhaps by Wedgwood himself, who

Fig. 43. *Left*: front of Whieldon-type dinner plate, cream-colored body, molded in the barley pattern and decorated with "clouded glazes" in gray, green, yellow, and brown. *Right*: the back of the same plate decorated with purple manganese "tortoise-shell" stipple. Staffordshire, c. 1760. Diam. 9½".

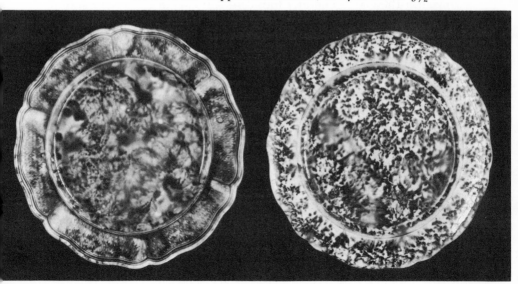

Fig. 44. Creamware dinner plate in the Queen's shape and decorated with a popular Liverpool transfer print in black. Staffordshire, c. 1770. Diam. 9¾".

Fig. 45. Creamware plate with feather-edge and chinoiserie decoration in underglaze blue. The house-and-willow motif was widely used on pearlware in the last years of the century. This plate with pseudo-Chinese mark on the back. Possibly from the Wedgwood factory. Staffordshire, c. 1770. Diam. 9½".

made that ware as late as 1772. In 1765, Wedgwood obtained, seemingly by default, an order to make a large tea service for the queen "with a gold ground and raised flowers upon it in green,"[1] and presumably it was after the delivery of it that he was able to style himself "Potter to Her Majesty." The date at which the "Queen's" and "Royal" shapes were so named is uncertain, but these and the "feather" and "shell" patterns (see below) are listed and identified in Hartley, Greens, and Co.'s design catalog published at Leeds in 1783.

In the early 1770's Wedgwood also produced a cockled-edged creamware with the rim underglaze-painted in blue, green, red, or very occasionally in "wine" purple, a style appropriately known as the "shell-edged" pattern. Although the blue-painted shell edge was used on Bow porcelain as early as c. 1755, this design is rare in creamware and belongs predominantly to a later period. Creamware plates were also produced prior to 1783 with entirely plain rims, but these are generally found in contexts of the 1790's and of the early nineteenth century. The problem of how early creamwares became popular in America has yet to be resolved. One would expect to find them appearing at least by 1765; however, I have yet to encounter them in Virginia inventories before 1769.

As a general guide it may be assumed that the earliest pieces are of a deeper yellow than are the later and that the difference has become pronounced by about 1785. This is by no means infallible,

---

[1] Ann Finer and George Savage, eds.: *The Selected Letters of Josiah Wedgwood* (London, 1965), p. 34; Josiah Wedgwood to John Wedgwood, June 17, 1765.

as Wedgwood himself admitted having difficulty in maintaining the same color from batch to batch.

Wedgwood had no patent on his creamware and anybody who knew how to make it did so in factories ranging all the way from Bovey Tracey in Devonshire to Leeds in Yorkshire and Glasgow in Scotland. However, the products of Wedgwood, and of the Leeds factory of Hartley, Greens, and Co. (later Humble, Hartley, Greens & Co.) are given most of the credit by collectors and curators. It is frequently difficult, even impossible, to tell the difference between the two, while few attempts have been made to pin down the peculiarities of the many other factories. An important exception is provided by the creamwares of William Coles's Swansea pot house (established 1764), which were often decorated in "scratch blue," the best-known pieces being tea jars incised with names and dates in the 1770's; e.g.,

the
Mary Evans : 5 : 1775

From 1765 to the early 1770's Wedgwood was experimenting with the production of a whiter ware than creamware which, in 1779, he termed "Pearl White." The body had an increased flint content and the glaze contained a small quantity of cobalt to negate its natural yellow tint. Wedgwood, himself, did not then think it was in his best interests to produce the ware in quantity, but other potters who were not so committed to creamware had fewer reservations, and by 1787 in Burslem alone there were no fewer than eight factories producing "china glaze, blue painted," and one "enameller and printer of cream colour and china glazed ware."[2] This last is of considerable importance in that it shows that transfer-printing on "china glaze" or "pearlware" had begun by 1787.

The art of mass production transfer-printing was claimed to have been perfected by Messrs. Sadler and Green of Liverpool in about 1756. However, prints in red and purple on white saltglaze plates that have long been attributed to them are now believed to have been made three years earlier by Messrs. Janssen, Delamain, and Brooks at York House, Battersea. Be that as it may, Sadler and Green are best remembered for their black prints on Liverpool

[2] See fn. 9, p. 122.

Fig. 46. Blue shell-edged serving dish, pearlware, with Chinese-house motif painted in underglaze blue. C. 1790–1800. Length 18¾".

delftware tiles and also for their black printing on creamware. (Fig. 44) But printing in underglaze blue on earthenwares does not seem to have become popular until the end of the century, though it had been used on Battersea enamels as early as 1753. Much more common was the continued use of hand-painted decoration (the design first stenciled in charcoal onto biscuit) in underglaze blue, most frequently in simple Chinese-house patterns borrowed from porcelain. This motif occurs on creamware before 1775 (Fig. 45) and continued on pearlware to about 1805 or 1810. (Fig. 46) From about 1795, pearlware was also decorated in underglaze polychrome colors usually in floral or geometric patterns. Examples of 1795–1815 are generally in soft pastel hues, but thereafter, and continuing to about 1835, directly stenciled floral patterns in bright blue, orange, green, and a pinkish red became the vogue among the poorer classes.

Pearlware is undoubtedly the most common ceramic item found

Fig. 47. Pearlware soup plate decorated with a fine quality "willow pattern" print in underglaze blue; the unusual rim print occurs on pieces attributed to Swansea. C. 1810–20. Diam. 9½".

on sites of the early nineteenth century; it can readily be distinguished from late creamware by the way in which the glaze appears blue in crevices of footrings and around handles. Creamware glaze, on the other hand, appears yellow or green in the crevices. It should be noted that the earliest transfer-printed "willow pattern" and related chinoiseries occur on pearlware. (Fig. 47) The "willow" design is thought to have been conceived by Thomas Milton at Chaughley; it was then shipped to China for use on export porcelain, and the first products arrived back in England in 1792, thus making all "willow pattern" Chinese porcelain later than that date. Its use as a transfer for pearlware seems to have occurred around the same time, though the only-known dated piece is marked "Thomasine Willey 1818." By 1820, pearlware was on its way out, being superseded by various forms of hard white wares and semiporcelain that are extremely difficult to date with accuracy (unless bearing factory marks) and which ran parallel to the "stonechina" produced by Spode in 1805 and Mason's celebrated "Ironstone China" of 1813.

Although pearlware had been used for everything from close-stool pans to eggcups, it is most commonly found in the form of shell-edged plates with rims painted in either blue or green. (Fig. 35) The early examples (c. 1780–95) are generally well painted, the brushwork being drawn inward to create a feathery edge (not to be confused with the molded creamware feather-edged pattern), but later, as the market swamped the craftsman, it was common to sweep the brush laterally around the edge to produce a mere stripe. Such debasement is usually found on examples dating later than 1800 or 1805, though it does occur earlier—just as better examples were made later. Sometimes the rims were embossed with feather-like devices, fish scales, floral garlands, and even human and animal figures, and although they were often better painted than their plain cousins they are unlikely to date prior to 1800.

Next to the blue- and green-edged plates, pearlware is most commonly found on early nineteenth-century sites in the shape of mugs, jugs, and bowls decorated in horizontal bands of color—black, green, light brown, pale blue, etc.—that were sometimes used to fill in broad, engine-turned grooves. Such products are collectively known as "annular wares" and were popular in the period 1795–1815. (Fig. 48) The technique, however, may go back as far as c. 1785 when found on a creamware rather than on a pearlware body. At the other end of the scale, a thicker and drab yellow ware, decorated with bands of light blue and with raised ridges in white, continued to be made both in England and America into the present century. Belonging to the earlier group, but continuing into the second half of the nineteenth century, was the ware known as "mocha," which is characterized by brown fernlike ornament on otherwise annular wares, the fronded device being created from a mixture of tobacco juice and urine. (Fig. 48, top left) The earliest-dated example is marked 1799. It should be noted that collectors frequently call all annular wares "mocha," though the latter term actually refers only to vessels decorated with the fern ornament.

Fig. 48. Examples of hand-painted pearlware from a privy pit at McKnight's Tavern in Alexandria, Virginia, and discarded c. 1810. *Top*: 1. mocha-decorated bowl in green and brown, with a blue rim border flanked by dark-brown lines; 2. engine-turned bowl with annular decoration, the cut body slip dark-brown, the rim border sienna-brown flanked by blue lines; 3. bowl with annular decoration, reddish-brown lines below a green band at the rim. *Bottom*: 1. saucer with typical Chinese-house motif in underglaze blue; 2. blue shell-edged plate with an American eagle rather crudely executed in polychrome colors, the wings, tail, arrows, and stars brown, the leaves green, the head and stripes golden-yellow, and the upper shield blue; 3. engine-turned mug with over-all blue slip cut through to expose the pearl body and alternating bands decorated with dashes of black or deep orange. All probably Staffordshire. Diam. of plate 7⅜".

Also occurring on banded pearlware are zones of cloudlike swirling lines generally in black, blue and white, and which are sometimes known as "finger-painted" wares. The technique was popular during the first twenty years of the nineteenth century. The effect was rather like marbling, which was yet another ornamental technique used on late eighteenth- and early nineteenth-century annular wares. This involved the swirling together of different colored slips, most commonly green and light-brown, and the result is generally known as "marbled" ware. It should not be confused with those wares that achieved rather similar effects by the mixing of two or more body clays of different colors to create veins that went right through the ware and could be seen both inside and out. These are known as "agate" wares and were used extensively by the Astbury-Whieldon partnership in the mid-eighteenth century, not only for such things as teapots but also for toys and mantle ornaments, and even for knife handles.

A much thicker agate ware combining a red and a yellow clay was common in the third quarter of the eighteenth century and much of it reached America. These light-brown bowls and dishes are often decorated with yellow bands at the rims frequently incised with rouletted impressions. (Fig. 49) The blending of two clays of different colors, however, was not always done for ornamental purposes; it could also serve to make a poor clay more workable. This

technique was characteristic of the potters of the Buckley district of North Wales, where vast quantities of coarse earthenware cream-pans, storage jars, and pitchers were made and shipped to the colonies from Liverpool. (Fig. 50) The vessels are characterized by their purplish-red bodies which, when broken, show an agatelike section of yellow and red clays, and which are coated with a thick, black glaze. The potting itself is as ponderous as the ware, and the body exteriors are frequently heavily ribbed, while the rims of pans are generally square and hammerlike. I have yet to see this ware in contexts dating earlier than 1720 (though I am told it has been found in one of the late seventeenth century), but it becomes increasingly common thereafter, the trade seemingly terminating at the time of the Revolution.

A second coarse earthenware exported to America in large quantities during the eighteenth century came from North Devon and was confined to creampans and to jugs and small storage jars, though the latter are uncommon after about 1720. The principal characteristics of this ware are a pink body (often with a gray core) heavily gravel-tempered, a light-brown to apple-green glaze and, on the creampans, gently curving folded rims. It is possible that this ware was being shipped over along with the sgraffito slipwares throughout the second half of the seventeenth century (*see* p. 104); however, fragments are uncommon on sites dating before 1680. It

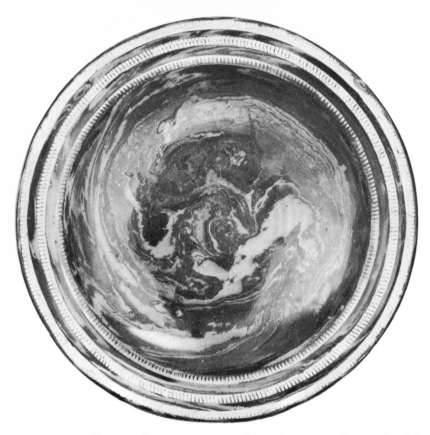

Fig. 49. Coarse agateware dish using pale-yellow and pink-firing clays beneath a lead glaze that turns them to a deep yellow and reddish brown. The same blend would eventually be used for 19th-century doorknobs. This dish is characteristically decorated around the rim with bands of rouletted pipeclay, which appear yellow beneath the glaze. Probably Staffordshire, c. 1760. Diam. 8⅝".

seems likely that the trade declined in the mid-eighteenth century and that it ended before that of the Buckley ware.

Falling between the coarse earthenwares and the refined table-wares of the Astbury-Whieldon class were the ornamental slipwares that continued to be imported into the American colonies up to the 1770's. The majority of these were buff- to yellow-bodied and decorated with combed lines in iron oxide or manganese under a clear to pale-yellow glaze. (Fig. 29) Mugs, pictures, posset cups, chamber pots and chambersticks were made in this ware in Staffordshire and also in Bristol, and it is virtually impossible to distinguish between them. These sources also made what might be termed the reverse style, covering the buff bodies with a black or dark-brown slip and trailing pipeclay designs over it before glazing. Both types were frequently decorated around the rims and necks with light or dark spots causing some collectors to dub them "dot" wares. The earliest versions go back to the last quarter of the seventeenth century in both Staffordshire and Bristol, at which time bowls and mugs were often straight-sided, while the combing was generally zigzagged or in panels of alternating combed scales and stripes. Although applied horizontally, the designs appeared vertical in the period c. 1680–1700, whereas, thereafter, the combing ran in more or less parallel lines around vessels that were invariably bulbous-bodied below straight collar necks with slightly everted lips.

There seems to be as yet no evidence that slipware dishes were made in Bristol in the eighteenth century. They appear to have been a Staffordshire speciality, the most common varieties being made from a buff to yellow clay thinly mixed with pink, and sweepingly combed in black over a white slip and beneath a lead glaze to create a wasplike effect of yellow and black stripes. As a rule of thumb it may be contended that the later the piece the straighter and wider the stripes. Other variations occur with light trailed

Fig. 50. Storage jar of black, lead-glazed Buckley earthenware, the body a mixture of pink-firing and yellow clays. The ribbing and thick, angular rim are typical of the ware. Found at Yorktown, Virginia. Imported from Flintshire, North Wales, Mid-18th century. Ht. 10⅝".

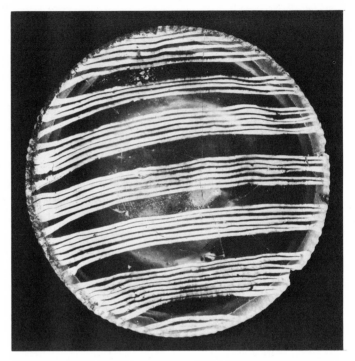

Fig. 51. Slipware dish, the body buff with inclusions of pink-firing grog clay, the decoration in dark brown under a trailed white slip appearing yellow under the leadglaze. Staffordshire, c. 1750. Diam. 13½".

stripes over a black slip (Fig. 51) or with a skillfully marbleized blend of white and dark- and light-brown slips. These dishes are difficult to date with accuracy, but they do not seem to have been imported after the Revolution.

The combed and marbelized Staffordshire dishes are common on American eighteenth-century sites, but they do not by any means represent the best of English slipwares. Those began in the late seventeenth century with the famous signed pieces by Thomas Toft and Ralph Simpson, decorated with lions, royal portraits, a mermaid, Adam and Eve, and other popular designs generally executed in trailed red-brown slip on a white ground. The Toft dishes are all attributable to the 1670's, while those of Ralph Simpson run as late as 1707. I know of no examples yet having been unearthed

on American sites. Another elaborate dish type does occur, however, both on American and West Indian sites, the pieces being
shaped over bat molds decorated with incised ornament that was
thus transferred in relief to the dishes. The latter were then painted
in brown slip over a white (yellow when glazed) ground. The
technique was used in the late seventeenth century on dishes with a
crude piecrust edge, the designs usually very "rustic" in the shape of
equestrian figures. The technique was revived in the second quarter
of the eighteenth century, when the designs ranged from standing
figures to clock faces and suns with human faces in the centers. (Fig.
29, bottom left) These later dishes usually have a notched rim similar to those of the combed dishes, and the decoration is much more
restrained than was that of the earlier examples.

I have said nothing about English porcelain on the ground that
anyone capable of recognizing the difference between it and the
ubiquitous Chinese export wares will already have referred to books
devoted wholly to the subject. It is enough to note that English
porcelains are generally less hard than the Chinese, that they are
often decorated with transfer prints in underglaze blue (while the
Chinese are always hand-painted), and that, in the ground, blue-
decorated Bow porcelain tends to lose both its surface and its
decoration—which Chinese never does.

The principal English porcelains found on American sites are
generally confined to tea wares handpainted in underglaze blue and
come from Bow, Worcester, Liverpool, and Caughley, nearly all of
it in the period 1755–75. The distinctions between the various factories are hard to comprehend without the specimens in front of
one, and when the piece is unmarked it is often possible to extract
different attributions from different specialists.

ANON.: *English Pottery Patents Specifications (1626–1863)*. London, 1863.
BEMROSE, GEOFFREY: *Nineteenth Century English Pottery and Porcelain*.
    London, 1952.
COOPER, RONALD G.: *English Slipware Dishes 1650–1850*. London, 1967.
GARNER, F. H.: *English Delftware*. London, 1948.
GODDEN, GEOFFREY: *Encyclopedia of British Pottery and Porcelain Marks*.
    New York, 1964.
——: *An Illustrated Encyclopedia of British Pottery and Porcelain*. New
    York, 1966.

HODGKIN, JOHN E., and EDITH HODGKIN: *Examples of Early English Pottery, Named, Dated and Inscribed.* London, 1891.

HONEY, W. B.: *English Pottery and Porcelain.* London, 1952.

JEWITT, LLEWELLYNN: *The Ceramic Art of Great Britain.* 2 vols. London, 1878.

LEWIS, GRIZELDA: *A Picture History of English Pottery.* London, 1956.

LUXMOORE, CHARLES F. C.: *"Saltglaze" with the Notes of a Collector.* Exeter, Eng., 1924.

MANKOWITZ, WOLF, and REGINALD HAGGAR: *The Concise Encyclopedia of English Pottery and Porcelain.* London, 1957.

NOËL HUME, IVOR: *Pottery and Porcelain in Colonial Williamsburg's Archaeological Collections.* Williamsburg, Va., 1969.

RACKHAM, BERNARD: *Early Staffordshire Pottery.* London, 1951.

RACKHAM, BERNARD, and HERBERT READ: *English Pottery.* New York, 1924.

RAY, ANTHONY: *English Delftware Pottery in the Robert Hall Warren Collection, Ashmolean Museum, Oxford.* London, 1968.

TAGGART, ROSS E.: *The Frank P. and Harriet C. Burnap Collection of English Pottery in the William Rockhill Nelson Gallery.* Kansas City, Mo., 1967.

TOWNER, DONALD C.: *English Cream-Coloured Earthenware.* New York, n.d. (c. 1959).

———: *The Leeds Pottery.* London, 1963.

WATKINS, C. MALCOLM: "North Devon Pottery and Its Export to America in the Seventeenth Century," *United States National Museum Bulletin No. 225,* Paper 13. Washington, D.C., 1960.

See also BOTTLES, Pottery; CHAMBER POTS; DRUG POTS; and TILES.

§ *CERAMICS, European*
(except STONEWARE, Rhenish, q.v.)

Prior to the introduction of the Navigation Acts of 1651 and 1660 requiring that foreign goods (including most ceramics) should be imported into England and her colonies only aboard English ships, pottery reaching America came from more or less any available source. Colonists fresh from England brought along many of their household wares, which included Netherlandish, Italian, and Iberian maiolica, Rhenish stonewares and slipwares, and Flemish earthenwares. Unfortunately, little close dating has yet been established for any of these early wares, save for the Rhenish stonewares and

Fig. 52. Dish decorated with heavy white slip, copper green, and with sgraffito detail in the central medallion cutting into the red body beneath, all under a leadglaze. Wanfried, c. 1625. Diam. 12¼".

one variety of slipware. The latter, the red-bodied sgraffito ware from Wanfried (often described as Hessian) was frequently dated and ranged from the 1580's to about 1625. (Fig. 52) Examples found at Jamestown are confined to deep dishes with short, vertical rims and two horizontal loop handles striped with pipeclay, as also are the interiors of the rims. The interior walls and base are coated with a white slip, cut through in designs which frequently include human figures in Elizabethan garb and which are filled in with copper green over the slip. Later versions from the Limburg area are more "peasant" in concept, though retaining the same basic shape. In place of the sgraffito ornament the potters made use of thickly trailed white slip in bands, swags, and crosses, some of which were overlaid with copper before firing under a lead glaze. Such wares are found on American sites prior to 1650.

Attributable to the same period is a group of red-bodied bowls, plates, and dishes with slightly rising pad feet, folded or everted rims, and decorated with marbleized patterns predominantly in white and green under the rich lead glaze. A few omit the green and appear as red and white; some use the latter on the outside and the more elaborate coloring on the inside, and others include touches of black-firing iron oxide. These all belong to the same class as the costrels discussed on p. 77 and are of French or Italian origin. The same ware and bowl forms were also coated with white slip and decorated with sgraffito motifs (usually birds or flowers) and with haphazard splashes and lines of green and a golden yellow.

Other imports belonging to this period include chafing dishes and cooking vessels in a coarse buff ware coated with a drab-green gallena glaze. These are considered to be Flemish. Much further up the ladder of elegance, and alongside the Dutch delftware, is the maiolica found at Jamestown and attributed to Lisbon. The designs are frequently in the classic Wan Li and Ming styles, but others belong to the simple geometric and floral motifs favored by the Dutch and English potters of the second quarter of the seventeenth century. The Lisbon ware seems to have been painted in rather darker blues than its northern counterparts, the designs often outlined in purple or black. Extreme caution, however, should be exercised in making such an attribution, for it is probable that a number of pieces hitherto claimed for Lisbon are actually Dutch.

The 1651 Navigation Act was re-enacted by Charles II as a further attempt to limit Dutch maritime influence, and it remained in force until 1685. In the meantime the Staple Act of 1663 had specifically stated that goods bound for the colonies could only be shipped through English ports after paying English duties. In 1672 a proclamation was issued banning the importation into England of "any kind or sort of Painted Earthen Wares whatsoever (except those of China, and Stone bottles and Juggs)."[3] Four years later the restriction was further defined, customs officers being ordered to seize and destroy all imported painted earthenwares "as well white

[3] Order in Council, July 22, 1672; quoted in Aubrey J. Toppin: "The China Trade and Some London Chinamen," *English Ceramic Circle Transactions*, No. 3 (1935), p. 40.

Fig. 53. Faïence dish, the tin glaze often with a blue tint, the decoration in pale blue outlined in dark blue to black, the back coated with a rich brown (iron-oxide) leadglaze. The type occurs on French sites before 1755, but on British colonial sites it is generally confined to the Revolutionary period. Rouen. Length 17″.

or Blew or any other colours."[4] Thus, the trade in European maiolica, faïence, or Delftware was prevented from reaching the British American colonies, for thenceforth it was not to be bought in English ports even if the ships were ready to carry it. The embargo remained in force until 1775 and served also to prevent any open trade in European porcelains. It is true that the London port records from 1697 to 1776 do show that some earthenwares, including "galley dishes," were imported from Europe in small quantities, but it is apparent that most of the trade was reduced to German and Flemish stonewares shipped from Holland. Nevertheless, to all intents and purposes it may reasonably be contended that, apart from stonewares, very little European pottery reached the British American colonies in the eighteenth century.

[4] Ibid. (Order in Council, November 24, 1676.)

141

Even though the embargo on "Painted Earthen Wares" was lifted in 1775, the taste for it had declined virtually to vanishing point. The British ceramic industry was in full gear, and even immediately after the Revolution it was busily designing specifically to feed the new American markets. The European potters really had no chance to step in. The only attempt of any consequence was made by the French potters of Rouen, whose once famous faïence industry was in a rapid decline. Newspaper advertisements in the period 1778–84 refer to the importation of "Rhoan" and "Deph and Roan wares," and there is little doubt that these relate to a heavy, red-bodied faïence, brown-glazed on the exteriors or undersides and white on the interiors of cooking wares and on the upper surfaces of dishes. Only the dishes seem to have been decorated, generally in purple or in blue outlined in black, the designs being limited to very simple baskets of flowers in the centers and bands of hatched and dotted zones divided by sprays of short, radiating lines around the rims. (Fig. 53) They are a far cry from the celebrated and highly complicated lambrequin motifs for which Rouen was famous earlier in the century. The late dishes were either round or oval and sometimes of large size, while the plain wares (their white tin glazes frequently pink-tinged) ranged from tubular-handled pipkins to pans, saucers, and strap-handled storage jars and mixing bowls.

Virtually no serious ceramic studies have yet been attempted on erstwhile French colonial sites in the United States, and therefore the dating of French pottery is extremely sketchy. It is reasonably certain that little or none came into the British colonies by sea from c. 1660 to 1775, but that does not mean that it did not filter down in that period from Canada or eastward from Louisiana. A few possible pieces of Moustiers faïence have turned up in contexts of the mid-eighteenth century, generally decorated in pale blue, while a few painted in bright yellow have been attributed to Marseilles. Most common among the anomalies encountered on sites having French contacts are plain white plates decorated around the rims with a single stripe of pale blue. Such plates are common on French colonial sites in contexts of the mid-eighteenth century, but their full date range is unknown. There are also numerous faïence cups with patterns below the rims similar to those found on Rouen dishes and having bodies decorated either with small foliate sprays or a checker pattern in blue, sometimes with small manganese crosses at the intersections. These, too, seem to occur in contexts of the mid-century. Plain white faïence plates, usually with shell-like edges, occur on Revolutionary sites, and these two are almost certainly French, though it is not known whether they came over with French troops or were merely the products of trade with France during the war years.

Fig. 54. Iberian storage jar with thickened rim and vestigial arched handles, coarse redware streaked externally with white slip, and lead-glazed on the inside. Common in the period c. 1745–80. Ht. 32½".

Spain's principal contribution seems to have been the manufacture of bulbous or carrot-shaped jars with small round necks and rims, and no feet, which were originally intended as containers for olives or olive oil. They range from the sixteenth century well into the eighteenth century, have a buff to yellow body and sometimes a thin, pale-green glaze on the inside. Another variety has a flat base, slopes up and outward to a generously rounded shoulder topped by a vestigial folded rim. The jars stand some 18″ in height, have a sandy-pink body, and were apparently sealed by flat clay discs of the same ware. The exact place of origin for any of these "olive" jars has not been determined, but it seems reasonable to classify them as Iberian, and the flat-rimmed variety seems to have been confined to the eighteenth century. The same may also be said of another group of much larger ollae which stand 3′ and more in height, have vestigial crescent-shaped handles on either side below the shoulder, and possess thick folded or rolled rims. The ware is generally a flowerpot red, sometimes coated on the outside with a buff or yellowish slip and on the inside with a clear (appearing brown) lead glaze. The body areas capped by the handles are sometimes decorated with molded relief medallions bearing initials or religious symbols; others have letters painted in pale-buff slip. In the latter instances the slips over the bodies are often confined to groups of vertically painted stripes. (Fig. 54) Although the shapes of the jars found on British colonial sites seem to be fairly standard, many variations of size and ornament are to be seen in the West Indies where they are still used by the peasants as water containers. We know that George Washington had six at Mount Vernon and kept soap in them, and two fine specimens have been recovered from British vessels sunk during the Battle of Yorktown. Most of the examples so far recovered seem to date in the period 1745–80. The prevalence of these large jars on British colonial sites has led some authorities to conclude that they are of English manufacture. But although examples are not uncommon in England, the only specimens with a known history that I have encountered there were brought back early in the present century from Portugal.

As already noted, any British-American trade in European porcelains in the eighteenth century was thwarted by the embargo on painted wares, but undoubtedly a few pieces came over amid the effects of European immigrants. A few pieces of yellowish and semidecomposed porcelain decorated in pale underglaze blue have been found in unstratified contexts in Williamsburg and are attributed to Tournai in Belgium, a center that began porcelain production in 1751. Fragments of marked German Fürstenburg blue and white porcelain have been found on the site of the glass factory built by John Frederick Amelung, who arrived in Maryland from Bremen in 1784, and it is highly probable that many more such people had similar wares. However, this is a very specialized field and it is unlikely that the average archaeological historian will be able to pin them down. I mention them only as a reminder that all porcelain found on American sites (particularly those of the late eighteenth century) does not have to be either Chinese or English.

DE JONGE, C. H.: *Oud-Nederlandsche Majolica en Delftsch Aardewark.* Amsterdam, 1947.

GOGGIN, JOHN: "The Spanish Olive Jar," in *Indian and Spanish Selected Writings.* Miami, 1964. pp. 253–98.

HAGGAR, REGINALD: *The Concise Encyclopedia of Continental Pottery and Porcelain.* New York, 1960.

HANNOVER, EMIL: *Pottery and Porcelain, a Handbook for Collectors.* 3 vols. ed. by Bernard Rackham. London, 1925.

LANE, ARTHUR: *French Faïence.* London, 1946.

NOËL HUME, IVOR: "Rouen Faïence in Eighteenth-Century America," *Antiques,* Vol. 78, No. 6 (December 1960), pp. 559–61.

RACKHAM, BERNARD: *Italian Maiolica.* London, 1952.

See also BOTTLES, Pottery; and STONEWARE, Rhenish.

§ *CHAMBER POTS, BEDPANS, and CLOSESTOOL PANS*

As happened in so many other areas, silver was initially the chamber pot style setter, and the silversmiths' designs were copied by both the pewterers and the potters. Both silver and pewter pots are naturally extremely rare, but those of pottery are among the most common items found on archaeological sites dating after about 1640.

Fig. 55. Coarse earthenware chamber pots with reeded handles and decorative cordoning below the rims. *Left*: buff body with apple-green glaze, discarded c. 1700; rim diam. 8½". *Right*: red body with tortoise-shell-brown leadglaze, discarded c. 1730.

The majority of ceramic pots were of course lead-glazed earthenware; and although they generally kept pace with popular taste their proportions and construction quirks are those of individual local potters, and they can only be accurately dated or associated with a particular factory when wasters are found in stratified contexts on the kiln sites. As a general rule of thumb, however, it may be said that, although the shapes varied widely in the seventeenth century, by 1700 styles had settled down and the majority of pots of the first half of the eighteenth century were squat-bodied with a small cordon about 1″ below the rim. (Fig. 55) The rim itself was flat, more than 1″ in width, and was angled slightly upward. Handles were generally attached to the underside of the rim and were drawn out as a strap and anchored to the lower body with no ornamental terminal. The better handles were usually given a little character by the addition of single or double reeding, but this was a purely ceramic technique not borrowed from metal and so was very much a matter of potter's choice. Body colors varied from buff coated with an apple-green glaze, to red covered with a purplish-brown tortoise-shell leadglaze. By the later eighteenth century the flat rim had generally been replaced by a simple folded or rolled lip.

The earliest delftware chamber pots date from about 1650, at which time they were broad-rimmed and very squat with the tin glaze having a marked pink tinge to it. (Fig. 56, left) By 1700, the pots had become taller and the flat rim had been replaced by a

Fig. 56. English delftware chamber pots. *Left*: a typical 17th-century form, the handle oval in section, discarded c. 1660. *Right*: with strapped handle and slightly everted rim, discarded c. 1730; ht. 5".

gently flaring lip creating an ogee curve projecting up and out above the belly of the bowl. The lip was generally neatly folded under. The handle was attached below the rim and looped out as a concavo-convex strap which was anchored at the lower end with a square, thumbed terminal. (Fig. 56, right) The majority of these pots were plain, but some were elaborately decorated in cobalt, the handles laterally striped, the rims sponged, and the bodies decorated in the Chinese manner. Both the plain and colored pots of this form can be dated in the period 1680–1735. Thereafter, delftware chamber pots lost their pleasing contours, the ogee curve being much reduced and the rim bending only slightly outward above a much taller body. The shoulder cordon present on most chamber pots up to 1735 is usually absent from these later examples, and the glazes, instead of being a pinkish white, lean toward a drab off-white with a hint of blue. Such pots seem to have continued to the end of the eighteenth century, probably being made (along with washbasins and cheap drug pots) at least ten or fifteen years after the production of decorative delftwares had ceased.

English white saltglaze chamber pots followed much the same eighteenth-century evolution as that of delftware. They appeared in the 1730's beautifully potted and with splendid ogee curves from rim to belly. Cordons at the shoulder and above the base were cleanly and dramatically formed, while the plain strapped handles produced a paradoxical combination of delicacy and strength. They were, in short, among the most splendid creations of the saltglaze potters' art. But by the 1760's the glory had departed, along with the ornamental cordons and the fine, sweeping rims. In their stead the bodies had become taller and the rims smaller. Later still, in the last quarter of the eighteenth century, the pots were made with rolled rims and with thick handles thinly reeded at the edges, a style apparently borrowed from creamware.

Creamware pots were extremely simple, having plain bulbous bodies, flat angular rims, and handles that were anchored at the top—not to the rim, but to the body itself (as also were those on the saltglaze pots)—while the lower extremity was pressed against the body and sometimes molded into a classical acanthus-leaf terminal. Most of these pots belong to the last quarter of the eighteenth century, and their shape was adopted more or less contemporaneously by the makers of pearlware—who were frequently one and the same. The majority of pearlware chamber pots were decorated around the body with rich blue transfer prints of pastoral scenes, with similar smaller scenes (or occasionally rude verses) on the interior bottoms and with floral printing around the flat rims. Such pots were common up to about 1835, by which time the more refined bodies of stone china with clearer glazes replaced the pearlware and its blue-tinged surface.

Although considerable quantities of coarse earthenware and delftware chamber pots were available for the public convenience in the first half of the eighteenth century, the potters of the Westerwald district of the Rhineland thought they saw a popular need and immediately proceeded to fill it. By 1710, large supplies of gray stoneware chamber pots were being shipped to England, all decorated with bands of cobalt at the shoulders and above the bases, the space between ornamented with three impressed and cobalt-filled rosettes and, between these, two facing, crowned, and bellicose lions, sprig-molded and encircled with cobalt. (Fig. 92, bottom left) This was the same combination that had previously been used to decorate the bodies of cheap gray stoneware bottles attributed to Bouffioulx in Belgium. It is possible that the ubiquitous Rhenish chamber pot was first manufactured at Bouffioulx, for an example in the collection of Colonial Williamsburg has an entirely different rim from those of all others I have encountered, and instead of

Fig. 57. Examples of ornamental chamber pots, red-bodied with pipeclay turned yellow under the leadglaze. "Metropolitan" slipware. The central example is inscribed PRAISE GOD AND HONOUR THE KING, and the right BE MERRY AND WIS . . . The inscribed specimens c. 1660 and the other possibly somewhat earlier. Ht. of right example 6¼".

being decorated with three stamped rosettes has a single armorial medallion flanked by the two lions, a characteristic of the Bouffioulx bottles. This pot with its armorial medallion (initialed IM)—and one in my own collection with oval wreaths in place of the usual rosettes (Fig. 92 bottom right), plus three comparable fragments found in Williamsburg—are the only examples out of the thousands I have seen that appreciably differ from the usual shape and pattern.

The new and hardy stoneware was an instant success, and Rhenish chamber pots were to be found in most British and colonial homes for at least the next fifty years. The rims of these pots were flat-topped and wedge-shaped in section, and the bodies, being mass produced, are often marked with the vertical "chattering" of the templates. The only change that occurred between c. 1710 and 1760 was that the later pots were slightly taller and had a smaller diameter than the early examples. Handles remained the same throughout this period, being heavy, decorated with multiple reeding, and having rolled or folded lower terminals.

By the 1760's, the English white saltglaze potters were awakening to the fact that the Germans were milking a sizable market that could well be exploited by home firms, and they proceeded to develop a coarse "scratch blue" technique (*see* CERAMICS, British, p. 117) which could serve for tavern tankards, pitchers, and chamber pots—the principal gray stoneware export products of the Rhineland. In place of the lions and stamped rosettes the English potters took the idea of the ornamental royal cipher medallions from the Rhenish jugs and stuck them on their chamber pots, surrounding them with incised foliate ornament filled and overflowing with cobalt. (Fig. 37) The majority of medallions bore the initials of George III, but some went further and used a profile relief portrait of the monarch. These patriotic pots were as successful as the Westerwald stonewares before them and they are to be found on most late colonial American sites—though it is possible that patriotism may not have been at the fountainhead of their popularity.

So successful was the new chamber pottery that the pearlware potters copied the same designs (painted instead of incised), using rather fatter portraits of the king or more crudely molded GR ciphers. Such pots may be dated in the period c. 1785–1810, but it is possible that they run even later, for a white earthenware example found in Jamaica still retains the earlier influence but bears a coronation portrait of Queen Victoria.

Cylindrical-handled bedpans dating from the first years of the eighteenth century are occasionally found in green-glazed coarse earthenware (copying a pewter form), but it seems that they were not particularly popular. Closestool pans resembling truncated cones some 18″ in height and with flat, everted rims, were made in both white saltglaze and creamware in the second half of the eighteenth century. The only American examples that I have yet encountered, however, were made at Yorktown, Virginia, in the second quarter of the century in a soft buff earthenware coated with a slightly orange-yellow glaze.

§ *CLOCKS and CLOCKCASES*

No archaeologist is very likely to excavate a complete clock mechanism, and the prospect of discovering an intact long-case standing in a hole in the ground is smaller still. Nevertheless, parts do turn up, and they are rarely recognized for what they are.

The common household timepiece of the seventeenth century

was the brass lantern clock, which normally stood about 16″ high from foot to finial and, until the latter part of the century, generally had only one hand. The hemispherical bell was suspended above it on four brass straps which anchored into as many finials atop the pillars that provided the supporting framework for the entire mechanism. The finials, usually identical to a fifth that projected above the bell, were frequently elaborately knopped and are sometimes mistaken for miniature andiron terminals. The feet at the lower ends of the pillars were usually ball-shaped with a small nipple projecting below. However, these clocks were more often hung on the wall than stood on a bracket. The space at the front and two sides, between the four capping finials, was occupied by ornamental, cut-out brass plates in the shape of a pair of dolphins or, occasionally, a lion and unicorn supporting a crown and shield of arms. The front plate was usually engraved, while those at the sides were not. The chapter rings on which the Roman numerals were incised were often silvered and became larger in the latter part of the seventeenth century, some of them extending beyond the flanking pillars. The dials themselves were generally elaborately engraved and bore the name of the maker and his place of work. These clocks were powered by weights and chains, and weights of considerable elaboration are sometimes found. The example shown in Figure 58, Number 3, was recovered along with part of the crown of a lantern clock by divers excavating in the submerged city of Port Royal, Jamaica.

The inconvenience of the weight-driven clock, which could not be moved from room to room, led to the invention of the spring-powered table clock, which appeared in the early sixteenth century and was refined in the seventeenth. In 1657 the pendulum was invented, and thereafter clocks became infinitely more accurate. By about 1660, they began to be housed in wooden cases and are called bracket clocks, regardless of the fact that they were meant to be stood on tables. At the same time the weight-driven lantern clock began to disappear inside a tall case, the dial being enlarged in the manner of the bracket clock and embellished with applied cast-brass ornaments to fill the corners of the square window outside the chapter ring. Such ornaments are known as spandrels, and the majority have the face of a cherub as their central motif. Those of the seventeenth century generally had wings; later types used filigree and

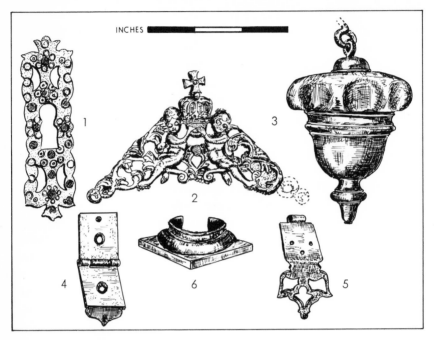

INCHES

1

2

3

4

6

5

Fig. 58. Clock accessories, all of brass. **1.** Keyhole escutcheon with stamped floral ornament; c. 1700–40. **2.** Rough casting for a spandrel, probably copied from one made in or near Philadelphia in the second quarter of the 18th century. **3.** Weight, perhaps for a small lantern clock; lost in 1692. **4.** and **5.** Hinges for clockcase doors; c. 1760–70. **6.** Capital or base for a pillar flanking the face on the hood of a long-case or bracket clock; c. 1740–70. Nos. 1 and 4–6 were found on the site of Anthony Hay's cabinetshop, and No. 2 is from the Geddy brass foundry, both in Williamsburg, Virginia. No. 3 was recovered by divers from what may have been a silversmith's shop at Port Royal, Jamaica.

foliate scrolls to flank the face, though such examples are known as early as 1695. In the 1740's a number of Philadelphia clockmakers were using locally made spandrels in the shape of two cherubs supporting a large crown, and an example of both this and the cherub's-face variety have been found in unfinished states at the Geddy brassworking site in Williamsburg, Virginia. (Fig. 58, No. 2, and *see* pp. 12–14) While the vast majority of spandrels, both American and English, were cast in brass, a few are encountered in gilded lead or pewter.

Any fragments of brass plates with numerous holes drilled in them, pivoting levers, cogs, wheels, drums, and spindles that are found in excavations are liable to be clock parts, and to a specialist they may be both significant and fairly closely datable. Weights for tall case clocks are sometimes found; as these were never visible, they are sometimes extremely crude, being no more than sausage-like lumps of lead with a hook at one end. Those of better quality were encased in copper or brass. I have never heard of a pendulum bob being found, but it may be useful to note that in the last quarter of the seventeenth century the cases were often made with circular windows in their doors so that the swinging pendulum could be seen. Bobs used during that period are therefore likely to have been gilded or painted in other metallic colors.

Most frequently encountered and easily recognizable are items of case hardware: finials, keyhole escutcheons, hinges, and the bases and capitals for hood orders. Bracket clocks generally had a locking door and consequently a keyhole escutcheon; those that had no pillars flanking the door usually embellished the frame by adding a matching blind escutcheon opposite the keyhole. The same was true of tall case clocks. The latter had a much larger escutcheon on the door of the body, usually tall and narrow and not to be mistaken for one from a drawer. They do not differ, however, from escutcheons used on the doors of secretaries and other cupboards. The styles follow those of contemporary furniture hardware—e.g., stamped ornament being common up to 1730 or 1740—but cast devices and entirely plain plates follow thereafter. Hood doors that had no locks were held shut by small brass or iron latches, the latter often painted to match the color of the case.

Hinges were generally of the butt variety but possessed a right-angled projection to one of the plates so that the thin door could be anchored by screws through both its thickness and its back. (Fig. 58, Nos. 4 and 5) Equally distinctive, but baffling when you have never seen one before, are the brass bases and capitals that decorated the hood orders, each having but three sides so that they not only enclose the projecting diameter of pillar but fit snugly into the corners of the hood itself. (Fig. 58, No. 6)

BAILLIE, G. H.: *Clocks and Watches, a Historical Bibliography*. London, 1951.
GOAMAN, MURIEL: *English Clocks*. London, 1967.

§ *COINS, TOKENS, and JETTONS*

The serious numismatist will not expect to find much in a book of this kind that will be either new or. helpful to him. Consequently, I have elected to address this section to the archaeologist, restricting it largely to those coins of low denomination which are most often encountered on British colonial sites of the seventeenth and eighteenth centuries. (Figs. 59 and 60) Recognizing, however, that later coins are frequently unearthed on colonial sites, and that when corroded they are hard to distinguish, I have strayed far beyond the bounds of the book's title to summarize the evolution of United States copper through the nineteenth century. (Fig. 61)

The quantity of English silver coins found in excavations is extremely small and I have yet to see a gold coin from a colonial site; indeed, coins of any sort were always in short supply. When the colonial period began, much Elizabethan silver was still in circulation and a number of sixpenny pieces (some cut in half) have been recovered. It is important to note that Elizabeth faced left and, except in rare instances, had a Tudor rose in the field behind her head. A shield bearing the arms of England occupied the reverse, with the date placed above it and within the legend.

Before going any further it may be well to explain the meaning of the various standard numismatic terms which I shall not only use here but which the excavator or collector will need to employ when describing his coins.

Blank:	The metal disc before striking.
Die:	The incuse impression on a metal block used to stamp the design onto the blank.
Graining:	Commonly called milling, the crenelation of the edges of some coins, a technique intended to prevent clipping.
Clipping:	The practice of trimming the edges of silver coins to obtain free bullion.

Coins, Tokens, and Jettons

Obverse (obv.): The front face of a coin, generally bearing the portrait of the monarch.

Reverse (rev.): The back of the coin.

Type: The central design.

Legend: The inscription, generally around the type.

Field: The blank area between the type and the legend.

Exergue: The area below the obverse or reverse type, usually containing the date.

AV: Gold.

AR: Silver.

AE: Copper or bronze.

mm: Mint mark (as distinct from mm: millimeters).

At the beginning of the seventeenth century, England was suffering from an alarming shortage of small coinage, and what there was was of silver so small and thin that it was in constant danger of being lost. In an attempt to solve this problem James I issued a license to Lord Harrington in 1613 to mint a quantity of copper farthings that were tin-plated to resemble the familiar silver. But their metal content was far less than a farthing and the public lacked confidence in them. The coins were about 15mm. in diameter and had a scepter and crown on the obverse and a crowned harp on the reverse. The license later passed to the Duke of Lennox (Fig. 59, No. 1) and, in the reign of Charles I, first to the Duchess of Richmond (1626) and then to Lord Maltravers (1634), all of whom produced little copper coins very similar to the original Harringtons (though without the tinning); it is difficult to tell the difference between them. In 1636 the licensed coinage was changed to put a rose on the reverse instead of the harp, and these "rose" farthings (13mm. in diameter) became the common small change of the nation. (Fig. 59, No. 2) In 1644, during the British Civil War, Parliament ordered that no more licensed coins should be struck, whereupon the English tradesmen began to produce their own token coinage bearing their names and addresses in the legend and their business signs as the type. (Fig. 60, Nos. 24 and 25) Examples of both the "rose" farthings and the slightly larger English tradesmen's tokens of the mid-seventeenth century have been found in excavations at Jamestown.

Realizing that the minting of coins by private individuals was not in the Crown's best interests, Charles II ordered the production of an official copper coinage, but this was not issued until 1672. The coins were halfpennies and farthings bearing the royal portrait to left on the obverse and the legend CAROLVS•A•CAROLO, with Britannia seated as the reverse type. The halfpennies measured approximately 31mm. in diameter and were issued in 1672, 1673, and 1675, while the more common farthings had a diameter of 22mm. and are dated 1672–5 and 1679. (Fig. 59, No. 4) In 1684, in an effort to encourage the flagging Cornish tin industry, Charles II issued farthings of tin, pierced through the center by a square copper plug to discourage forgeries. The date was moved from the exergue and was embossed on the edge along with the Latin inscription to read NVMMORVM + FAMVLVS + 1684. Silver penny, twopenny, and threepenny pieces continued to be minted during the reign of Charles II, but they were still small and thin and are not nearly as common as the smaller denominations of copper and tin. It should be noted that, contrary to the opinion of many archaeologists, no copper penny was issued in England until the advent of the "cartwheel" pennies of 1797. (Fig. 60, No. 20)

Because copper coins remained in fast circulation for considerable periods of time they are often extremely worn when found in archaeological excavations; they are also generally heavily encrusted with copper salts, a combination making them difficult to identify and date without cleaning and careful study. The portrait of the monarch, however, is generally the most easily discernible feature,

Fig. 59. British low-denomination coins, James I to George II. Examples all copper and obverse unless otherwise stated. 1. James I "Lennox" farthing. 2. Obv. and rev. Charles I rose farthing. 3. Commonwealth pattern pewter farthing. 4. Charles II farthing, 1673. 5. Charles II Scottish bodle. 6. James II tin farthing, date illeg. 7. William and Mary tin farthing, 1690. 8. William III farthing, 1699. 9. William III rare tin halfpenny, 1697. 10. William III halfpenny, 1700. 11. Obv. and rev. George I halfpenny, 1720. 12. Obv. and rev. George I Irish "Wood" halfpenny, 1723. 13. George I farthing, 1720. 14. George II young-head farthing, 1734. 15. George II old-head farthing, 1754. 16. George II young-head halfpenny, 1733 (forgery?). 17. Obv. and rev. George II old-head halfpenny, 1744 and 1757. All full size.

1

2

3

4

5

6

7

8

9

10

11

12

13

14

15

16

17

and some clue to his or her identity can be obtained from determining which way the profile faces. They were as follows:

Monarch	Reign	AV and AR	AE and Tin
Elizabeth I	1558–1603	left	—
James I	1603–25	right and left	—
Charles I	1625–49	left	—
Commonwealth	1649–60	Cromwell left	—
Charles II	1660–85	right	left
James II	1685–8	left	right
William & Mary	1688–94	right	right
William III	1694–1702	right	right
Anne	1702–14	left	left
George I	1714–27	right	right
George II	1727–60	left	left
George III	1760–1820	right	right
George IV	1820–30	left	left
William IV	1830–7	right	right
Victoria	1837–1901	left	left

Fig. 60. British low-denomination coins, all copper unless otherwise stated, George III; British tokens; and German jettons. **18.** Obv. and rev. George III halfpenny, 1772 and 1775. **19.** Obv. and rev. George III Virginia halfpenny, 1773. **20.** Obv. and rev. George III "Soho" penny, 1797. **21.** Obv. George III "Soho" twopence, 1797. **22.** Obv. and rev. George III penny, 1807. **23.** George III halfpenny, 1806. **24.** Privately minted tradesman's token inscribed [obv.] R.K.B. AT THE WINDMILL, [rev.] WITHOUT TEMPLE BAR, 17th century. **25.** Rev. brass tradesman's token inscribed [obv.] ISAAC WARDOCK. OYLEMAN. I. I., [rev.] IN SVFFOLK STREET. 1666. HIS HALFE PENNY. **26.** James II pewter token coinage apparently minted for use in the West Indian and American colonies; equestrian portrait on the obverse; shields with the arms of England, Scotland, Ireland, and France all chained together on the reverse, with the legend VAL. 24 PART. REAL. HISPAN. **27.** Rev. typical late 18th-century tradesman's halfpenny token, with the legends [obv.] LONDON & MIDDLESEX. HALFPENNY, [rev.] JOHN BEBBINGTON. FOR. CHANGE. NO. FRAUD. **28.** Obv. and rev. typical brass jetton by Hans Crauwinckel of Nuremberg, c. 1580–1610. **29.** Brass jetton of superior quality, same maker and date as No. 28. **30.** Rev. brass jetton by Wolff Laufer of Nuremberg, 1618–60. All full size, and all (except No. 19) found in the River Thames at London.

18   19

20   21

22   23

24   25   26   27

28   29   30

James II followed in his brother's numismatic footsteps and issued tin halfpennies and farthings, the halfpennies only having the
copper plug. These were issued in 1685–7 and the farthings in
1684–7. (Fig. 59, No. 6) William and Mary did the same, issuing
both tin halfpennies and farthings from 1689 to 1692 (Fig. 59, No.
7), some having one date on the edge and the next in the exergue.
They also issued copper halfpennies and farthings in 1694. After
the death of Mary, William is generally supposed to have issued
only copper halfpennies (1695–1701) and farthings (1695–1700),
though I have a tin halfpenny of 1697 in my own collection of coins
from the River Thames. (Fig. 59, No. 9) It should be noted that
some of the copper coins of 1698 and 1699 have the date at the end
of the reverse legend rather than in the exergue.

No copper coins were issued in the reign of Queen Anne, although a 1714 farthing was in production at the time of her death.
A good deal of gold and silver, however, was produced in all denominations from five-guinea pieces down to silver pennies. After
the Act of Union with Scotland in 1707, the royal arms on the
reverses were changed, the English leopards and the Scottish lion
being emblazoned together (per pale) on single shields at top and
bottom. (*See* p. 306.) Thereafter the coinage should be termed British rather than English.

Following the design adopted for the belated Queen Anne
farthings, the copper coinage of George I was characterized by a
pronounced ridge encircling the legend of both obverse and reverse
as well as by prominent crenelation beside the edge. The first issues
of both halfpennies (1717–19) and farthings (1717–18) were
thicker and smaller than any that came afterward, and these are

Fig. 61. Examples of United States half- and one-cent copper
and copper-alloy coinage. *One-cent*: (Nos. 1–7 obv. and rev.,
8 and 9 obv. only.) 1. Fugio type, 1797. 2. Wild-haired Liberty,
wreath type rev. (as opposed to chain), 1793. 3. Liberty-cap
type, 1794. 4. Draped bust, 1794. 5. Turban head, 1808. 6.
Coronet type, 1817. 7. Braided hair, thin features, 1844. 8.
Flying eagle, 1858. 9. Indian head, 1860. *Half-cent*: (Obv.
only.) 10. Flowing-haired Liberty facing left, with cap, 1793.
11. Similar design facing right, 1794. 12. Draped bust, 1803.
13. Turban head, 1809. 14. Coronet and braided hair, 1854.
All full size.

1

2

3

4

5

6

7

8   9

10   11   12   13   14

known as the "dump" series. The same design features continued throughout the reign on slightly larger and thinner pieces minted in each year from 1719 to 1724. (Fig. 59, Nos. 11 and 13) For the next five years no copper was issued, and when the mint began to pour again, George II had been on the throne for two years. It was to be a long reign requiring two coinage portraits of the king, the "young" and the "old" heads. The young-head halfpennies were issued through the years 1729–39 and the farthings through 1730–7 and in 1739. (Fig. 59, Nos. 14 and 16) The old-head halfpennies were minted in every year from 1740 to 1754 with the exception of 1741, but the farthings were much more sporadic, appearing only in 1741, 1744, 1746, 1749, 1750, and 1754. (Fig. 59, Nos. 15 and 17) Because both the young and old heads of George II face left it is often difficult to distinguish between them when they are badly worn—and the total absence of new copper coins from 1755 to 1770 ensured that most of them endured long, hard use. Two pointers are worth remembering, however: the ribbons on the laurel wreath at the neck are short and more or less straight on the young head, while they are long and more "ribbony" on the old. The second clue is provided by the spacing of the letters R E X on the obverse of the young-head coins and REX on the old.

The first copper issue of George III was similar in style to that of the old-head coinage of his predecessor, but owing to a shortage of copper and its resulting high price, none was issued until 1770. Halfpennies were then minted in each year up to and including 1775 (Fig. 60, No. 18), while farthings began in 1771 and missed 1772. From 1775 until 1797 there was no further minting of copper, and once again the lack of official small change prompted merchants, manufacturers, cities, and counties to issue their own tokens (Fig. 60, No. 27), occasionally in denominations as high as the half crown. In addition to momentary tokens, merchants also began to issue purely advertising pieces, a practice also adopted in America, and early nineteenth-century Boston tokens have been found as far south as Virginia. Most of the English tokens were produced for use as money to fill the gap left by the royal mint. The most vigorous gap filler, however, were the forgers who copied (in brass or underweight copper) the regular issues of Georges II and III. It has been estimated that by 1775 approximately 60 per cent of the copper coins then in circulation were forgeries; the large number of them found on colonial sites tends to support this surprising proportion. While the majority were straight copies of the official issues (sometimes using dies stolen from the mint), others exhibited minor changes, such as replacing the GEORGIVS•III•REX legend with the name BRVTVS SEXTVS, thus enabling the forger, if caught, to plead that his was a token and not a forgery of the king's coinage, the latter an offense punishable by death.

In 1797 a second and entirely new copper issue appeared. It had two revolutionary features: being struck in James Watt's new steam-powered presses and being worth almost its weight in copper. These huge coins were known as "cartwheels" and were issued in two-penny (Fig. 60, No. 21) and penny denominations; halfpenny and farthing patterns were also struck but never issued. They were made under contract at the Soho refinery in Birmingham and have the word SOHO amid the waves beneath the shield of Britannia on the reverse. The legend on both the obverse and the reverse is incuse on a raised collar surrounding the field. In 1799 the Soho mint produced both a halfpenny and a farthing, both with a grained line around the edge giving the coins a sandwich appearance. The obverse bears the extended legend GEORGIUS III DEI GRATIA REX. On the halfpenny the date is in the usual place beneath the seated Britannia, but on the farthing it was moved to the obverse, replacing it with the legend 1.FARTHING.

A fourth and final issue for the reign of George III (the third from Soho) had the same graining on the edge as the 1799 issue but reduced DEI GRATIA to •D:G• on the obverse, placing the date beneath the bust, and leaving the reverse exergue blank. Pennies were minted in 1806 and halfpence and farthings in 1806 and 1807. (Fig. 60, No. 22)

As few British coins dating after 1775 are likely to be found on United States sites, our Canadian neighbors must forgive me for not pursuing the subject beyond the reign of George III. Instead, I must go back to the earlier mintings designed for use in Scotland and Ireland, for both are liable to be found on American colonial sites.

The Scottish low denominations were the bawbee, or sixpence, and the bodle, or twopenny piece (Fig. 59, No. 5); these were minted in the reign of Charles II with a left-facing portrait on the obverse and the Scots thistle on the reverse (bawbee 1677–9 and bodle 1677–8). William and Mary also faced left on bawbees of 1691 to 1694, but the bodles (1691–4) had the royal cipher instead of the portraits on the obverse. The William III bawbees (1695–7) had the obverse portrait to left while the bodles (also 1695–7) replaced it with a crossed sword and scepter beneath a crown. The date on all these Scottish coins is to be found at the top of the reverse legend and not below the type, as occurs on most of the English. Although Scottish silver ten-shilling and five-shilling pieces were issued in 1705, no copper was minted, and after the union with England only the standard London copper issues were circulated. It is worth remembering, therefore, that any coin bearing a thistle as the reverse type must date prior to 1707.

The history of Irish upper coinage is rather more complicated, for most of the denominations circulating in the seventeenth century were produced under royal licenses. The small copper coinage of England (Harrington, Lennox, Richmond, Maltravers) was used in Ireland during the first half of the seventeenth century and when, in 1660, Charles II issued his first license to Sir Thomas Armstrong, the farthing thus produced bore a striking similarity to one of the Maltravers designs, having crossed scepters and a crown on the obverse and a harp on the reverse. The obverse legend, however, spelled out the name of the monarch CAROLVS II, whereas the English farthings of his father said only CARO, CARA, CAROLV, or CAROLVS. Another presumably licensed minting of Charles II was the so-called "St. Patrick" money in copper halfpence and farthings which showed the saint preaching on the reverse—driving away snakes on the farthings—and with King David accompanying him on the harp on the obverse. There are numerous die variations and none is dated. They are of some significance, however, for in 1682 they were authorized to be used as official currency in the New Jersey colony.

The official regal copper coinage (still under license to Armstrong) began with the minting of Irish halfpennies in the years 1680–4 with the portrait of Charles II facing right on the reverse and a harp under a crown on the obverse. The dates, divided in half, were placed in very small numerals above the harp and flanking the crown. Similar halfpennies were minted in the reign of

James II (1685–8), but no farthings, possibly because Armstrong and his successor Sir John Knox continued to produce the small farthings authorized in 1660.

In 1689–90 James II issued what has come to be known as "gun money" to pay his troops invading Ireland after his abdication in England. These coins were made from any available base metal (melted bells, guns, etc.) and were minted in Dublin and Limerick in denominations from crowns to sixpences. The obverse shows the King's head to left, while the reverse carries the crown and crossed scepters of the Armstrong farthings. The value is shown above the crown—xxx: half crown; xii: shilling; vi: sixpence—with the date above it. In addition, a three- or four-letter abbreviation for the month occurs in script below the crown. I would have been inclined to suppose that these rather specialized coins had little American relevance were it not for the fact that one such sixpence was dug up a few years ago by a laborer laying a foundation for a motel in Williamsburg.

In addition to the gun money, James II also issued some pewter coins in crown (1690), groat (1689), penny (1689–90), and halfpenny (1689–90) values. Some of the halfpennies had copper plugs, and all of them carried the obverse royal portrait to left and the crowned harp as the reverse type. In 1691, during the siege of Limerick, however, gun-money shillings were restruck as halfpennies and farthings, the reverse types showing an extraordinarily skinny-legged Hibernia seated and resting on a harp.

Regal halfpennies were issued in the reign of William and Mary (1692–4) with the usual obverse: double royal portraits to right and a crowned harp on the reverse. Similar coins, with the omission of Mary, were minted for William III in 1696.

No more copper was produced for Ireland until 1722, when William Wood obtained a patent for producing Irish halfpennies and farthings. But as this was done without reference to the Irish parliament the Irish did not warm to the new money, and as a result the Wood money was sent on to America as general currency. They may be distinguished from the "dump" British coins of George I by the fact that the obverse legend includes the words DEI·GRATIA and most obviously by the reverse legend HIBERNIA followed by the date. But even if the legend has been worn smooth it should be possible to tell whether the seated female figure is leaning on a harp (Hibernia) or on a shield (Britannia). Halfpennies were issued in 1722, 1723 (Fig. 59, No. 12), and 1724, and farthings in 1723 and 1724. There was also a rare copper halfpenny of 1722 that shows Hibernia sitting to the front with her body twisted to her right and holding a harp beside her.

The reign of George II produced both halfpence and farthings with the royal portrait to left (both young and old heads) and with the crowned Irish harp on the reverse. Young-head halfpennies were minted in the years 1736–8, 1741–4, 1746–53, and 1755, and farthings in 1737, 1738, and 1744. Unlike the British copper designs that changed to the old head in 1740, the Irish did not receive it until 1760, the year of the king's death. There was, by then, a considerable shortage of small change, and in the same year a series of curious copper halfpence and farthings appeared with a right-facing bust (George III?) on the obverse, with the legend. VOCE POPULI, and Hibernia on the reverse holding a spear in her left hand (as did Britannia) and with her harp leaning unsupported behind her. This extraordinary and unflattering coinage may have prompted the London mint to come to the rescue with an official regal halfpenny in 1766 (four years before it did as much for England). The obverse showed the royal profile to right and with the familiar crowned harp on the reverse. These continued to be issued in 1769, 1774–6, 1781–2, and possibly in 1783, but at no time during that long period were any Irish farthings minted. It was not until 1806 that the Soho mint produced an Irish farthing, one year after it had issued pennies and halfpennies. They all have obverse types rather similar to the British copper of 1806–7, except that the king is shown with long hair flowing over his right shoulder. They differ, too, in that the date appears on the reverse below the crowned Irish harp and not beneath the bust. No further Irish copper was minted in the reign of George III.

The need for coinage of small denominations in the American colonies had been felt as early as 1636 when the Virginia Assembly petitioned the Crown to supply "farthing tokens" as there was "little or no money in the colony";[5] we may suppose that the presence

---

[5] W. Noël Sainsbury, ed.: *Calendar of State Papers, Colonial Series, 1574–1660* (London, 1860), pp. 238–9; Sir John Harvey to Secretary Windebank, London, June 26, 1636.

of Charles I "rose" farthings on archaeological sites at Jamestown are the product of that request. In 1652 silver coins bearing the denomination in Roman numerals (shilling, sixpence, and three-pence) on one side and the letters NE (New England) on the other were minted near Boston. In the same year these were refined to produce less easily counterfeited pieces, the obverse type depicting one of three trees, the willow, the oak, or the pine. The legend read (with a lisp?) IN:MASATHVSETS; while the reverse type comprised the date 1652 over the value XII, VI, or III encircled by the legend NEWENGLAND:AN:DOM.

In 1658, Cecil Calvert, 2nd Lord Baltimore, began issuing silver shillings, sixpences, and fourpenny pieces for use in his Maryland proprietorship. The obverse type comprised a shaggy-haired and popeyed left profile of himself with the legend CÆCILIVS:DNS:TER-RÆ-MARIÆ:&CT. On the reverse was the coroneted Baltimore shield of arms flanked by the denomination and surrounded by the legend CRESCITE:ET:MVLTIPLICAMINI.

During the reign of James II, a token "Plantation" coinage was issued for use in the West Indies and on the continent. These coins were of tin with an equestrian figure of the king as the obverse type and on the reverse four crowned shields of the English arms linked together by chains. The broken legend between the crowns stated that the value was one 24th part of a real (Spanish). They are undated and being of soft metal are generally in very poor condition when found.

In 1694 the Proprietors of Carolina issued a copper halfpenny token having on its obverse an elephant and on the reverse an incription in four lines calling on God to preserve Carolina and the Lords Proprietors. These tokens are thought to have been struck in London along with another similarly dated "elephant" token calling for divine protection for New England.

I have already mentioned the "St. Patrick" tokens that were legal currency in New Jersey in 1682, and the William Wood Irish coinage of George I that was shipped over for general circulation. At the same time (1722), Wood also produced a copper twopence, penny, and halfpenny specifically for the American colonies. The obverse shows the royal portrait to right, the twopenny pieces having a more lengthy legend than usual, GEORGIUS•D:G:MAG:BRI:FRA:

ET•HIB:REX•, for which there was hardly room. The reverse type for all three denominations took the form of a handsomely designed Tudor rose, while the legend read ROSA•AMERICANA•UTILE•DULCI• 1722. In the case of the twopenny piece, however, the UTILE•DULCI (the useful with the pleasant) was placed in a scroll below the rose. This treatment of the legend was utilized for the reverses of subsequent issues (1723 and 1724) for all three denominations, along with the addition of a crown above the rose. None too surprisingly, the Wood coins are known as the Rosa Americana series.

The shortage of copper coinage in the first half of the eighteenth century continued to be a nuisance to shopkeepers dealing in cheap "for ready money" goods, and it seems likely that some colonial merchants copied their English brothers and struck their own tokens. One of these (only two examples are known) seems to have been issued by Richard Dawson in Gloucester County, Virginia, in 1714. The copper token has his name and the date on the obverse around a five-pointed star made from entwined triangles, with a story-and-a-half building (Gloucester Courthouse?) as the reverse type plus the legend GLOUCEST CO [?] VIRGINIA, while in the exergue is the value XII (presumably meaning a shilling).

In 1769 the Virginia General Assembly authorized the purchase of £2,500 worth of current English copper halfpennies, but perhaps because this was the end of the fourteenth-year period in which no English copper was minted, Virginia did not get its money. Instead, the colony began negotiations for the minting of a special Virginia halfpenny, negotiations which dragged on for years. The coins were finally struck in London in 1773, and five tons of them were shipped in September of that year. They were not issued, however, until late February or early March of 1775. Large quantities were immediately bought up and taken out of circulation by people expecting a steep rise in the value of copper. Nevertheless, a great many were circulated in Virginia and beyond, and they are common on sites of the Revolutionary period and seem to have continued in circulation for some years thereafter. On the obverse is the royal portrait to right with the legend GEORGIUS III • R E X (there are numerous minor die variations and associations), while the reverse type comprises a large, almost square shield bearing the arms of the colony: a St. George's cross dividing the royal Hanoverian quartering. To the right are the letters VIRGI and to the left

NIA, while above the shield a crown divides the 17 from the 73 (Fig. 60, No. 19).

Between 1785 and 1787, when the first Federal coinage was issued, a number of enterprising states produced their own small change. Vermont issued copper cents in 1785 with a plough, mountains, and a rising sun on the obverse and a reverse type with rays and stars projecting from a central eye. In the following year it produced another with a profile bust on the obverse and a seated figure resembling Britannia on the reverse. A series of similar cents was issued in Connecticut between 1785 and 1788, the obverse "Georgian" profile facing either left or right with the legend AUCTORI:CONNEC:, the reverse with the seated "Britannia" figure to left with the legend INDE:ET LIB:, and with the date in the exergue. A number of privately minted cents were also circulated in New York; some were similar to the Vermont and Connecticut effort but had the obverse legend NOVA EBORAC, with VIRT.ET.LIB.1787 on the reverse. Another of the same date, but more in step with the times, bore an armed Indian on the obverse and on the reverse an eagle with spread wings. Massachusetts issued cents and half cents bearing similar design motifs from its own state mint in 1787 and 1788. New Jersey, on the other hand, devised its own—a horse's head over a plough for the obverse type with the legend NOVA CÆSAREA, but with the United States shield in the reverse and the legend ★E★ PLURIBUS★UNUM★. In addition, there were many privately circulated tokens which, like the British issues of the same period, were often of high artistic quality.

The first American copper cents issued by Federal authority appear in 1787 using a design described as having on one side:

> . . . thirteen circles linked together, a small circle in the middle, with the words "United States," round it; and in the center, the words "We are one"; on the other side of the same piece the following device, viz: a dial with the hours expressed on the face of it; a meridian sun above on one side of which is the word "Fugio" [meaning: "Time flies"], and on the other the year in figures "1787" below the dial, the words "Mind Your Business."[6]

[6] Journal of Congress, April 21, 1787; quoted in R. S. Yeoman: *A Guide Book of United States Coins* (Racine, Wis., 1967), p. 56.

(Fig. 61, No. 1) These coins are sometimes known as "Franklin" cents on the grounds that the designs have been attributed to Benjamin Franklin, but they are more commonly known simply as "Fugio" cents. They were struck in New Haven, in New York City, and elsewhere; the first products of the official U.S. mint did not appear until 1792, and the first regular issue of cents and half cents followed in the next year.

The large one-cent pieces were slightly smaller than an English halfpenny and went through a rapid evolution in the first year of issue, beginning with a wild-haired "Liberty" to right on the obverse and a linked-chain device on the reverse encircling the inscription ONE CENT over 1/100 and with UNITED STATES OF AMERICA (or AMERI) in the legend. (Fig. 61, No. 2) These soon gave way to a more sedately coiffured "Liberty" with a liberty cap behind her left shoulder, the word LIBERTY above her head, and the date below her neck. The reverse retained the same legend as before, but the chain had been replaced by a wreath, below the knot of which was set the fractional value. (Fig. 61, No. 3) The general design continued until 1796, in which year Liberty acquired a draped bust and lost her cap (Fig. 61, No. 4); she remained thus until 1807. In the following year Liberty turned left, discarded her drapery, and acquired a band bearing her name around her hair. (Fig. 61, No. 5) The date remained beneath the bust, but thirteen stars were added to the field, seven in front of the head and six behind it. The reverse remained essentially the same as before save for the elemination of the fraction, a detail that never reappeared. In 1816 the obverse was refined still further, the headband turning into a coronet, the hair being drawn back into an empire knot, and the stars being evenly spaced around and over the head. (Fig. 61, No. 6) This type survived, with minor variations, until 1857. In that year the first large minting of a new smaller cent began, the obverse design being a flying eagle over the date, confined from beak to tail feathers within the legend UNITED STATES OF AMERICA, this having been moved from the reverse and replaced by a broader wreath encircling the value. (Fig. 61, No. 8) The design was short-lived and was replaced in 1859 by the famous Indian-head cent that continued until 1909 (Fig. 61, No. 9), when it was succeeded by the Lincoln penny.

The half cent evolved in much the same manner as the cent, beginning in 1793 with a wild-haired Liberty to left with the cap behind her (Fig. 61, No. 10) and then, in the same year, turning her around to face right. (Fig. 61, No. 11) The draped bust to right first appeared in 1800 and continued until 1808 (Fig. 61, No. 12); the next year it was followed by the banded head to left with flanking stars. (Fig. 61, No. 13) The latter was the first issue without the 2/100 fraction on the reverse. The new design continued in general production until 1835; thereafter there was no further large-scale minting of half cents until 1849, when the coroneted Liberty occupied the obverse. (Fig. 61, No. 14) These were issued until 1857, when the half-cent denomination was discontinued.

Although I have no space even to summarize the range of European coins that was circulating on colonial American sites, it must be noted that the shortage of small change encouraged the use of foreign silver, particularly that of France and Spain. In the eighteenth century the one, two, four, and eight reals of Philip V of Spain were widely used and many of them were quartered or halved to create proportional denominations.

Returning to the beginning of American numismatic history, it is important to note that many very thin brass pieces are found in sixteenth- and early seventeenth-century archaeological contexts. (Fig. 60, Nos. 28–30) These are frequently mistaken for continental European coins, but were actually jettons or casting counters originally intended as mathematical aids, but which were frequently traded to the Indians, who strung them onto necklaces. The majority were made in Nuremburg and frequently bear the names of their makers in the legends—Hans Krauwinckel (c. 1580–1610); Hans Schultes and Hans Laufer (both early seventeenth century); and Wolf Laufer (c. 1618–60). The most common variety has as its obverse (?) type three crowns and three fleur-de-lis surrounding a rosette, with a legend such as WOLFF:LAVFER•NVRNBERG⋆, and as its reverse type a cross surmounting an orb and enclosed within a border of two lines alternating between three arcs and three v's. The reverse legend for this example reads: ⋆RECHA•PFENIG:MACHER•IN. Nine out of ten jettons belong to this general class, though they vary in diameter from about 10mm. to 25mm. (Fig. 61, No. 28) But some produced by the same makers are

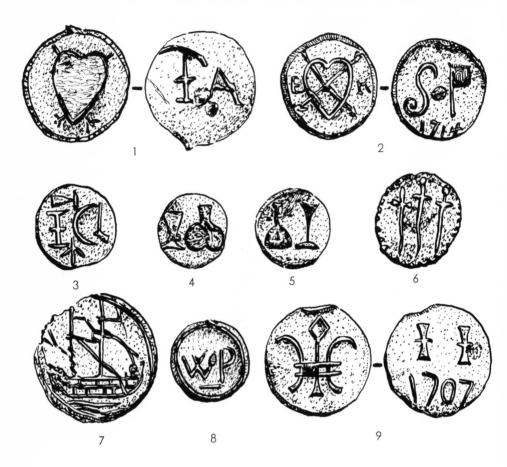

Fig. 62. Examples of 17th- and 18th-century lead tokens, all English. **1.** and **2.** Arrow-pierced heart types. **3.** J. C. with drinking glass and tobacco pipe. **4.** and **5.** Bottle and glass. **6.** Three swords. **7.** Ship. **8.** W. P. **9.** Stylized fleur-de-lis, and possible J. J. over the date 1707. All full size.

splendid examples of the German medalists' art. Hans Krauwinckel is particularly known for his classical and allegorical designs (Fig. 61, No. 29), and Wolf Laufer produced jettons specifically for the foreign markets, notably for the French, these having the portrait of Louis XIV on the obverse with the legend LDV:XIIII•D G:FR:ET•NAV: REX and the crowned fleur-de-lis of France on the reverse. (Fig. 61, No. 30) One might be prompted to take it for a French counter were

it not for the reverse legend ••★WOLF•LAVFER•RECHPF:MACH•IN•N:B••★.
Both the simple and the elaborate forms have been found in
excavations at Jamestown, and it is reasonable to expect that they
are still buried on many another early colonial site.

Although practically all the jettons found in archaeological contexts date prior to the mid-seventeenth century, I should note one
exception that I found inside an eighteenth-century shoe on the
foreshore of the River Thames. It bears a portrait of Queen Anne
(1702–14) on the obverse and on the reverse a fair representation of
the back of the British gold coinage with the legend identifying the
piece as a product of Johann Jacob Deitz, maker of counters. That
this brass counter might have been accepted by the uneducated as a
gold half guinea may not have been entirely accidental. Thicker
brass counters in direct imitation of the famous "spade" guineas
were produced in large quantities in England in the reign of
George III and used to entrap the unwary at fairgrounds.

In conclusion, a word must be said about that least-understood
item in the numismatic field, the lead token. These vary in size
from 10mm. to 35mm. and are decorated on one or both sides with
a great variety of devices ranging from meaningless groups of lines
to owners' initials, anchors, swords, fleur-de-lis, castles, horsemen,
stags, and even a crow. (Fig. 62) I have encountered three dated
specimens, 1635, 1707, and 1714, and datable devices from the arms
of Elizabeth I to a portrait of Edward VII. The earliest-recorded
date is 1624. The purposes to which these tokens were put were
doubtless varied and are certainly debatable. Some, decorated with
a wine bottle and a glass (Fig. 62, Nos. 4 and 5), may have been
communion tokens, but those with an additional tobacco pipe certainly were not. (Fig. 62, No. 3) It may be that both types were
associated with taverns. Because the majority of these lead tokens
bear no identifiable names or signs, it must be supposed that they
were not widely circulated and therefore had no monetary value as
did the copper and brass tradesmen's tokens of the seventeenth and
eighteenth centuries. The only reasonable alternative would seem
to be that they were given to workmen in exchange for piecework,
who then cashed them at the end of the job. Because so many have
been found near wharves, it is possible that they signified units of
merchandise carried or loaded. While their original purpose re-

mains in question, the final use to which some of them were put is in no doubt at all. Two holes were punched close to the centers and they were thus transformed into buttons.

BARNARD, FRANCIS P.: *The Casting Counter and Counting Board*. Oxford, Eng., 1916.

BOYNE, WILLIAM: *Trade Tokens Issued in the 17th Century in England, Wales and Ireland by Corporations, Merchants, Tradesmen, etc.* George C. Williamson's edn. London, 1889 (reprinted 1967).

CALDECOTT, J. B., and G. C. YEATS: "Lead Tokens," *British Numismatic Journal* 1st Ser., Vol. 4 (1907), pp. 317–26.

CRAIG, WILLIAM D.: *Coins of the World 1750–1850*. Racine, Wis., 1966.

DALTON, R., and S. H. HAMER: *The Provincial Token-Coinage of the Eighteenth Century*. London, 1910 (reprinted 1967).

MONTAGU, H.: *The Copper, Tin and Bronze Coinage and Patterns for Coins of England from the Reign of Elizabeth to That of Her Present Majesty*. London, 1885.

NEWMAN, ERIC P.: "Coinage for Colonial Virginia," *Numismatics Notes and Monographs*, No. 135, American Numismatic Society, 1956.

SEABY, HERBERT A.: *The English Silver Coinage from 1649*. Rev. edn. London, 1957.

————: *Standard Catalogue of British Coins*. Rev. edn. London, 1968.

SEABY, HERBERT A., and MONICA BUSSEL: *British Copper Coins and Their Values*. Rev. edn. London, 1968.

YEOMAN, R. S.: *A Guide Book of United States Coins*. Rev. edn. Racine, Wis., 1968.

§ COMBS

Most of the examples found in excavations are common hair combs of a type that persisted throughout the seventeenth and eighteenth centuries, being rectangular in shape with teeth of different sizes along two opposite sides. They were known as head combs, double-tooth combs, or close and narrow-tooth combs, and were made from black thorn, box, horn, ivory, bone, or tortoise-shell (hawksbill turtle), and occasionally in lead (*see* p. 37). The double-edged comb continued to be used by the poor until the very late nineteenth century, generally in bone and later (c. 1860) in vulcanite, and was then often known as a lice comb. Beard combs of the seventeenth century were similar to those for the head except that they were shorter, being more or less square. Wig combs were made with teeth rather widely spaced, each one rounded instead of being rectangular in section as were those of the normal hair combs.

HOLME, RANDLE: *An Academie or Store House of Armory & Blazon*, pp. 12–13. London, 1905. Manuscript completed in 1682.

§ *COOKING VESSELS of Iron and Copper Alloys*

While this heading could embrace a great many varieties of pots, there is space to consider only the two most common types, the bulbous, iron cooking pot or cauldron and the single-handled copper-alloy skillet. Unfortunately, neither of them can be dated at all closely, as traditional shapes continued to be made in a great many places over a long period of time.

Both types had a common ancestor in the fourteenth century, a tripod-legged bronze pot, having a flaring collar neck and with two earlike handles projecting from it and anchored to a shoulder. Such pots were suspended over the fire by means of a pair of hinged iron hooks. The skillet evolved from this by simply removing the ear handles and substituting a single straight handle projecting from one side. In early examples (fifteenth and sixteenth centuries) the handle was reinforced with a loop beneath it which gave it the appearance of retaining one of the original ears and simply projecting the top of it outward into the long handle. These early copper-alloy pots invariably had one or more molded cordons around the body, while the legs, which were sometimes as long as the pots were high, ended in zoömorphic feet.

In the seventeenth century the skillet body began to resemble a modern saucepan, straightening the sides and replacing the flaring rim with another that was no more than a thickening or slight everting of the upper wall. A reinforcement beneath the handle still occurred from time to time, but was usually very angular and no longer resembling the ear. Feet continued to be shaped and the legs were sometimes fluted. In the seventeenth century, and possibly later, the upper surfaces of skillet handles were often decorated with molded inscriptions giving either the name of the founder or some pious reminder, such as Yᵉ•WAGES•OF•SIN•IS•DEATH•. Many of these vessels seem to have been made in Kent and Devonshire. They continued to be used throughout the eighteenth century, but the legs were generally plain and tapered almost to a point.

One other skillet type should be mentioned, though I have only encountered a single example in a well-dated archaeological context. This was a sheet-copper or brass pot similar in shape to the body of the later skillets, but which seated in an iron collar to which the legs and handle were welded. The detachable pot usually had its everted rim rolled over an iron wire or rod, while the iron legs had flat, everted feet and the handle ended in a loop or hook to enable it to be hung on the kitchen wall. The excavated example was thrown away in the mid-seventeenth century.

Tripod-legged copper-alloy cauldrons continued to be made in the seventeenth century, but the majority were of small size. By this time the cast-iron cooking pot of the same general shape was used in most homes and avoided the much-feared dangers of copper poisoning. It should be noted that pots and skillets of copper, bronze, bell-metal, or pot-metal were invariably tinned on the inside to minimize that danger.

The iron pots ranged in capacity from half a gallon to ten gallons and more, and were made in both England and America well through the nineteenth century. As they became later, the collar necks grew shorter, and the body cordons less pronounced; the ear handles also developed into something resembling cow horns, tapering upward from the shoulders and with a much lighter crossbar returning to the rim. Nineteenth-century cauldrons are frequently embossed with capacity numbers in Arabic figures. Until the early eighteenth century, the legs tapered downward and then expanded again into a bifid or trifid foot. Thereafter, the leg simply tapered until it came to the end and then stopped. By the last quarter of the eighteenth century the legs were often no more than short, triangular stumps no deeper than the sag of the base, serving merely to prevent the vessel from rolling over. Such pots were therefore designed only to be hung over the fire and not stood in it, though, of course, for centuries suspension had been the principal method of using the caldrons.

LINDSAY, J. SEYMOUR: *Iron and Brass Implements of the English and American House*. London, 1964 (first pub. 1927).

§ *CUTLERY and SPOONS*

The seventeenth-century manufacture of knives was divided into four operations theoretically undertaken by four different crafts-men, the bladesmith, the hafter, the sheather, and finally the cutler who assembled the components and sold them. It is, however, the work of the seventeenth-century bladesmith that is of greatest in-terest to the archaeologist, in part because more blades survive than do handles, but also because cheaper and more common varieties of handle are less readily datable. It is important to remember that it was not until well into the century that the fork was used for any-thing other than serving or anchoring the food to the plate while cutting it. The use of the fork to transport the cut food to the mouth did not filter down to the lower classes before the third quarter of the seventeenth century, and therefore the medieval pointed knife continued in common use.

The typical table knife of the first half of the seventeenth cen-tury had a narrow, straight blade and long, solid shoulders that were often faceted and inlaid with brass or precious metals. (Fig. 63, No. 1) Although these heavy shoulders became smaller among the more costly cutlery of the second half of the seventeenth cen-tury, they continued to be used for cheap table knives of the first thirty years of the eighteenth century, though I have yet to encoun-ter any that were inlaid.

As the fork gained in popularity among the wealthy, the points of the spearing knives were rounded off; in the third quarter of the seventeenth century fashionable knives had their blades square-ended, looking almost as though the points had been snapped off. (Fig. 63, No. 3) In the same period a round-ended blade, wider than the medieval style, was introduced. This became the forerunner of the table knife as we know it today. The next stage (c. 1670) saw the new blade slightly concave at the back and proportionately convex along the cutting edge; the round end now became slightly bulbous. (Fig. 63, No. 4)

By 1700, the curved blade had acquired a dorsal ridge about a third of the way along the blade, which gave it the appearance of a round-ended scimitar. The new blade shape which was to continue almost to the end of the eighteenth century was almost invariably associated with a new-style handle whose butt curved down to balance the bulbous and upswept blade end. (Fig. 63, No. 5) Such hafts are known as pistol-grip handles. By about 1770, the blade's cutting edge had lost its convexity and became a direct extension of the handle. These later eighteenth-century knives were frequently made with handles having bone or ivory plates anchored to a flat tang by brass rivets and gripped at the end of the haft by a metal cap. In contrast, the majority of seventeenth-century and early eighteenth-century handles were attached over a spiked tang which, in the former century, extended right through and was beaten over a terminal washer. However, the flat, rivet-pierced tang can be traced back to the Bronze Age, and its presence or absence can therefore never be an inviolable dating factor.

In the second and third quarters of the seventeenth century many knife handles were made from stone and crystal sections ground and polished by lapidaries to fit neatly together when mounted in series on the tang. Tapered, cylindrical bone or ivory handles of the second half of the century were frequently elaborately inlaid in floral designs using small brass tubes. (Fig. 63, No. 4) The same technique was sometimes employed on the later, plated pistol-grip handles in much simpler patterns in an attempt to disguise the purely practical brass rivets. Silver and silver-plated handles of the first half of the eighteenth century were made in two cast sections joined down the middle, but in the second half the entire handle was often machine stamped in very thin silver and filled with plaster composition which gave it weight but little durability. Staffordshire potters of the mid-eighteenth century produced excellent pistol grips in their popular, blended-clay "agate" ware, while the porcelain makers of Bow and other factories made them in their medium, decorated in underglaze blue or overglaze enamels. Porcelain handles are attributable to the third quarter of the eighteenth century. At the other end of the scale, being cheapest of all, were wooden handles which were made in both plain and pistol-grip forms. For obvious reasons, few of them survive in the ground, and being little prized by their original owners they rarely lasted long enough to become antiques.

There were two principal centers of cutling in England: London and Sheffield. In the seventeenth century the London craftsmen were superior, and although in the eighteenth there was little reason to choose between them, London knives continued to command better prices than did those from Sheffield. Through both centuries, and even into the early 1800's, Sheffield bladesmiths were wont to pirate London makers' marks. Throughout the sixteenth century, cutlers working in England had struck only their personal marks into the blades (inlaid with copper until the mid-century), but in 1606 the London Court of Cutlers ordered that all London bladesmiths should add the "dagger" (sword of St. Paul) symbol of the City to their marks, a practice that continued into the eighteenth century. In using this helpful guide, it should be noted that bladesmiths of Solingen in Germany used a similar mark, though their dagger's blade was longer than that of the London symbol.

Blade marks should be examined with care, for they are not always what they seem. I recall one which at first glance appeared to be the London dagger under the letter L, but which turned out to be a pistol. I later discovered that this was the mark of James Bernardeau (or Bernardo), whose eighteenth-century trade card revealed that he was a "Razor Maker, at the Pistol & L in Russell Court, in Drury Lane," London, who also made and sold "Siszors, Penknives, Lancetts, and all other Instruments. Also Silver, Chiney, Ivory, Ebeny, Handled Knives & Forks &c."[7]

---

[7] Ambrose Heal: *London Tradesmen's Cards of the XVIII Century* (London, 1925), Pl. LXXXI; reprinted New York, 1968.

The earliest-recorded English silver fork is two-tined and bears the date letter for 1632/3, but slightly older French, Italian, and Spanish specimens are known. The silver fork, however, did not become popular in England until the end of the seventeenth century, at which time it generally had three tines. By the mid-eighteenth century it had acquired a fourth and closely resembled the style that has persisted into the present century. It should be noted that Spanish silver forks had four tines by the early eighteenth century; examples (one bearing a Mexico City mark) of these were aboard the plate fleet wrecked off the Florida coast in 1715. Four tined French forks in brass and iron have been found in contexts of the 1730's and '40's at Louisbourg, Nova Scotia.

Silver forks are rarely found in excavations, but those of steel are common and range in their two-tined form from the last quarter of the seventeenth century to the beginning of the nineteenth, though a wider-shouldered variety with three tines became popular in the second half of the eighteenth century. Very long and thin tines occur on some forks of the late seventeenth and early eighteenth centuries, and they should not be confused with the much larger and heavier double-tined carving forks that have been made with few changes ever since the late seventeenth century, at which early date the folding guard first appeared.

Fork handles were invariably similar in shape to those of the knives they accompanied, though the majority were slightly smaller. The shanks of steel forks were somewhat balustroid in shape, a style sometimes transformed into a midsection bulge (Fig. 63, No. 8); this seems to occur more often in the third quarter of the eighteenth century than in the first half of it.

The evolution of the spoon is readily traceable through dated silver examples, for the same styles were religiously followed (with some minor time lag) by makers of brass, latten, and pewter. Latten, it should be noted, was an alloy of copper, zinc, and iron (approximate proportions: 73, 25, and 2 per cents) which, from the second half of the seventeenth century and when used for spoons, was usually tin-plated, giving the appearance of silver. The makers of latten (and other tin or tinned products) were known as whitesmiths.

From the fifteenth to the mid-seventeenth century all spoons had fig-shaped bowls, being rounded at the end and curving weakly up to their junction with the stem. The stems were usually rectangular in section and extended out as a very slightly tapering shaft to an ornamental finial, the latter being the spoon's principal feature and the one by which the type is now identified. The earliest are probably those ending in a female head; they go back at least to the fifteenth century, as is evidenced by the elaborate bifid headdress with which they are capped. All the female-headed spoons are known as maiden heads; the earliest-known literary reference to them occurred in 1446, while the latest-dated example that I can find bears the letter for 1549. (*See* SILVER.) It is quite possible, however, that such spoons may have found their way to the colonies in the early seventeenth century. Less likely to be found are those with acorn and diamond-point finials, for neither of these seems to have occurred much after the end of the fifteenth century. More elaborate finials in the shape of a lion seated (sejant) began that early but continued at least to the late sixteenth century. Much better known are the "Apostle" spoons that began to be made around 1500 and which continued to at least 1642. These take the form of a robed human figure capped with a disc halo and were made in sets of twelve, plus a thirteenth "Master" spoon; they were frequently given as christening presents. Yet another variety also ended in a flat disc, generally over a baluster or ball knop. These are known as "seal-top" spoons, and I have located dated examples ranging from 1494 to 1699. A latten specimen has been found at Jamestown and another of the same metal has been recovered from an Indian grave at East Dennis in Massachusetts. Others omitted the seal and ended only in the knop, sometimes writhen ornamented, and these belong mostly to the sixteenth century.

As a general rule, it may be deduced that spoons with any of the foregoing terminals date prior to 1670. But not all spoons were that elaborate, and by about 1500 the straight shaft was sometimes cut off at an oblique angle. These are, quite logically, known as "slipped ends" and were made at least as late as 1657. One such silver spoon bearing the owners' initials $^W E^C$ has been unearthed at Jamestown.

In about 1660 the silver spoon bowl became broader at the shoulders and thus more oval; at the same time the straight, flat stem became a little wider and was square cut at the end, eliminating the necessity to thicken the shaft toward the terminal to permit

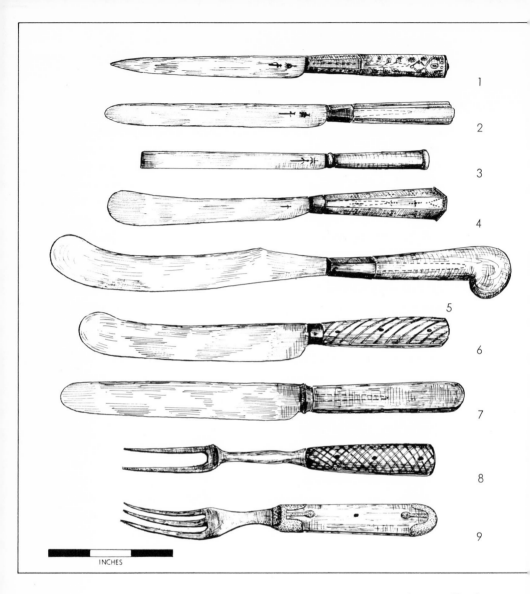

Fig. 63. Examples of English and American cutlery. **1.** Shank inlaid with brass, handle bone with incised ornament; early 17th century. **2.** Ridged bone handle; mid-17th century. **3.** Blade deliberately square-ended, handle silver; late 17th century. **4.** Octagonal bone handle inlaid with brass tubes and with iron cap; late 17th century. **5.** "Pistol grip" bone handle; early 18th century. **6.** Riveted bone plates for handle with incised decoration; mid-18th century. **7.** Polished bone or ivory handle; late 18th to 19th century. **8.** Steel fork type comparable to No. 6. **9.** American iron fork with bone-plated handle held together with pewter mounts (knives are similar); c. 1850–80? Nos. 1–4 have marks of the London Cutlers' Company.

the angular cut of the slipped end. The new shape is known as "Puritan"; it was soon replaced by a spatulalike terminal which was generally notched to create a trifid end. The "Puritan" bowl was retained, though deepened, and the junction with stem and bowl was reinforced with a spinal rib which extended down the back of the latter and was known as a rat tail, thus giving this class of spoon its generic name. The rat tail continued to be used on silver until the second quarter of the eighteenth century and considerably later on pewter. Latten spoons were most common in the rat-tail period, usually with trifid stem terminals, though often without the rat tail itself. (Frontispiece) Their popularity was greatest in the second half of the seventeenth century, but lost out to the pewter spoon in the early 1700's. Although there is irrefutable archaeological evidence that rat-tailed latten spoons were still being made in Williamsburg, Virginia, as late as the 1740's, there can be no denying that pewter became the common American spoon metal of the eighteenth century. So simple was it to work that householders frequently cast their own spoons.

Although the rat tail continued well into the eighteenth century, it was generally associated with an evolved egg-shaped bowl (by c. 1710) and a handle which, by 1715, had abandoned its trifid terminal in favor of a rounded, upcurling spatula which was usually thickened at the edge. It was a stem style that would remain popular almost to the end of the eighteenth century. By about 1740, the rat tail had been replaced by a single or overlapping double, scale-like junction ornament, and that, too, continued late in the century. In the second half of the century, however, it was generally associated with a much more pointed bowl, in fact almost the reverse of the early fig bowl. In the 1760's yet another change occurred, for the stem terminal which hitherto turned up now turned down and was shorn of its ornamental, thickened upper edge, though this detail was sometimes transferred to the back. Another new feature that occurred in the third quarter of the eighteenth century was a widening of the stem to provide two, small, earlike projections above the bowl. Although this was absent from most silver in the last quarter of the eighteenth century, it reappeared in the nineteenth and has lasted into our own time.

A few additional pointers are worth remembering. The so-called

Sheffield plate was invented by cutler Thomas Bolsover in 1742, and, as previously noted (p. 90), it was superseded in England almost exactly a century later by electroplating, the latter being marked EPNS—electroplated nickel silver. Pewter also fell before the advances of technology, being at least partially superseded by Britannia metal, which was developed in about 1795 and which contained 90 per cent tin and 10 per cent antimony. In the nineteenth century this new alloy was generally plated, but at first it was used simply as an improved pewter. Spoons and other household items made from Britannia metal were generally so stamped. It may also be noted that Britannia-metal spoons were often reinforced by an iron wire around which the handles were cast. This also occurred in some pewter spoons, but not, as far as I can determine, before the 1770's.

HAYWARD, J. F.: *English Cutlery.* H. M. Stationery Office, London, 1956.
PRICE, F. G. HILTON: *Old Base Metal Spoons.* London, 1908.

§ *DRINKING GLASSES and DECANTERS*

Drinking glasses in delicate and elaborate forms were well known to the English before the first of their colonists set foot in America, but the glasses themselves were rarely of English manufacture, the best of them having come either from Venice or Antwerp. However, an English glass industry had existed since the thirteenth century, though its products had been confined largely to window glass and bottles. It was not until 1571 that the first successful venture into the making of Italian *cristallo* was launched in England by the Venetian Giacomo Verzelini. His products were direct copies of current European styles, having stems molded in the shapes of lion masks (Fig. 64, No. 1), or inverted balusters, some of the latter vertically and horizontally ribbed and known as "ladder" stems.

The bowls were either funnel- or bell-shaped, and the extant examples are usually elaborately diamond engraved, probably by Anthony de Lysle, the only known glass engraver working in England in the late sixteenth century. Verzelini retired in 1592, at which time Sir Jerome Bowes was granted a patent to be the sole maker and importer of glasses into England. In 1615 a similar patent was granted to Sir Edward Zouche, on whose board of directors sat Admiral Sir Robert Mansell, who thus became interested in glass and who, in 1623, obtained letters patent from Charles I authorizing him to carry on where Zouche had left off. The glasses produced in London in this early period were frequently extremely tall, standing on elongated inverted balusters known as "cigar" stems (Fig. 64, No. III) or, alternatively, on very small chestnut-shaped balusters. (Fig. 64, No. II) The soda metal was very thin and therefore very fragile; it inclined to a pale straw color. Although more complicated designs were attempted during the period of the Mansell monopoly (1623–c.1649), the elaborate dragonesque and butterfly stems using entwined clear rods and applied wings in other colors which are occasionally found on early colonial sites must be classed as either Venetian or Flemish.

A certain amount of Rhenish glass was also imported into England in the first half of the seventeenth century and some of it also came to America, though whether it did so in trade or among emigrants' personal possessions is uncertain. The principal types were cylindrical-stemmed goblets ornamented with "raspberry" prunts and with conical feet encircled by thin glass trails. These vessels with their balloon-shaped bowls were produced in a deep-green metal characteristic of the German *Waldglas*, or forest glass. The second form was that of a cylindrical beaker (humpen) with a padlike base slightly conical in the middle and surrounded by a notched or "rigaree" trail; such pieces were often elaborately enameled with heraldic devices, wedding processions, or scenes of rural crafts. Dated examples run through most of the seventeenth century.

The Mansell glass industry came to grief during the English Civil War, and little or nothing was done to revive it until the restoration of the monarchy in 1660, whereupon various patents were issued, the most important being that granted to the Second

Duke of Buckingham in 1662. By then the old Venetian styles and metal were no longer as popular as they had been, and there was a pressing need for something new and exciting. It was for this reason that the London Glass Sellers Company sponsored researches into the making of a new and more brilliant "Christall de roache," first by Frenchman Jean de la Cam and then by the Englishman George Ravenscroft. Under contract to the Company, Ravenscroft produced a new clear metal of considerable promise, but unfortunately it was subject to crazing, or "crizzling" as it was termed. By reducing the proportions of salts and adding lead oxide, Ravenscroft was able to solve this problem, and in June 1676 the Glass Sellers Company issued a certificate of excellence for the new "flint glasses." These new glasses were subsequently marked on their stems with a small glass seal, first plain, and then embossed with Ravenscroft's rebus, a raven's head. Although fewer than forty such sealed vessels are yet recorded in England, either broken or intact, at least one example has been unearthed at Jamestown, and three other seals found there are too decayed to be safely identified. A fifth seal is clearly stamped with a bell; this has tentatively been identified as the rebus of John Bellingham, who managed the Duke of Buckingham's glass factory at Vauxhall from 1671 to 1674. It is reasonable to suppose that any glasses found with a single glass seal (not to be confused with decorative prunts) are likely to be English and of the period c. 1670–81, ending with the death of Ravenscroft. The majority of Ravenscroft's drinking glasses possessed simple, more or less conical bowls over an inverted baluster stem, the baluster pinched into four segments and known as a "quatrefoil" stem. (Fig. 64, No. VI) The feet would seem always to have been folded at the edge. Unfortunately, Ravenscroft did not entirely overcome the crizzling problem. After his death his factory at the Savoy in London was run by his manager, Hawley Bishopp, and glasses believed to have been made there in this later period are sometimes badly crazed.

In the years of experimentation prior to Ravenscroft's alleged perfection of the lead crystal, London glass sellers imported considerable quantities of glasses from Venice (Murano), and fortunately the records of one of these importers, the firm of Measey and Greene, are preserved among the Sloane Manuscripts in the British

Museum. The papers include carefully measured drawings of the designs (popularly known as the Greene designs) which were sent as patterns to be used by their Murano manufacturer, Allesio Morelli. They began in 1667 and ended in 1673, by which date Measey and Greene had arranged to have their glass made for them in London. Plentiful among the Greene designs are glasses whose principal stem feature is a vertically ribbed knop (Fig. 64, No. IV), sometimes drawn up into a baluster, though both types were described simply as "wrought buttons." They were also made with "pla[in] ring & button,"[8] the ring being the trailed band around the base of the bowl which was otherwise ornamented in a rigaree pattern. The bowls of most of the knopped-stem glasses were generally wide, truncated cones, except in the case of beer glasses, whose bowls tapered almost to a point at the junction with the stem and whose mouths were almost as wide as the bowls were deep. As far as can be determined from the drawings and from excavated examples, the feet were never folded and were therefore made thicker to give the necessary strength—strength which Greene specifically demanded. Examples of both the beer- and wine-glass forms are common on colonial sites of the period c. 1670–85. Also encountered from time to time are fragments of tumblers or beakers with small, molded, diamond-shaped bosses patterned over the walls, presumably as an aid to gripping the vessel. Such beakers were included in Greene's designs of January 1668 and were there ordered to be made in two thicknesses, for beer and for French wine.

Plentiful and seemingly popular though the Greene-type glasses were in the years up to about 1680, the Ravenscroft revolution successfully ousted them in very short order. By 1690, the new lead crystal was well established in the American colonies, and one finds fragments in archaeological contexts every bit as handsome as the best available in England. Romers having raspberry prunts on their stems and with bulbous bowls with trailed threads tooled into a

---

[8] Papers in the British Museum (Sloane MSS 857) relating to the Glass Sellers Company, 1670–1690; and John Greene's correspondence and drawings, 1667–1672. Illustrating letter of January 26, 1668.

network of diamond-shaped ridges (a technique described in 1679 as "nipt diamond waies"[9]) were among Ravenscroft's more distinguished products, and although I have yet to see a fragment from an American site, the quality of other pieces found certainly suggests that they may have reached here.

The glass made by Hawley Bishopp and by other London and provincial glassmakers in the 1680's and early 1690's is impossible to pin down to any one factory, and it runs the gamut from magnificent to dreadful. On the one hand we find elaborately gadrooned glasses with complicated balustroid stems in a heavy and brilliant icelike metal, while on the other we encounter many quatrefoil-stemmed glasses whose mix was so poor that they have broken down into a substance little more stable than sugar. It may be noted that this collapse of the glass structure seems to be confined (as far as English glass is concerned) to examples made in the period 1685–1700. English pieces thus decayed generally have a yellow or brownish appearance that spreads inward from the fractures. A rather similar effect occurs among excavated French glasses dating as late as the second half of the eighteenth century, but in these the fractures and "sugar" areas tend to be pink.

With the advent of lead crystal the English glass industry clambered to its feet and launched into the eighteenth century freed from the shackles of patents and monopolies. By 1696, there were already twenty-six glasshouses in the London area alone, though not all of them were making table glass. Thus, it becomes impossible to attribute the products to individual factories, for they all catered to the popular taste of the time. We can do no more than to follow these trends through the eighteenth century (Fig. 64) trying to determine an approximate date at which each began. It is important to note, however, that there is reason to believe that taste in glassware developed more slowly in the colonies than it did at home. Thus, styles losing favor in England in, say, the 1740's may have continued to be popular in America until ten or even fifteen years later. It is uncertain, whether (if this is true) the English factories continued to produce for the colonial taste or whether

[9] W. A. Thorpe: *History of English and Irish Glass* (London, 1929), I, 127.

those markets were served from glass sellers' existing stock. Indeed, it is possible that the English merchants deliberately manipulated the colonial trade to enable them to dispose of their outdated inventories. It may well be significant that no style time lag is discernible from the study of glass found in dated contexts of the seventeenth century. It is not until the eighteenth century that it becomes noticeable, by which time the potential colonial market for glass had been appreciated by the English traders.

While bowl shapes are certainly significant to the student of glass, so few are found intact that I do not propose to devote space to them here. Similarly, feet exhibit differing characteristics, but they cannot be dated with any accuracy. As a rough rule of thumb it may be said that plain and folded feet are equally common on glasses of soda metal during the seventeenth century up to about 1680, that glasses of lead metal generally had folded feet up to the mid-eighteenth century, and that in the second half of the century plain feet gradually increased in popularity, particularly for the cheaper glasses. It is the stem form, however, that is the most datable part of any glass, and fortunately they are the most substantial and therefore the best preserved when found on archaeological sites.

The more elaborate products of Ravenscroft and his immediate successors reflected the "busyness" inherited from the earlier Venetian tradition, the stems being put together from a combination of balusters, inverted balusters, knops, and collars of all shapes and sizes. But just as the elaborately turned furniture styles of the late seventeenth century settled down into the simpler and cleaner lines of the Queen Anne period, so the stems of drinking glasses did likewise. Plain inverted balusters, either solid or containing a single large tear and with a collar separating it from the thick base of the bowl, appeared in about 1690 and by 1700 had been somewhat elaborated upon, the baluster often being constructed to give the top a mushroomlike appearance while the bottom spread out either into a ball knop or into a true baluster. The latter resembled a pear as it hangs from the tree, while the vastly more common inverted baluster was turned the other way up. (Frontispiece) These heavy baluster stems are found on most colonial sites up to the 1740's, though their popularity in England had waned some years earlier.

By about 1710, the inverted baluster appeared in a molded pedestal form, most commonly with four sides, but often with six, and with round or diamond-shaped bosses molded onto the shoulders. (Fig. 64, Nos. XV and XVI) The period of popularity for these glasses was c.1710–30; a number were made to commemorate the accession of George I (or possibly George II) and are molded on the shoulders or sides with such slogans as GOD SAVE KING GEORGE or sometimes merely the initials GR. These molded pedestal stems (as purists prefer to call them) are popularly known as "Silesian" stems, though they have nothing to do with Silesia. Although the form lost favor as a wine-glass stem around 1730, it did continue much later as the stem for sweetmeat glasses and even for large

Fig. 64. Examples of drinking-glass stems likely to be found on colonial and early Federal sites. **I.** Lion mask. **II.** Invested baluster. **III.** "Cigar" stem. **IV.** Greene design, ribbed knop with "rigaree" decoration at base of bowl. **V.** Solid, truncated and inverted baluster. **VI.** Quatrefoil. **VII.** Heavy, inverted baluster with tear. **VIII.** Waisted and inverted baluster. **IX.** Solid, inverted baluster with knop above. **X.** Heavy, inverted baluster with ball knop parted by a collar, hour glass tear within. **XI.** True baluster with ball knops above and below, the latter separated from the baluster by a narrow collar; single tear. **XII.** Solid, inverted baluster separated from a large, annulated knop by a collar. **XIII.** Acorn knop with tear, plus flattened knops above and below. **XIV.** Inverted baluster with large tear and with marvered ball knop below. **XV.** Molded "Silesian" stem, four-sided with diamonds in high relief, plus embossed crowns on the shoulders. **XVI.** "Silesian" stem, octagonal, and with embossed diamonds on the shoulders. **XVII.** Drawn stem with elongated tear. **XVIII.** Straight stem with tear in base of bowl. **XIX.** Straight stem with an angular knop in its midsection, generally classed as balustroid. **XX.** Drawn stem decorated with air twist. **XXI.** Balustered air twist. **XXII.** Straight stem decorated with opaque-white ribbon twist. **XXIII.** Straight stem cut with hexagonal faceting. **XXIV.** Short, drawn stem of a type seemingly produced in quantity by the Amelung factory in Maryland. **XXV.** Typical early 19th-century stem form with angular (often bladed) knop and stepped junction with faceted bowl. The dates given cover the range of the general types and are not necessarily the same as the terminals for the life of the illustrated examples.

1580-1620

III.1620-50

I.1590-1630

IV. 1665-75

V. 1675-85

VI.1685-1705

VII.1690-1710

VIII.1695-1710

IX.1700-25

X.1700-30

XV. 1710-20

XI.1700-20

XII. 1705-15

XIII.1710-25

XIV. 1710-40

XVI. 1715-50

XVII. 1725-60

XVIII.1730-60

XIX. 1745-70

XX.1735-60

XXI.1745-65

XXII.1755-75

XXIII.1760-70

XXIV. 1780-1805

XXV. c.1815

INCHES

pedestal-based salvers made in sets of decreasing size to be stacked as "pyramids." These later examples generally have a triple- or quadruple-ringed collar at the base of the molded stem, which itself is usually eight-sided and somewhat fluted. Examples of such late "Silesian" stems have been found amid a cargo of glass discovered on a wreck site off Bermuda dating no earlier than 1784.

In the second quarter of the eighteenth century, taste prompted the glassmakers to move away from the heavy lead stems of the early years and to produce balustroid forms of greater delicacy. This trend was given an economic push in 1745–6 with the passage of the Glass Excise Act taxing glass by weight. Whereas the baluster glasses were built up from a number of welded components, the second quarter of the century saw the development of the drawn stem, which extended down in one piece from the bowl and whose only separate attachment was the foot. (Fig. 64, No. XVII) The stems of such glasses were plain except for the frequent insertion of a single large tear, and the majority of the examples found in excavations seem to have had trumpet-shaped bowls. Such glasses run the gamut from the extremely delicate (often classified as toasting glasses) to the monumentally heavy. The latter are common on tavern sites, and nearly all of them have thick, plain feet, the majority dating in the period 1740–60. It should be noted that the same drawn stem and more or less trumpet-shaped bowl continued in smaller sizes through the eighteenth into the nineteenth century. It figured prominently among the products of the Amelung glass factory in Maryland (1784–95), the first American glasshouse to compete in quality with the comparable products of English and Irish houses.

The popularity of the straight, drawn stem wooed most English glassmakers away from the hollow balusters, but they were not long content with the new simplicity and they soon began to ornament the solid stems with round and flattened knops at the top, base, or midsection (Fig. 64, No. XIX), and sometimes at all three. These are known as balustroid glasses and are sometimes indistinguishable from late examples of the baluster group discussed earlier. The balustroid glasses belong roughly to the period c. 1725–60, and the later they got the worse they became. The stems became increasingly heavy and the knops were distributed with little obvious consciousness of design. These, too, became common, cheap tavern glasses of the mid-eighteenth century.

The desire to decorate plain stems with something other than a single tear prompted glassmakers to insert more air traps into the glass and to draw them out into spiral patterns, creating what are known as "air-twist" stems. (Fig. 64, Nos. XX and XXI) There is disagreement as to the date of their introduction, but current thinking puts them back to c. 1730 and perhaps even five years earlier; they continued to be made until about 1760. The later air twists are frequently contained within elaborate balustroid stems. (Fig. 64, No. XXI) In the eighteenth century these air-twist glasses were known as "worm'd" glasses and were advertised in that way in the *Boston News-Letter* of March 13, 1746.

In the mid-eighteenth century another internal stem ornament was developed, or rather redeveloped, adapting the Venetian *latticino* technique of decorating the walls of vessels with opaque white threads and using them to create spiral and gauze designs within the stems. These opaque or "enamel twists" appeared in the early 1750's but achieved their greatest popularity in the period c. 1760–75. (Fig. 64, No. XXII) Although plain white patterns were by far the most common, colors were also occasionally included, and examples combining green, blue, and red have been found on colonial sites dating from the years immediately prior to the Revolution.

Although, in Europe, the ornamental cutting of wine-glass stems can be traced back to the early years of the eighteenth century, it did not become common in England until about 1760, when stems were decorated with either diamond or hexagonal faceting. (Fig. 64, No. XXIII) Shortly thereafter, these facets were elongated into flutes which often extended the full length of the stem and ran up onto the base of the bowl, the latter characteristic being known as bridge-fluting. In the mid-1760's the straight stem was joined by a knopping or expansion of the midsection and the fluted cutting was deftly adapted to emphasize these contours. Cutting in much more elaborate forms continued through the nineteenth century on all sorts of English and Irish glassware, though it was confined largely to the glass of the wealthy, the lower orders being admirably, though later, served by the pressed "cut" glass invented in the United States in about 1827.

Enamel decoration had been popular in Europe since the fifteenth century, but it never found much favor in England, though the celebrated Beilby family of Newcastle-on-Tyne produced many handsomely ornamented pieces in the period c. 1762–78. In the same period Michael Edkins was decorating opaque white glass in enamel colors at Bristol. I have yet to see, however, any English enameled glass from a colonial site. Nevertheless, enameling does occur on glass from American sites and most of the examples (generally light tumblers and flasks) are claimed as products of the Henry William Stiegel glasshouses at Manheim, Pennsylvania (1763–74). However, the style of ornament, the colors used (white, yellow, blue, green, brick red, and black), and the German inscriptions make it impossible to visually distinguish with certainty between the Stiegel products and those from Bohemia, the Rhineland, or the northern Netherlands.

Wheel-engraving became a popular English form of decoration in the mid-eighteenth century and is best remembered by the large number of surviving glasses engraved with the rose and bud, thistle, or oak tree motifs of the Jacobites. Few excavated glasses are engraved, however, and the majority of those that are date no earlier than about 1770. One normally expects to find them in contexts of the period c. 1780–1820, though at least one elaborately engraved tumbler with a ship design has been found in a mid-eighteenth-century context in Virginia, and, according to the *Boston Gazette*, "best engrav'd flower'd wine glasses and decanters" had reached Boston by June 1761.

It is often suggested that eighteenth-century Americans were content to receive and use whatever glassware their English agents cared to buy for them or whatever happened to be in the local colonial shops. While doubtless this was true of the majority of colonists, there were notable exceptions. In September 1771, the Virginia lawyer and plantation owner Peter Lyons wrote to John Norton & Sons in London ordering a great variety of goods ranging from a pound of "Jesuits Bark powder'd in two ounce Bottles" to a Dutch oven, and amongst them were listed "Two dozen wine glasses (as pr pattern sent by Captn Robinson)." A postscript to the covering letter read:

Colo. Snelson & myself have an inclination to taste some good Burgundy & Champaign Wine, and therefore shall be obliged to you to purchase for me two dozen Bottles of each sort the best that can be had in London, and have it carefully packed and sent by the first of your Ships. I have given Captn. Robinson a Wine Glass as a pattern for two dozen mentioned in the Invoice to be sent me.[1]

It is evident, therefore, that Peter Lyons knew what he liked in glass and went to considerable trouble to get it. It is unfortunate that he had a sample to send, otherwise he might have drawn or described what he had in mind and thus revealed whether it was the shape or style of decoration that he was trying to match.

In the last quarter of the eighteenth century a new fashion in table-glass design captured the English market and spread to America in the 1790's and thereafter. These glasses were longer in the bowl than in the stem and wider at the mouth than at the foot, and because of their proportionately massive bowls were known as "rummers," being reminiscent of the German *roemer*s of the seventeenth century. Nothing else about them harked back to anything, and they mark the end of elegance in English glass. The bases are generally thick and almost flat—some are square—and the stems often feature a central angular or bladed knop, while the bowls are generally truncated cones. Such glasses are often engraved with ships, masonic emblems, and similar devides, but not with sufficient frequency to make them common on archaeological sites. The rummer is most often found in contexts of the early nineteenth century, but it actually spans the period c. 1780–1830. Molded examples (the marks visible on stem and foot) continued through to the mid-nineteenth century.

Not to be confused with the late-eighteenth-century rummer are the earlier firing glasses that are common on colonial tavern sites of the third quarter of the century. The principal characteristic of these small, thick-stemmed glasses was their remarkably heavy feet, which were sometimes as much as $\frac{1}{2}''$ in thickness. Such glasses are said to have been used in responding to toasts by banging them on the table to produce a noise like musket fire. They were much used

[1] Francis Norton Mason, ed.: *John Norton & Sons, Merchants of London and Virginia* (Richmond, Va., 1937), pp. 189–91.

195

by masonic lodges, and a number of extant examples are engraved with the symbols of freemasonry.

Colored glass became popular in the 1750's and continued to be so through the third quarter of the century. The technique of making it, however, can be traced back to Egypt before 3000 B.C., and it was being used and made in England in the sixteenth century. The principal "colors," blue and opaque white, were specialities of Bristol, though both were produced elsewhere, notably at Birmingham, Stourbridge, Newcastle, and London. The so-called "Bristol blue" is said to have been developed in 1763 when a supply of fine cobalt (smalt) from Saxony became available to Bristol glassmakers. The English blue metal is so closely akin to the first American products that it is generally impossible to distinguish between them. The latter were made in the Manheim, Pennsylvania, factory of Henry William Stiegel between 1769 and 1774.

Although it is true that colored metals did not become major features of English glass production until the mid-eighteenth century, there is evidence that they were being made and exported earlier, if only in small quantities. On January 24, 1731/2, Mrs. Rebecca Abbot of Boston advertised in the *New England Journal* that she had for sale "fine white Glass Japann'd." Six months later she was selling "Tea Setts of White, Blew and Japann'd Glass." Opaque-white, derived from the inclusion of a small quantity of tin oxide in the mix, was being made in the London borough of Southwark in 1743; but it is Bristol that became famous for it, and production seems to have commenced there in about 1745, with the output accelerating during the following twenty years, perhaps in an effort to compete with the rapidly developing English porcelain factories. Opaque-white, sometimes described as "enamel," was made in other centers, but their products lacked the density of whiteness achieved at Bristol and more closely resembled the *Milchglas* imported from Germany. Like porcelain and white salt-

Fig. 65. 18th-century, lead-glass decanter shapes with stopper types commonly associated with them. Nos. 1–4 and 6 are without grinding; 5, wheel-engraved Jacobite; 9 and 10, wheel-engraved "label" decanters; 11, 12, and 14, cut. Nos. 1, 4, 5, and 12–14, ht. 9½". Nos. 2 and 3, ht. 7½". Nos. 6 and 7, ht. 8½". Nos. 8, 9, and 11, ht. 11". No. 10, ht. 12".

1	2	3	4	5
1700-20	1720-40	1745-60	1730-50	1745-50

6	7	8	9	c.1760
1710-20	1720-35	1745-70	1755-70	

10	11	12	13	14
1755-70	1745-80	1760-80	1780-1800	1780-1800

glazed stoneware, opaque-white glass was frequently decorated with enamel colors, notably at Bristol by Michael Edkins, who had come there in about 1762 from Birmingham, where he had been an apprentice enameler. His surviving ledger shows that he enameled opaque-white wares and gilded blue, while an undated list reveals that he supplied cases of both for shipment abroad.

In studying opaque-white products one should beware of accepting contemporary documentary references to "white glass" or "White Flint Glass" as necessarily referring to opaque-white. "White glass" simply distinguished between clear and green metals; thus John Frederick Amelung notified in the *Maryland Journal and Baltimore Advertiser,* February 11, 1785, that he made "white and green Bottles." The term "White Flint" seems to have been coined by a Bristol glassmaker, Humphrey Perrott, who, in 1736, obtained a patent for a new and hotter furnace that imparted a greater brilliance and clarity to the metal than had hitherto been possible. When Perrott died in 1752, he was described as being the proprietor of "the White Flint Glasshouse at Bedminster,"[2] and there is reason to suppose that "White Flint" referred to his improved clear lead metal, a belief supported by the fact that by the end of the century there were several "white or flint glass houses" in and around Bristol; yet there was no great quantity of opaque-white being made at that time. Just to add a final note of confusion, it is worth remembering that the term "flint white" was used to describe English white salt-glazed stoneware.

The evolution of the decanter was far less involved than that of the drinking glass, though it too developed through a combination of improved technology and a lingering reliance on tradition. (Fig. 65) The first decanters, or serving bottles, were no more than green-glass wine bottles with green-glass handles, and their evolution progressed exactly as did their prototypes. Such handled wine bottles are known from the 1660's to about 1720, by which date they were replaced by decanters in clear, flint glass. The flint- or lead-glass forms do go back earlier, however, back in fact to the bottle shape of the period 1650–70 which was given, in addition to a handle, a gadrooned lower body and a thin and purely decorative string rim

---

[2] W. A. Thorpe: *English Glass* (London, 1949), p. 203.

well below the lip. Regardless of their antiquated shape, such bottles could not date much before 1680 and possibly as late as 1700. Belonging to the same period are a group of flint jugs with gadrooned or "nipt diamond waies" bodies and pan-shaped mouths that may have been made by Ravenscroft.

Ravenscroft advertised his decanters as being available with and without handles, and fragments of flint-glass carafes without handles or string rims have been found in archaeological contexts of the period 1720–35. These bottles have bulbous bodies and straight necks with slightly flaring mouths, and are known as the shaft-and-globe form. It is reasonable to assume that such bottles (perhaps with handles) bridged the gap between Ravenscroft and the same types of bottle which became common in the mid-eighteenth century. (Fig. 65, Nos. 1–5) Unfortunately, very little is known about these early decanters other than that they were made and sold. In August 1710 *The Tatler* advertised that the "Flint Glass-House in White Fryars" in London had available "all sorts of decanthers of the best Flint."[3]

At some date in the first quarter of the eighteenth century a very distinctive decanter form appeared, having a molded, six-or-more-sided body slightly broader at the shoulder than at the base and with the long neck and low string rim of its predecessors. The body somewhat resembled a carpenter's mallet, and they are consequently known as mallet decanters. (Fig. 65, No. 6) In the period c. 1730–45 the molded mallet took another step and became cruciform in plan, the idea being to enable its wine contents, when set in water or an ice cooler, to come in as close contact as possible with the cooling agent. (Fig. 65, No. 7) The cruciform type are usually decorated on their otherwise plain necks by the application of a triple-ring collar placed well below the lip. Although the form is generally supposed to have been obsolete by 1750, fragments of a less angular version are present in the large quantity of glass recovered from the c. 1784 wreck off Bermuda previously cited in connection with the "Silesian" stems. (Fig. 66) Mallet decanters are usually quite thick-walled and when found in small fragments

---

[3] H. J. Powell: *Glass-Making in England* (Cambridge, Eng., 1923), p. 81; quoting *The Tatler*, August 9, 1710.

might be mistaken for pieces of wet battery cases. Stoppers allegedly associated with mallet decanters were generally ball-finialed, the balls ornamented with numerous carefully arranged tears. (Fig. 65, No. 7)

By the mid-eighteenth century, the square shoulders characteristic of the earlier mallet decanters had weakened and the body had become taller, much in the manner of the French wine bottles of the period; the neck had become shorter and had lost its string rim. (Fig. 65, No. 8) Such decanters were usually fitted with a faceted conical stopper, and both the interior of the neck and the walls of the stopper were ground—a technique known as early as 1675 but apparently little used prior to c. 1718. The range of such vessels may tentatively be placed in the period c. 1745–75. Decanters of this type were often wheel-engraved; in about 1755 it became fashionable for them to be decorated with wine labels surrounded by floral and botryoid motifs, and with linking lines running around the necks simulating the chains from which silver labels were suspended. (Fig. 65, No. 9) Such fine pieces were not for the gentry alone, and an excellent example of less than half-bottle size (known as "one-go" decanters) marked MADEIRA has been found in excavations at Wetherburn's Tavern in Williamsburg. The next step in the decanter's evolution was for the shoulder/base relationship to be reversed, the latter becoming broader than the former; at the same time the body became considerably taller. This development had occurred by about 1760. (Fig. 65, No. 10) Shortly thereafter, the shoulder disappeared altogether and the neck simply flowed uninterrupted into the body. (Fig. 65, No. 11) The type was common in the last quarter of the eighteenth century, when a great many examples were decorated above the base with vertical-cut fluting and with wheel-engraving on the upper body in foliate and floral festoons. Some of these are attributed by collectors to Amelung (1784–95), and it is likely that he did produce decanters of this then-popular shape. Most of these late eighteenth-century vessels sport a slightly outturned and flattened lip, a characteristic not common before 1770. Stoppers were generally conical or disc-shaped, the latter often decorated at the edge with cut facets known as lunar slicing. (Fig. 65, No. 11)

By the last quarter of the eighteenth century one had come to

Fig. 66. A late mallet decanter developed from the cruciform type, Fig. 65 (No. 7), and similar to fragments from a cargo of glass lost off Bermuda in the 1780's. English, probably third quarter of 18th century. Lead metal. Ht. 10¾".

the age of Irish glass, the decanters of which were among the most impressive of their period. The bodies were shorter and more bulbous than the previously discussed shoulderless variety, and the lips were broad and flat. (Fig. 65, No. 14) The bodies were decorated from base almost to midsection with vertical fluting, while around the necks were three broadly spaced rings. Some examples are helpfully molded on the base with the words, CORK GLASS CO., a firm in business from 1783 to 1818. It should be noted that the prosperity of the Irish glass industry really dates from about 1780, at which time the British ban on exporting it was lifted. Very similar decanters to those from Cork were made at both Belfast and Waterford and it is hard to distinguish between them. A possible clue is provided by the fact that Waterford necks taper slightly toward the top, whereas those from Cork are virtually straight. Stoppers for Irish decanters are similar to those of the comparable English forms from which they were copied—by English workmen. The most common styles are variations on the flat vertical disc, either cut or molded in target or sunflower patterns. (Fig. 65, No. 13) Also encountered from this period are stoppers with flat, horizontal discs cut in radiating grooves or convex with ribbing spreading out and down like the spokes of an umbrella, the latter known as "mushroom" stoppers. (Fig. 65, No. 14) Another variant of the mushroom has the disc rising to its convexity by means of a triple step.

Before leaving decanters, a word must be said about the simple, straight-sided, square lead-glass bottles that were stored in cases and were commonly used as containers for gin or medicines. Such bottles generally had a rough pontil scar on the gently rising base, were thick-walled and short-necked (little more than a collar), and possessed an everted, flat rim sometimes thickened with an additional trail of glass, the mouth usually ground on the inside. Such bottles were being made by 1740 but seem to have been most common in the third quarter of the century. They did, of course, continue well into the nineteenth century, when they were often elaborately cut and housed in wooden cellars holding three, and sometimes more, bottles. Much thinner, square bottles in soda glass, roughly wheel-engraved with tulip designs, are frequently described as being of "Stiegel type," though they could equally well be European. Case bottles heavier than these, with bolder shoulders and decorated with much neater engraving in the form of floral wreaths, were made at New Bremen by Amelung between the years 1788 and 1795.

ASH, DOUGLAS: *How to Identify English Drinking Glasses & Decanters 1680–1830.* London, 1962.
BARRELET, JAMES: *La Verrerie en France de l'Époque Gallo-Romaine à Nos Jours.* Paris, 1953.
CHAMBON, RAYMOND: *L'Histoire de la Verrerie en Belgique.* Brussels, 1955.
FROTHINGHAM, ALICE WILSON: *Spanish Glass.* New York, 1964.
HARTSHORNE, ALBERT: *Old English Glasses.* London, 1897.
HAYNES, E. BARRINGTON: *Glass Through the Ages.* London, 1959.
HUGHES, G. BERNARD: *English, Scottish and Irish Table Glass.* London, 1956.
MCKEARIN, GEORGE S., and HELEN MCKEARIN: *American Glass.* New York, 1941.
NOËL HUME, IVOR: *Glass in Colonial Williamsburg's Archaeological Collections.* Williamsburg, Va., 1969.
THORPE, W. A.: *A History of English and Irish Glass.* 2 vols. London, 1929.
———: *English Glass.* London, 1949.
VAVRA, J. R.: *5000 Years of Glass-Making.* Prague, 1954.
WILLS, GEOFFREY: *English and Irish Glass.* London, 1968.

§ *DRUG POTS, JARS, and PILL TILES*

When Jasper Andries and Jacob Janson petitioned Queen Elizabeth for a patent in 1567 they described themselves as makers of "Gally Paving Tiles, and Vessels for Apothecaries and others."[4] The latter products had been popularly known in England as gallipots since the fifteenth century. The etymology has been explained as pots brought by galleys from the Mediterranean, presumably made from the tin-enameled maiolicas of Italy and Spain. Regardless of the validity of this debatable interpretation, the fact remains that the earliest delftware potters to set up their kilns in and near London devoted much of their energies to producing vessels for apothecaries. These ranged from jars for storage some 7″ or 8″ in height to miniature versions of no more than 3″ or 4″, in which salves and elixirs were sold. Such vessels resembled cylinders constricted above the base and below the rims, in the manner of the Italian *albarelli*, and were decorated over their white tin glazes in polychrome, generally blue, orange, purple, and occasionally green. (Fig. 67, No. 1) For many years these colorful pots and jars were considered to date from the late sixteenth and very early seventeenth centuries, but more recent archaeological evidences recovered both in England and in Virginia indicate that they continued to be used (and probably made) as late as c. 1640. While the small English pots of this early period were generally taller than they were broad, the storage jars were squat and wide—unlike their Italian and Netherlandish counterparts that followed the same proportions in all sizes.

English polychrome pots and jars of the period c. 1580–1640 were commonly decorated in the manner of Figure 67, Number 1, but some were adorned in the midsection with a zone of interlock-

[4] John Stow: *A Survey of the Cities of London and Westminster and the Borough of Southwark.* 6th edn. (London, 1755), II, 327; first pub. 1598.

ing arcs of chain ornament. The latter feature was often painted in purple or orange, while the lines above and below were blue, as also were narrow bands of dots or dashes at the shoulder and above the base. The same design combination in blue alone continued to be used for apothecaries' storage and dispensary jars until at least the mid-eighteenth century. In its most degenerate form, probably dating in the period 1755–80, the decoration was reduced to a series of plain blue encircling bands extending up the entire body or leaving a blank zone in the midsection where the earlier chain pattern would have been. A few of these late jars are glazed in a pale duck-egg blue as a background to the darker bands, though it is uncertain whether this was intentional.

It should be noted that while the jars were originally intended for apothecaries' use, contemporary paintings show them in numerous other contexts. They are found on most seventeenth- and eighteenth-century British colonial sites, and it by no means follows that their discovery is automatically evidence of the presence there of an apothecary.

By the mid-seventeenth century the costly and time-consuming practice of decorating the small ointment pots had ceased, and they were thenceforth produced in plain white and in ever-increasing numbers. (Fig. 67, Nos. 2 and 3) The earliest plain white pots were of the same shape as their decorated predecessors, i.e., cylinders pinched in above the base and below the rim, the latter step being necessary to enable a paper lid to be tied down. This shape persisted into the late seventeenth century, though the height and diameters of the vessels varied widely. In the last decades a change began to develop, the bases of the pots becoming smaller and the concavity below the rim being created, not by constriction but by everting the mouth outward beyond the wall. (Fig. 67, No. 4) This style persisted throughout the eighteenth century, and although some very small pots remained more reminiscent of the previous century, the majority were more cup-shaped than cylindrical. By 1730, an anomalous type began to appear, a pedestal-footed vessel with a bowl shallower than that of the normal pot but retaining its everted rim. (Fig. 67, No. 6) Variations on this last shape became increasingly common toward the end of the eighteenth century and were used for dry salves such as eye ointments and cosmetics. Some of

INCHES

1   2   3

4   5   6

Fig. 67. Delftware pharmaceutical-ointment pot shapes. 1. Decorated in blue, orange, and purple; c. 1590–1640; this shape also occurs in plain white in the second quarter of the 17th century. 2. and 3. C. 1640–90. 4. and 5. 1690–1780. 6. The pedestal type appears in various forms from c. 1730 to 1830, the later examples often for eye ointments and cosmetics, usually small, thick, and shallow.

these pedestal forms were little deeper than artists' paint palettes and were less than 1″ in height. They are occasionally found bearing inscriptions in blue giving the names and addresses of the shops from which they came, and research has shown that some of those inscriptions relate to firms not in business before the second or third decades of the nineteenth century.

Although the manufacture of delftware continued in these mundane forms much later than many people suppose, it was by no means the only ware from which drug pots were made. Delicate white saltglaze examples with rolled rims and bodies resembling Figure 67, Number 4, without its foot, were common in the late eighteenth century; so also were similar shapes in what appears to be a poor-quality creamware. These last have been found in Virginia in contexts of the 1780's, usually coated inside and out with a greenish-yellow glaze covering the cream-colored earthenware body beneath in an extraordinarily uneven manner. It is tempting to suggest that such pots might be early American attempts at copying English creamware.

The evolution of the apothecary's storage jar did not follow that of its smaller cousin. In addition to the *albarello*-derived jars previously discussed, two new forms appeared in the third quarter of the seventeenth century, one normally for dry compounds and the other for liquids. The former began in the 1650's as a barrel-shaped vessel with the usual construction at top and bottom and was decorated with a ribbon scroll in blue identifying the contents. Others of the same shape were adorned with a blue-outlined panel for the same purpose, the ends of which were embellished with satyr masks whose tongues curl out and upward—causing some authorities to extend their imagination to the point of describing these faces as men smoking pipes. The barrel-like shape of both these jar styles was emphasized by the inclusion of ridges or narrow bands above and below the decorative devices; the form is safely attributable to the years c. 1650–65.

By the late 1660's the two ridges had disappeared, the bodies had become a little less bulbous, and the ribbon scroll had been transformed into an angel whose wings spread above and behind a panel describing the contents. These continued until about 1700. In the early eighteenth century the shape changed somewhat, the lower body tapering inward to leave the shoulder as the dominant feature, with the foot sometimes being reduced to a mere downward extension of the sides. Such jars were often elaborately decorated, though the devices had become smaller and busier, giving greater emphasis to the label. The adornments frequently included a pair of winged angels at the upper ends of the label, with flowers and a scallop shell between them. Below the label and under the scallop there was usually a winged cherub with a flower or tassel hanging below his chin, the device flanked by stylized flowers. Such jars continued to be made as late as the mid-eighteenth century. (Fig. 68) A rare polychrome example is dated 1723. A footed version of this general type has a pair of birds in place of the flanking angels,

Fig. 68. Delftware drug jar decorated in blue, with "angels" and scallop shell above the inscription, and a tassled cherub below; found in Williamsburg. C. 1720. Ht. 7". Miniature drug jars of this general shape (though wider at the shoulder than the midsection) occur in the later part of the 17th century.

and dated examples range from 1702 to 1763. Thereafter delft was in decline, and its place in the apothecaries' shelves began to be taken by tin-lidded jars of creamware, later still of pearlware, with bald identifying labels painted in overglaze black.

The containers for liquids (usually syrups) were entirely different, though they seem to have developed alongside the dry-content jars in the 1660's. The shape was simply a spherical container atop a hollow pedestal foot, with an everted mouth, a tubular spout projecting from beneath it, and opposite the spout a strapped handle. All these features underwent evolutionary changes. The early feet were more or less flat with a stem rising above them to the bowl, but toward the end of the seventeenth century stem and foot had merged into one another to create a gently flaring slope. This degenerated in the early eighteenth century into a virtually conical foot with a very small section of stem dividing it from the bowl. Spouts of the early 1660's possessed a wide flange at their midsection and tapered inward from it to the mouths. Although these characteristics are to be found on specimens dating as late as 1678, a new spout form had begun to appear at least four years earlier. This diminished the taper between mouth and flange and transformed the latter's originally angular shape into a new, bulbous knop. By about 1700 all the early spout features had disappeared and had been replaced by a straight tube with an everted lip over which a cork or paper cover could be tied. Handles, too, underwent a datable change; throughout the second half of the seventeenth century they were deeply dished on their upper surfaces so that the edges seemed to stand up like small walls, but by 1700 that feature had almost disappeared and thereafter was no more than a gentle concavity similar to that found on delftware chamber pots of the same period.

Decorative labels painted in blue on these pedestal-footed jars closely followed the evolving styles of those previously discussed, beginning with the spread-winged angel and going through—in the early eighteenth century—to the cartouche flanked by angels. The labels, however, do possess one step that seems to have been their own, for in the late seventeenth century many of those labels embraced by angel wings also had a scalloplike device below the inscription. In some cases, dating from about 1700, the angel had degenerated into a human-faced bird, while the scallop below had turned into something resembling a bird's spread tail.

It is uncertain as to how long these spherical-bodied vessels continued to be made in delftware, and I have seen none in the ware's obvious successor, white saltglaze. However, the shape was later produced in creamware and is illustrated in Josiah Wedgwood's c. 1810 pattern book, where it is listed as "Syrup pot with pipe - qt - plain 1/9, labelled 2/1."

Before passing on from these seemingly easily recognizable jars, a word of warning is necessary. Feet and plain white body fragments are often found in excavations. It would be a mistake to assume that all such pieces come from apothecaries' jars, for the same foot and spherical body coupled with a similar shallow and slightly everted rim were used in the second half of the seventeenth century to create flower vases. These usually had three tubular spouts placed equidistantly around the shoulder and between them three decorative scroll handles or lugs, but in fragments the bases and bodies may be indistinguishable from syrup jars. The same conical foot that one associates with the later jars was also used as the base for a popular type of standing salt in the mid- to later seventeenth century. The bowls of such salts were *tazza*-like, with wide cockle-edged rims atop which were three scrolled lugs similar to those ornamenting the flower vases. The bases of this type of salt were generally open, as were those of the English syrup jars. Dutch syrup jars, on the other hand, had bottoms to their feet (often with a small central hole like that of a flowerpot), while English flower vases had completely bottomed feet providing a reservoir for the bulbous bowl above.

Seemingly, all the jar types produced in English kilns were paralleled in Dutch delftware, though specialists are generally able to distinguish between them. However, I have yet to see Netherlandish pieces on British colonial sites dating later than the mid-seventeenth century. On the other hand French faïence ointment and mustard pots occur in contexts dating within the period c. 1780–1830. Such pots have no feet and are cylindrically walled with either a slightly everted mouth or a small constriction below a straight rim. The ware varies from pale yellow to a rich pink and from very thin to enormously thick. The white tin glaze is heavy and prone to crazing; it is frequently adorned with identifying inscriptions (including Parisian addresses) stenciled on in black or orange.

Another delftware item of the apothecary's equipment was his pill tile or slab on which ingredients were mixed and rolled. The shapes varied from hearts or shields to octagonal, the former always dating in the second half of the seventeenth century. The surviving, identifiable examples are decorated in blue or polychrome with the arms of the Worshipful Society of Apothecaries—a rhinoceros crest, unicorn supporters, and on the oval shield Apollo holding a bow and arrow and straddling a dragon or, more properly, a serpent. Beneath, in a ribbon, one finds the Society's motto, OPIFERQUE PER ORBEM DICOR ("I am called Help-Bringer throughout the world"), a quotation from Ovid's story of Apollo and Daphne. Fragments of such tiles have been found in Williamsburg excavations, but they are naturally uncommon, being items that were not considered expendable. These armorial tiles were frequently hung up as shop signs (they are pierced for that purpose), and it is likely that many an apothecary rolled his pills on plain white delftware tiles, a usage which cannot now be identified. An order for medical supplies for the Continental Army written by Dr. William Brown on March 11, 1778, listed "6 dozen delft ware tiles for mixing Bolus, etc., on,"[5] but there is no knowing whether he expected them to be plain or decorated. Later pill tiles (c. 1790–1860) were made in heavy creamware, and fragments have been found that are decorated at one end with a spread-winged American eagle in a black transfer print. Intact examples are known with a printed ribbon below the eagle proclaiming that the tile is REAL WARRANTED WEDGWOOD. A Philadelphia advertiser was offering them as late as 1834.

In conclusion, a word may usefully be said here about another type of tile sign that had no relationship with the apothecary—the more or less triangular (actually pentagonal) bin and shelf labels for wines and other commodities. Wine labels were common in delftware in the mid-eighteenth century, generally with the lettering in manganese. They were subsequently manufactured in creamware; Wedgwood's catalog of c. 1810 listed two varieties of wine label, plain and lettered. The latter began with Port and ended with Pale Sherry, with seventy-seven varieties of beverage in between. The same catalog also listed forty lettered labels for household commodities from black-currant jelly to apple jelly—on the face of it, not too wide a gamut, until one recalls that the labels in between ranged from cucumbers to hartshorn shavings.

LOTHIAN, AGNES: "Angels in the Design of Seventeenth Century English Delft Drug Jars," *The Chemist and Druggist* (London), June 25, 1955, pp. 732–6.

————: "Cherub Designs on English Delft Apothecary Ware," *The Chemist and Druggist* (London), June 30, 1956, pp. 609–13.

————: "English Delftware in the Pharmaceutical Society's Collection," English Ceramic Circle *Transactions*, Vol. 5, Pt. 1 (1960), pp. 1–4.

WITTOP KONING, D. A.: *Delftse Apothekerspotten.* Deventer, Neth., 1954.

[5] George Griffenhagen: "Tools of the Apothecary, 5. Pill Tiles and Spatulas," *Journal of the American Pharmaceutical Association*, Vol. 17, No. 7 (July 1956), p. 464.

§ *FIREARMS and GUNFLINTS*

Gunlocks, being the most temperamental, most easily broken, and most readily replaceable of firearm parts, are frequently encountered on archaeological sites. They are invariably heavily rust-encrusted when found, however, and cannot be identified with accuracy until they have been carefully cleaned—at which time one will need much more detailed reference sources than the brief notes to be found here. I can do no more than help to indicate a few basic characteristics that are sufficiently obvious to be seen prior to cleaning and can thus enable the excavator to decide which class and to which century his lock belongs. (Fig. 69)

The simplest of all locks used in the American colonies was the matchlock, but although it came with the first settlers, it continued to be in general use until the end of the seventeenth century. Indeed, it was still the standard infantry arm of the British army until 1690. The most obvious feature of the matchlock is a bificated arm attached toward the right end of the straight, rulerlike lock plate (Fig. 69, No. 1). The head of the arm was often shaped like a snake's head and so was known as a serpentine. This gripped the burning, saltpetre-soaked match which, when the lever or tricker was pulled, was swung down into the priming pan, whose lid had previously been manually opened to reveal the powder. The earliest form was operated by a lever attached directly to the sear (interior moving arm) of the lock, but the improved matchlock common in the seventeenth century had a tricker (trigger) separate from the sear and protected by a guard attached to the wooden stock. By the 1670's the rectangular lock plate had become more sophisticated and resembled that of the flintlock that followed it, while the pan, which had originally been welded to the barrel, was now attached to the lock.

The matchlock musket, or arquebus as it was called in the sixteenth century, was an extremely heavy and clumsy weapon, and one that could be equally injurious to friend as to foe. The presence of the constantly burning match not only revealed one's position to the enemy but was also liable to ignite the powder prematurely. The first big improvement in the musket lock was the adoption of the wheel lock which, as practically every writer on the subject has pointed out, worked on the same principal as the cigarette lighter. (Fig. 69, No. 2) A revolving, serrated wheel struck sparks from a piece of pyrites into the pan, an operation much more complicated than it sounds. A thick, V-shaped mainspring was linked to the wheel by a small chain which, when the lock was wound up, was compressed and the chain wrapped around the spindle. When the spring was released it pulled the chain, so rotating the wheel; at the same time the pyrites (gripped in a miniature vise known as a "dog head") was thrust down onto the moving wheel, thus causing the sparks to be poured down into the pan atop the wheel. When found in excavations most wheel locks have lost their dog heads, but they are readily identifiable by the circular bosslike housing for the wheel in the midsection of the plate. Such locks did not have a long popularity and are unlikely to be found in archaeological contexts later than the mid-seventeenth century.

Neither the matchlock nor the wheel lock can claim to be the direct ancestor of the eighteenth-century flintlock; that distinction belongs to the snaphaunce lock. (Fig. 69, No. 3) The term is now used to denote a mechanism whereby a flint held in a cock was struck against a steel or battery that was separate from the pan cover. Experts on the subject have pointed out that in the seventeenth century the word *snaphaunce*, or snapping lock, meant any type of gun using the cock and steel relationship. However, excavations on sites of the first half of the seventeenth century have revealed a surprising preponderance of the locks which are thus named today. The obvious characteristics of the snaphaunce are its battery, an arm-supported, rectangular piece of steel anchored toward the right end of the plate with, to the left of it, a trough-shaped pan having a circular end plate. When rusted, this feature often resembles half a cotton reel. The cock is generally S-shaped with a small tail at the lower end, under which the nose of the sear rests after protruding through the plate. In front of the forward curve of the "S" is a mallet-shaped block known as a buffer. Because of the doubtful interpretation of the name, it is uncertain just how late snaphaunces continued in use. Two examples, however, have been found in an early eighteenth-century context in Williamsburg.

By about 1620 the obvious step had been taken of coupling the steel with the pan cover, so producing the first single-action flintlock. This pan cover and steel combination is generally known as the frizzen, though that, like most terms used by gun collectors today, has been coined in comparatively recent times. Because the new mechanism could not be carried in the cocked position without fear of its discharging accidentally, a latch was anchored behind the cock to hook over its tail and prevent it from moving forward. (Fig. 69, No. 4) This safety catch was known as a "dog" and so gave the mechanism the name "dog lock." The earliest dog locks (c. 1630–50) had long plates very similar to those of the snaphaunce, but later forms were shorter, while the S-shaped cock became solid in the lower curve, though with a notch cut in the back edge into which the dog engaged. The final step was the abandonment of the dog in favor of a notch in the tumbler between sear and mainspring, enabling the flint to be carried at the half cock and then be pulled back for firing. It will be appreciated that without either dog or sear catch, the cock was either in the firing position or lying forward, having pushed the frizzen open. The latter position, of course, meant that the priming powder could fall out.

Although a dog catch is occasionally found on percussion guns dating as late as the mid-nineteenth century, its principal period of popularity was confined to the years 1625–70, and it is rare on English muskets after about 1715. Nevertheless, two dog locks (one of about 1640) have recently been found amid a Williamsburg gunsmith's waste dating from the Revolutionary period. It is deduced that they were removed from old guns brought to the shop to be modernized. This raises the interesting probability that when in an inventory one sees listed "1 old musket," it may be much older than one might suppose.

The dog lock's successor, the half-cockable flintlock, did not become common in England until the last quarter of the seventeenth century, though the mechanism had been in use in France since about 1610. Once accepted, the flintlock became the standard English and American weapon until the second quarter of the nine-

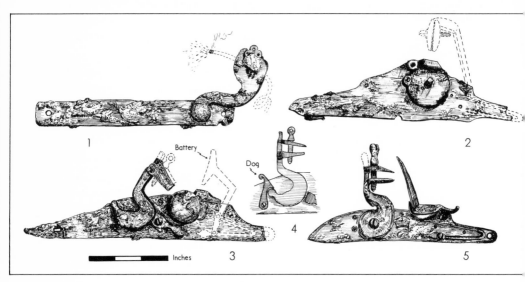

Fig. 69. Examples of excavated gunlocks. 1. Matchlock. 2. Wheel lock. 3. Snaphaunce. 4. Cock with "dog" catch. 5. British Brown Bess lock, Revolutionary period. Nos. 1–4 date from the early to mid-17th century.

teenth century. Indeed, many were still in use during the American Civil War. There were innumerable variations to the flintlock, only a few of which can be readily distinguished and dated when the lock is badly rusted. As a general rule it may be claimed that English flintlocks of the first half of the eighteenth century were more likely to have slightly convex plates prior to 1750 than thereafter, when flat plates with beveled edges became more common. Furthermore, in the period c. 1690–1740 the rear section of the plate (starting at the cock) was slightly downcurved, somewhat resembling the end of a banana. By the mid-century the lower edge of the plate had become virtually straight. (Fig. 69, No. 5) A looped reinforcement at the neck of the cock (the form known as a throat-hole cock) occurs on many English muskets of the first quarter of the eighteenth century, but it did not become common again until the first quarter of the nineteenth century, at which time the loop was integrated more solidly into the design. However, the throat-hole cock was used on French firearms of the Revolutionary period and many were carried by the Continental Army. They were also used on

214

American Springfield and Harpers Ferry locks of the late eighteenth and early nineteenth centuries.

Numerous attempts were made to find safe detonating powders for use with firearms, and intensive experimentation went on in the latter years of the eighteenth century, but it was not until 1822 that the first American patent was taken out for a reliable percussion cap. All cocks with hollow hammers in place of flints must belong to subsequent dates, as must all barrels fitted with a vertical nipple screwed into the breech. The majority of such locks, however, do not date earlier than the 1840's, though sometimes older guns were adapted to receive them.

In addition to the locks, items of brass gun furniture are often recovered from excavations (Fig. 70) and include butt plates, trigger guards, trigger plates, side or key plates, escutcheons, and thimbles. These last are sometimes known as pipes and were small tubes, often of ribbed, sheet brass with the ends drawn up into a pierced strip or lug. Three of them were attached to the underside of the barrel stock to house the rammer. On regulation military muskets the thimbles were of cast brass, and by the mid-eighteenth century the first and third were made flaring at the forward end. However, in the latter years of the century all three thimbles were expanded at one end. It should be noted that, until the mid-eighteenth century, rammers were generally of wood with a brass head; thereafter, steel with an expanded "button" end became standard for military muskets.

Peanut-shaped escutcheon plates with a nipple at the broad end, and with a single sleeve nut on the underside, were mounted on the stocks of Brown Bess muskets between butt and breech until 1775. Escutcheons of more elaborate designs were used on pistols and sporting guns, and these are best dated on the evidence of their decorative styles as they related to the taste of the times.

The original Brown Bess had a forty-six-inch barrel, but in the third quarter of the eighteenth century it began to be made 4" shorter. At the same time, changes occurred to the brass furniture; the side plate was no longer convex, the butt-plate tang was considerably shortened and lost its earlier nipple terminal, and the escutcheon was discarded. These amendments were standard after 1775 and until 1797. At the latter date a musket initially built for

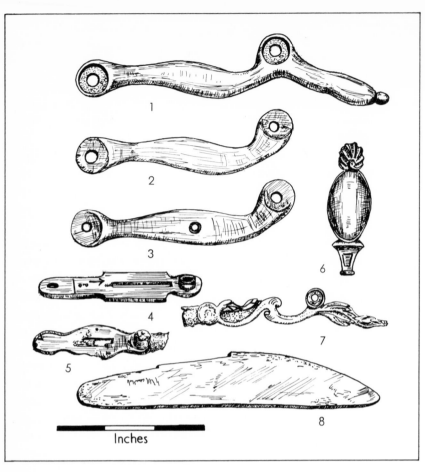

Fig. 70. Brass gun furniture. 1. Brown Bess side plate, First Land Pattern. 2. British military musket side plate, India Pattern. 3. Ditto, New Land Pattern. 4. Brown Bess trigger plate. 5. Rough casting for pistol trigger plate. 6. Escutcheon plate for a sporting gun. 7. Rough casting for a pistol side plate, with sprue still attached. 8. Lead pattern for a musket side plate. Nos. 5–8 are all relics of gunsmithing undertaken by the Geddy family in Williamsburg, and were found in contexts of the third quarter of the 18th century.

the East India Company was adopted by the British army and was known as the India Pattern. Its barrel was only 39″ in length, the tang of the butt plate was made narrower, and the tailed side plate was replaced by another that terminated at the rear screw hole. (Fig. 70, No. 2) As early as 1802, moves were begun to replace the India Pattern with another called the New Land Pattern; its side plate was similar in shape, but it possessed a small central hole to house a wood screw. (Fig. 70, No. 3) The new-pattern flintlock was produced intermittently until about 1838, by which time the percussion lock was taking over; existing Indian and New Land Pattern weapons were thereafter slowly converted to this more modern form.

The Brown Bess side plate had first been held in place by three screws, one at either end and the third in the middle, though only the front and middle screws extended through into the lock plate. With the standardization of the First Land Pattern in 1720 the rear screw was abandoned and the section of the side plate behind the central screw became nothing more than a decorative tail ending in a nipple. (Fig. 70, No. 1) This plate was markedly convex and the thick heads of the screws were recessed into it. With the introduction of the so-called Second Land Pattern, the flattened side plate was no longer thick enough to provide recesses for the screws. Subsequently, as already noted, the introduction of the India Pattern resulted in the shortening of the side plate to the second screw.

Trigger guards on regulation British muskets were consistently of brass after 1720 (before that some were of iron), and until the introduction of the India Pattern in the last quarter of the eighteenth century they possessed a terminal nipple at both ends and had one screw hole just behind the loop of the guard. The new guard was shortened, dispensed with the nipples, and had a second screw hole close to the end of the tail. Both styles of guard were drilled through the fore edge of the loop to receive a sling swivel.

It is important to remember that the evolution of musket hardware described above applies only to British regulation weapons, and then only to the Land and India Patterns. The criteria are not applicable to cavalry, light infantry, and officers' carbines, or to wall guns, blunderbusses, or pistols, all of which have dating characteristics of their own. For those I can do no better than to refer the reader to the bibliography.

Rifles, fowling pieces, and pistols made in or for colonial America, followed the European styles in brass furniture, being decorative as well as functional. (Fig. 70, Nos. 6 and 7) Their decoration was both cast and engraved, and even country gunsmiths were capable of producing ornament of elaboration and beauty. The best known of all decorative devices used on Early American muskets was the dragonesque side plate that characterized the weapons dispensed by the Hudson's Bay Company and by the North-West Fur Company of Montreal. Something akin to this motif occurs on a

Florentine pistol of 1695, on a French musket of c. 1700, on a few English examples of the first decades of the century, and on a German specimen of about 1740. These are all isolated examples, however, and there is no knowing which, if any, of them provided the inspiration for gun side plates of the later Indian trade. The earliest of them (perhaps dating in the third quarter of the eighteenth century) were engraved; but the vast majority were cast with the heads and scales in relief and, unlike the usual British musket side plates, the tail of the dragon or serpent curled around into a purely ornamental circle above the trigger. These cast plates are not likely to date before 1785, and all but a handful belong to the first half of the nineteenth century.

The principal firm of gunsmiths making the later North-West trade guns was that of Barnett and Co. of London, and the locks bear that name on the plate behind the cock, along with the mark of the Hudson's Bay Company (a seated fox within a circle) stamped between cock and pan. The earliest-recorded example is dated 1805, but it lacks the fox stamp. So popular were Barnett guns with the Indians that in the period 1828–35 the American Fur Company ordered guns bearing the Barnett name to be manufactured by gunsmiths in Pennsylvania. Others made for the Company in Belgium also traded on the Barnett name and were sometimes marked BURNETT.

Marks on barrels and locks are particularly helpful dating guides, but there were a great many of them and there is room here to mention but a few. English musket barrels usually have two stamps, the view and proof marks. The first was applied following the firing of a double-load test charge after the barrel was first bored, and comprised a v beneath a crown. The second mark, a ligatured G over P (gunmaker's proof) also under a crown, was stamped after the successful firing of another test charge when the barrel was completed. These marks were first used by the Gunmakers Company of London in 1637 and were contained within a pear-shaped punch. From 1672, when the London Company was granted a new, nation-wide charter, the marks were set in an oval. Until 1702, however, the crowns were divided into four segments and thereafter into only two. The London marks are easily mistaken for eighteenth-century private marks used by Birmingham gunsmiths, which differ only in that the proof mark contains the letter P—as opposed to the London G P. In 1813 the Birmingham smiths were allowed official stamps for both viewing and proofing: crossed sceptres under a crown and, over the letter v or P, the proof accompanied by the initials B and C to left and right of the sceptres. Royal Armory view and proof marks were entirely different, the former being a crowned GR over a broad arrow and the latter crowned sceptres without any letter. This last was also available for privately made guns brought to the Tower for proofing.

Musket locks were also marked, the Brown Bess series being engraved on the plate between cock and pan with a crowned AR or GR, the latter standing for George I, II, or III. From 1720 until 1764 these regulation locks were stamped on the tail of the plate behind the cock with the name of the maker and the date of manufacture; thereafter only the word TOWER was used, i.e., the official proofing house at the Tower of London. The locks of government arms were also stamped with a small crown over a broad arrow. East India Company weapons, on the other hand, were stamped on the barrel or stock with a heart-shaped merchant's mark containing the company's initials.

Gunflints are more common on archaeological sites than are parts of the weapons themselves, and although they cannot be dated with much accuracy a few deductions are possible on the basis of the presence or absence of one type or another. Initially, of course, one can deduce from the finding of any sort of gunflint that the weapons used on the site were more advanced than either the matchlock or wheel lock.

The true flint gunflint comes only from beds of chalk: in England, predominantly from Suffolk around the villages of Brandon, Tuddenham, Lavenham, and Mildenhall, where an industry that survives to the present day had been established in the late seventeenth century. Previously the "flints" had been made from *chert*, a general name given to any siliceous stone similar to flint but originating in rock other than chalk, and the "flints" struck from them are known as gunspalls. (Fig. 71) Whereas the eighteenth-century mass-produced gunflint was cut from previously prepared blades of flint, the gunspall was struck straight from the chert nodule and its shape was therefore largely dictated by the way in which the siliceous stone flaked. Thus, the back of the spall dropped sharply away from a single bulb of percussion and was generally rounded by secondary flaking. Such spalls had virtually no sides but sloped gently away from the bulb to three edges. However, seventeenth-century spalls took all sorts of forms, many of them fashioned by unskilled knappers from any available nodule, and it is common to find examples that are little more than slightly tapering chunks of stone.

The eighteenth-century English East Anglian flints were obtained by first striking the nodules into long cores having a flat or slightly concave bed (underside), sloping sides, and a flat face (upper surface), which were then broken into sections of appropriate width for use with the various sizes of guns from pocket pistol to cannon. The sides of the blade then became the interchangeable blade and back, and the cuts across the blade were then struck laterally (though not always) to slope the new sides of the gunflint, thus creating the finished prismatic form.

English flints from the East Anglian mines were invariably either gray or black and are easily distinguishable from the French, which are variously described as honey-colored, blond, or brown. The French flints also differ from the English (Fig. 71) since their shape is much more reminiscent of the spall in that they are rounded at the back, a feature carefully emphasized by secondary flaking. Although the majority have a rectangular flat face immediately in front of the rounded back, no small number of French flints are actually spalls having a bulb of percussion in place of the face. Unfortunately the French literature on the subject shows the backs of the flints to be much more square than the many archaeologically excavated examples would lead one to expect, but that may be the result of the draftsmen's desire to depict a neat and tidy product.

The vast majority of gunflints found on eighteenth-century colonial and Revolutionary sites (be they British or American) are French, for these were universally considered to be superior to the English. By the War of 1812, however, the British were using at least as many English flints as French, and in the first half of the nineteenth century western traders—both American and British— were selling only the English product. In short, therefore, the more common the English black prismatic gunflint, the later may be the date of one's site.

Flints were inserted into the cock grip with either base or face upward, but never without first being enfolded at the back with a

Fig. 71. Gunflints. 1. Gunspall. 2. English gunflint, gray prismatic type. 3. French gunflint, round-backed and pale-brown.

strip of leather or lead. The latter strips are frequently found on archaeological sites, sometimes still adhering to the flints. The grips were cut from sheet lead that was often scored so that they could be first cut into pieces of the right width for the various sizes of gun. Thus, rectangular strips of lead measuring approximately 1″ x 1½″ with one or two scored lines running down one side can reasonably be identified as flint grips.

The round, lead ball of various sizes was the only type of bullet used in America during the colonial period. It was not until the early nineteenth century that the French undertook sustained research to produce a bullet that fitted snugly enough in the barrel to prevent the exploding gases from escaping past it and at the same time loose enough to be inserted without forcing. The answer is generally attributed to Claude-Étienne Minié, who produced a slightly tapering-nosed bullet with a hollow at the base so that when the powder exploded the gases entering the concavity expanded the walls around it to the fullest extent permitted by the bore of the barrel before driving the bullet out. By 1850 the United States, and most European armies, had adopted the Minié principle. But, largely because it was easier to cast, the traditional round ball continued in use alongside the Minié bullet until late in the century.

The round, lead ball was available in gunsmiths' and other merchants' shops throughout the seventeenth, eighteenth, and nineteenth centuries, but a great many were made by gun owners who considered a bullet mold to be part of their kit. Seventeenth-century English bullet molds were generally of iron, shaped either like a pair of scissors or a pair of nutcrackers. The scissor type usually made only one ball at a time and was often fitted with a pivoting knife that trimmed off the waste lead or sprue that extended up through the pouring hole. Less time-consuming were the nutcracker molds which were capable of making up to a dozen balls of different sizes at one time. The seventeenth-century examples had comparatively thin leaves and could produce only the smaller ball sizes, these generally for use in sporting guns. In the eighteenth century this mold type became general, was made of brass, and was much thicker. A rectangular channel extended along the top when the leaves were closed to enable the lead to flow easily into each of the holes. Thus, when opened, the balls remained linked together by stalks springing out from the sprue like pigs from a sow of iron. The sprue strips are frequently found in excavations. It should be noted that this is much the same technique that was used in the making of solid pewter buttons.

In addition to molds of iron and brass, mention must also be made of those fashioned from stone (usually steatite) and also from pottery. Both types were made in two blocks that married together by means of pegs inserted at the ends and were usually held in wooden grips. Steatite (soapstone) examples have been found on eighteenth-century colonial sites, though not as yet in very closely dated contexts; they are known to have continued in use well through the nineteenth century. The only pottery example that I have encountered was probably made by the Pamunkey Indians of Virginia in the third quarter of the eighteenth century; but such molds were so simply manufactured that they could date from more or less any period.

BLACKMORE, HOWARD L.: *British Military Firearms 1650–1850*. London, 1961.
HAMILTON, T. M.: *Early Indian Trade Guns: 1625–1775*. Museum of the Great Plains, Lawton, Okla., 1968.
———, ed.: "Indian Trade Guns," *The Missouri Archaeologist*, Columbia, Mo. Vol. 22 (1962). A primary source for data on flints.
NEUMANN, GEORGE C.: *The History of Weapons of the American Revolution*. New York, 1967.
PETERSON, HAROLD L.: *Arms and Armor in Colonial America*. Harrisburg, Pa., 1956.
RUSSELL, CARL P.: *Guns on the Early Frontier, A History of Firearms from Colonial Times Through the Years of the Western Fur Trade*. Berkeley, Cal., 1959.
WITTHOFT, JOHN: "A History of Gunflints," *Pennsylvania Archaeologist*, Vol. 36, Nos. 1 and 2 (June 1966), pp. 12–49.

§ *FLOWERPOTS and BELL GLASSES*

Living as we do in a world that makes a fetish of change (even if it is for the worse), it is reassuring to find that there are still a few man-made objects around us that have remained virtually unaltered for centuries. Prominent among them is the common red-earthenware flowerpot. In its simplest form, it is still shaped like a truncated cone with a thickened rim and a small hole in the bottom. Heartening though this may be to those who find comfort in such islands of stability, to the archaeologist or the collectors (all eleven of them) of antique flowerpots, the pots' consistency over the years makes them extremely difficult to date with accuracy.

Flowerpots, once thrown, are among the easiest of all ceramic objects to manufacture, for they are fired at low temperatures and can be made from the poorest clays. It was ever thus, and consequently they were generally made locally rather than imported from some well-documented factory in England. Thus, minor variations and decorative eccentricities are likely to be meaningful dating guides only within a cart's travel of a single kiln.

The simple, utilitarian flowerpot of the colonial period seems to have been much the same both in America and in England, the body being without decoration and the rims everted and rolled. They came in a variety of sizes, all with a central basal hole, though some had an additional three holes equidistantly spaced around the sides immediately above the base. The latter pots, as today, were presumably used to raise young trees and shrubs, and were buried to their rims in the nursery bed. An example of this pot type, found in excavations on the site of John Custis's famous garden in Williamsburg, had been converted to a one-holer, the three in the side having been plugged with pitch.

Alongside the rolled-rimmed flowerpot, eighteenth-century Virginians used others of which the rims were simply folded over and pressed to the walls with two fingers, thus giving the rim exterior a "3"-shaped profile. Examples have been found in uncertain contexts at the Governor's Palace in Williamsburg and also at the site of the Travis House, the latter fragments thrown away c. 1780. While the rolled-rimmed type has persisted to our own times, straight-rimmed pots were common in Virginia in the nineteenth century (though how early in it has not been determined) and these gave way in the present century to the machine-made, square-collared pots which are now fighting a losing battle with similar shapes in plastic.

In addition to the purely utilitarian pots that were kept in the greenhouse or bedded in the ground, there were others, intended to be seen, which housed small plants and shrubs that were stood around paved yards, beside steps, or mounted on pilasters. Though made from the same low-fired red earthenware, these pots were often fitted with earlike loop handles and some were decorated with incised or applied ornament. Ornamental pots, apparently of two sizes, are clearly to be seen in Henry Danckerts's celebrated picture of Charles II being presented by his gardener with what is allegedly the first pineapple grown in England. There is some doubt as to whether the setting is actually English; nevertheless, it clearly dates from the third quarter of the seventeenth century and shows large and smaller pots, both bulbous and decorated with applied foliate festoons with semihuman masks at the junction of each. The large pot stands on a pillar and was probably two feet in diameter, while smaller versions are set out in a ring around a circular fountain trough. Pots of conventional shape but with applied winged cherubs linked together with swags of thumb-pressed clay strips have been found at the Governor's Palace in Williamsburg. They possessed unusually elaborate rims, having a square-cut but slightly down-bent flange ⅜″ below the straight lip and a V-sectioned cordon ¾″ below the flange. These decorative pots (rim diameter 10″) were not found in well-dated archaeological contexts, but the history of the site is such that they would not have been installed later than 1775.

The previously mentioned Custis garden (unlikely to have been improved after 1749) also yielded fragments of decorative flower-pottery in the shape of fragmentary pedestal urns of the usual red earthenware but adorned on the upper body with applied ("sprigged") medallions depicting the English royal arms supported by the lion and unicorn. In their plain earthenware state these urns

Flowerpots and Bell Glasses

must have been extremely attractive, but they had subsequently been painted gray (an undercoat?) and then a particularly revolting pink. The medallions also had the gray ground coat, but over it the arms were painted black and the supporters yellow.

There is no doubt that the better colonial gardens made use of potted plants in ornamental earthenware containers, a fact that should be borne in mind by restoration landscape architects. Whether wealthy American colonists went further and used the marble and lead pots, tanks, and urns that were popular in eighteenth-century England is uncertain; at least I know of no good archaeological evidence. They did, of course, have readily available a class of massive earthenware jar that is still seen in use in English gardens. This was the ubiquitous Iberian olive jar that is found on most colonial sites of the second half of the eighteenth century. (*See* p. 143.) It makes an excellent container for ferns and trailing plants, and it seems unlikely that colonial gardeners would have neglected to use it.

The excavator of a colonial American garden site can expect to find fragments of containers both *in* which and *under* which plants were raised. The glass domes used to protect seedlings were known as bell glasses; being of large size, they were fragile and when broken often shattered into a multitude of pieces. English bell glasses were blown from the same green metal used for making bottles and, as the name suggests, were shaped like a bell. Excavated examples have been found to measure approximately 2′ in diameter, but it is known that they were made in at least two sizes. The inventory of Governor Botetourt's possessions made in 1770 after his death at the Palace in Williamsburg, listed "22 Large Bell glasses, 1 Small Bell glass."[6] It would seem, however, that to most people a bell glass was a bell glass; when Peter Lyons of King William County, Virginia, wrote to England for a long list of items in 1771, it included "three Bell glasses for the Garden"[7] with no mention of size.

[6] Botetourt Papers, Archives Division, Virginia State Library, Richmond, Va. Inventory recorded October 24, 1770.

[7] Norton Mason, op. cit., p. 191.

English bell glasses flared at the mouth, the rims of which were folded outward onto themselves to form a band about 1¼″ in width. The thickness of the glass itself ranged from about ⅛″ in the midsection to more than ½″ at the dome. To the top of the latter a heavy glass knob was attached, crudely trailed around itself to create a shape resembling a doughnut; it measured about 3½″ in diameter and about 1½″ in height. Examples are occasionally found whose knobs have parted company revealing the pontil scar at the top of the dome, for the covers were made in much the same way as was crown window glass. (*See* p. 234.) It is not known how early bell glasses were manufactured in England, but examples of the type described above appear in an engraving of a kitchen garden in Richard Bradley's *New Improvements in Planting and Gardening,* published in 1726. About a quarter of a century later Diderot's *Encyclopédie* illustrated three varieties, one of straw (to protect flowers from direct sunlight), another made from flat panes of glass held together with a frame of iron or wood, and the third a cover having a mouth similar to that of the English bell glass but with the top flattened instead of domed and terminating in a much more practical handle shaped like a round doorknob.

The dome-shaped bell glass continued to be made through the nineteenth century in both England and America, but the metal was generally a paler, sometimes bluish, green and did not become iridescent in the ground as did the poor-quality bottle-green glass of the eighteenth century. The later examples possessed more neatly applied knobs, either round balls or stemmed as were those of the French glasses, and the walls of the bells were generally thicker, the thickness increasing toward the rim, which differed from the eighteenth century types in that it was not folded back on itself.

It is worth remembering that panes of glass found in a garden area need not have come from a dwelling; they could equally well have been used in greenhouses, cold frames, or in the paneled bell glasses illustrated by Diderot. Jane Webb Loudon, the English author of *Instructions in Gardening for Ladies* (first published in 1840) called Diderot's angular covers "hand-glasses" and described them as follows:

Portable frames or covers, formed of iron, zinc, or wood, and glazed. These glasses differ from bell-glasses in being longer, and composed of numerous small pieces of glass, which are fastened together by narrow strips of lead. Hand-glasses are generally square, but they may be made of an octagon, or any other shape that may be found convenient; and they are sometimes made with a pane to open to admit air, or with the upper part to take off.[8]

The previously cited 1726 engraving of an English kitchen garden showed a more permanent variation, a row of twelve framed panes set at a forty-five degree angle, each with a smaller piece of glass above that could be removed as described by Mrs. Loudon. That lady's reference to the panes of "hand-glasses" being seated in lead serves as a reminder that, just as all window glass need not have come from conventional windows, not all "turned lead" (*see* p. 233) was used for glazing houses.

§ *FURNITURE HARDWARE*

Although datable wooden fragments of furniture are rarely found on archaeological sites, examples of their brass fittings are common and, theoretically, are fairly easily datable. Among the earliest such fittings were the brass upholstery tacks used to ornament and anchor the leather of straight-backed side chairs of the second quarter of the seventeenth century; these were either circular or lozenge-shaped, concavo-convex, and with a welded brass shank. The large tacks measured up to 1" in diamter and were also used as harness ornaments, though the latter can sometimes be identified by the fact that the shanks are clenched over to grip the back of the leather instead of being driven straight into the wood. However, seemingly identical large-headed tacks were used to retain and ornament the

[8] Quoted in J. Didsbury: "18th Century Garden Bell Glasses," *The Chronicle* of the Early American Industries Association, Inc. (Williamsburg, Va.), Vol. 16, No. 3 (September 1963), p. 36.

Fig. 72. Examples of furniture and related brass hardware.
1. Teardrop handle and relief-molded plate; c. 1685–1720.
2. Loop handle sometimes used with plate similar to No. 1. **3.**
Torque-like bail handle with incurving knobbed terminals,
with typical split tang or cotter pin and thin, stamp-decorated
plate; c. 1690–1720. **4.** Everted-ended bail handle with balusters
and central knop, with nut and screw-ended mounting post
and early "bat's-wing" plate with stamped decoration; c.
1720–50. **5.** Bail handle with bulbous center section, and plain
plate of typical Chippendale type; c. 1750–75. **6.** Elaborately
cast bail handle usually used in association with relief-cast
foliate plates for each post, reminiscent of No. 1; c. 1765–75.
7. Bail handle, oval in section and with in-turned ends, used
with oval plates (see No. 8) of the Hepplewhite period; c.
1785–1800. **8.** Thin, relief-stamped plate of the Hepplewhite
period, used with bail handles comparable to No. 7; c. 1785–
1800; angular plates stamped from thin sheet brass with bail
handles having comparable outlines belong to the Sheraton
period (c. 1800–30). **9.** Cast-brass catch housing with iron
mechanism for tilt-topped tables; c. 1750–90. **10.** Brass swivel
caster with iron axle and central post, caster held in place
with screws through the flat collar, often used on armchairs;
c. 1750–75. **11.** Stamped cover for bed bolt; c. 1785–1830. **12.**
Coat hook with iron screw, the ornamental terminal sometimes
hexagonal, conical, etc.; c. 1745–75.

exterior leather of eighteenth-century coaches and sedan chairs, and
so the presence of an oversize tack need not necessarily suggest a
seventeenth-century context. Smaller tacks were used around the
skirts of seventeenth-century chair seats, and it is impossible to distinguish between these and the common upholstery tacks of the
eighteenth century.

Pendant loop handles appeared as early as the reign of James I,
when they were used for drawers and cupboard doors, but by and
large few brass handles were used on English furniture before about
1660. During the latter part of the seventeenth century and on to
about 1720, solid teardrop handles backed by a round or diamond-
shaped plate and anchored by an iron or brass tang or cotter pin
were used on the smaller pieces of furniture. (Fig. 72, No. 1) For
heavier drawers, bale handles curving inward at the tops were used;
these were also anchored by cotter pins but were backed with more
elaborate plates. (Fig. 72, No. 3) The latter were very thin, with

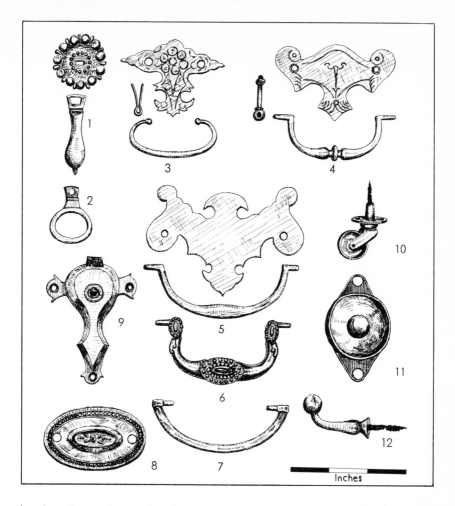

intricately sculptured edges, and generally were stamped with numerous crescents which together created foliate patterns.

From about 1720 to 1750 heavier "bat's-" or "angel's-wing" plates accompanied bale handles that turned outward at the top. Handles common to this group in its early years were still held by cotter pins and were often cast with a pair of balusters parted by a central disc knop. (Fig. 72, No. 4) But by mid-century the bales were anchored by means of hollow-headed posts with threaded shanks that were gripped by brass nuts on the insides of the drawers. The bales themselves had lost their knops and the two balusters had joined together to produce a bulging midsection. (Fig. 72, No. 5)

The plates of the third quarter of the eighteenth century developed from the older bat's-wing style, though their wings had a general tendency to lift the eye upward rather than down. (Fig. 72, No. 5) These are typical of the Chippendale period (1750–75), and many of them were lattice-stamped in the manner of the popular chinoiserie fretwork styles. The bale handles and their posts remained unchanged. Belonging to much the same period, though going on to the end of the century, a vogue for lighter hardware resulted in the elimination of the full brass plates for drawer handles; instead, handles were given circular collars surrounding only the posts, similar to those that had been used in conjunction with teardrop handles in the late seventeenth century. Rosette discs in the rococo manner were also used, though in conjunction with ornamentally molded bale handles. (Fig. 72, No. 6) However, these decorative styles were short-lived and more attributable to the years c. 1765–75.

From 1785 to 1800 the influence of Hepplewhite dominated English and American furniture, and handle plates again extended from post to post, though they were now oval and stamped out of very thin brass, ornamented in concentric loops or frequently with American eagles. The handles had lost their central bulge and exactly followed the line of the oval backs; instead of turning out at the tops to enter the posts, they now turned abruptly in and approached them from the outside. (Fig. 72, No. 8) Next came the influence of Sheraton (1800–20), and the thin cast plates became rectangular with the corners cropped, the handles following the same lines. Variations on this style predominated through the first thirty years of the nineteenth century, though they were also accompanied by a revival of the pendant loop, this time held in the jaws of a cast-brass lion mask or anchored to a post passing through a stamped-brass rosette.

Lock escutcheons followed almost exactly the same evolutionary steps as those of the drawer-handle plates. They began, however, in the first half of the seventeenth century as the front plates of locks which were inserted from the front into small chests, Bible boxes, and jewel caskets, rather than from the back as was common in later years. Early seventeenth-century brass lock plates were often extremely elaborately cut at the edges and were frequently stamped to resemble clockfaces. In the later years of the seventeenth century, when the lock was attached from behind and the escutcheon from the front, the latter became diamond-shaped and was chased with rosette patterns. By about 1740, the decorative touches had been

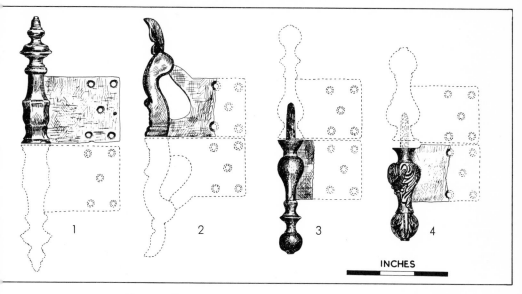

Fig. 73. Parts of ornamental-brass coach hinges found in Williamsburg; mid-18th century. The two matching units pivoted on an iron pintle that was normally anchored to the lower section and which, in turn, was attached to the jamb.

abandoned and plain brass was the fashion. But in the 1760's the desire to lighten furniture hardware slowly brought about the demise of the large, ornate escutcheons and replaced them with much smaller, oval keyhole plates or—alternatively—with small but elaborately molded rococo pieces to match the rosette discs and foliate handles. The large escutcheons never came back; during the Hepplewhite and Sheraton periods they were reduced to small ovals, rectangles, and often to no more than a brass sleeve to the keyhole.

Armchairs, light tables, and sofas of the third quarter of the eighteenth century were often fitted with brass casters. These generally pivoted on posts passing up through a sleeve into the leg and secured on the bottom by a circular plate held in place by three screws. (Fig. 72, No. 10) In the late eighteenth century the plate was replaced by a square cup or ferrule held by a pin that passed through the side. This cup next became cylindrical and was common during the first forty years of the nineteenth century. A variant of this type with a ball at the bottom of the cup was popular on chairs in the years 1805–20, while a caster offset under a cast-brass paw (in use alongside the ring handles and lion-mask plates) occurred in the years 1810–30.

Iron furniture hinges of solid, butterfly style were common on cupboards of the first half of the seventeenth century, but by 1650 they had been largely superseded on good quality furniture by H-hinges of elaborately zoömorphic forms whose curling terminals often resembled the heads of cockerels or dragons. These were followed by straight H-hinges whose decoration was confined to trifid ends at top and bottom; these were common in the later years of the seventeenth century and in the first half of the eighteenth century. Strap hinges with butterfly pintles and spearhead terminals were used for trunks and boxes throughout the seventeenth century, as also were long iron bale handles that turned abruptly up and outward at the ends and were held by cotter pins. The handles are usually identified as coffin handles, but they were actually used on all sorts of boxes and trunks and persisted unchanged, though in smaller sizes, through the eighteenth century on cheap, leather trinket boxes.

Hinges came to full and exotic flower in the late seventeenth century when they were cast in heavy and elaborately chased brass (sometimes tin-plated) and were used to decorate already heavily ornamented japanned cabinets. Such hinges frequently resemble Bible clasps and are occasionally mistaken for them. Book clasps (not only for Bibles) were common in the first half of the seventeenth century; they are always too thin to be mistaken for furniture hinges, and the majority are stamped with rosettes, acorns, thistles, and other such pastoral devices. At the other end of the scale, there is an eighteenth-century brass hinge form too heavy to be correctly associated with furniture but which is often so described when found in excavations. (Fig. 73) These offset butt hinges with elaborately cast exterior finials were intended for carriage doors, but the metal was often too brittle and they were prone to snapping at the point where the flat plate projected beyond the jamb. There are numerous examples to be seen on carriages of the mid-eighteenth century in the Museu Nacional dos Coches at Lisbon, the director of which has noted that the majority are anchored with two, three, or four screws per plate and only very rarely with five. It is significant that three broken examples have been found in excavations close by Williamsburg roadsides, presumably having fallen when coach doors were thrown open too vigorously. A lighter, two-screw version is illustrated in Diderot's *Encyclopédie,* and a close parallel found in Williamsburg is stamped with the maker's name, L. RENEL.

NUTTING, WALLACE: *Furniture Treasury.* New York, 1954.
ORMSBEE, THOMAS H.: *Field Guide to Early American Furniture.* Boston, 1951.

See also CLOCKS and CLOCKCASES.

§ *GLASS, Window*

Although fragments of window glass are liberally scattered around most colonial and nineteenth-century domestic sites of any consequence, such glass is impossible to date within anything but the widest brackets. As a rule the fragments are too small to give much idea of pane sizes or of the methods of manufacture; however, both (if discernible) can offer small dating guides. In the seventeenth century those windows that were glazed used glass cut into small diamonds, rectangles, and squares, known as "quarries," which were mounted in grooved strips of lead anchored to iron frames that in turn were nailed to wooden casements. It should be noted that the strips of lead are frequently found on sites dating anywhere in the seventeenth century and on into the first half of the eighteenth century, though by that time double-hung sash windows were well established. The lead strips are often erroneously described as "cames," but this term belongs to the cast H-sectioned lead rods (12" to 14" in length) prior to being drawn through a vise by the glazier to produce the flexible strips used in the window; thereafter, they were known as "turned lead," and so they should be by the archaeologist who must distinguish between the raw rod and the finished product.

The "broad" glass used in leaded windows was of indifferent quality, being either greenish-blue or greenish-yellow in color and made by blowing a long, tubular bubble, cutting off both ends to create a "muff," slicing this down one side, and laying it on an iron plate in the furnace mouth. As the glass was heated it was encouraged to open out along the cut until it lay flat on the plate, at which point it was known as a table. By the late seventeenth century, a new method of manufacture had been imported from France whereby one blew a large bubble, transferred it from the blowing iron to a pontil iron, and—while still workable—enlarged the orifice with a wooden tool, at the same time constantly rotating the bubble. By rolling it back and forth on the arms of the gaffer's chair the open-mouthed bubble spun out into a disc. The edge was thicker than the inner areas and, being curved, had to be trimmed off and wasted. The center of the disc, to which the pontil iron had been affixed, could be up to 1″ in thickness and was scarred with the mark of the iron. This central area was known as a "bullion" or "bull's-eye" and was usually thrown away, although it could be cut square and used in basement or transom windows, through which no one needed to look. The circles of glass are known as "crowns" and were generally shipped to the colonies in crates, to be cut to size by the purchaser. There does, however, seem to be a modicum of confusion regarding the techniques of making crown glass, for Chambers' *Cyclopaedia* (1738) was at pains to describe the method, after noting that other writers had it wrong, and proceeded to describe the technique of making broad glass! At the same time Neve's *Builder's Dictionary* (1736 edition) listed the various types of window glass, naming Ratcliffe and Lambeth in London as the sources of crown glass, while referring later to Newcastle glass as "the glass most used in England," the edge of which "as they stand in the Cases or Frames, is circular, about the 4th or 5th part of a Circle . . ."[9] This indicates that the sheets were cut from discs which could only have been made by the crown process described above.

Neve described the Newcastle glass as being "subject to Specks and Streaks in it, and . . . very often warped and crooked." These traits are to be seen to a greater or lesser degree in most panes made by the crown method. Because the disc achieved its shape by being spun, any bubbles, stress lines, and other imperfections were also

[9] For full citation, see fn. 9, p. 36.

drawn around in curves, whereas in broad glass they were elongated in straight lines as the bubbles were drawn out to create the cylinder. Thus, it may be assumed that glass with curving bubbles and stress lines (the latter are accentuated when the surface is decayed) will date after about 1690.

No further major changes occurred in the making of English window glass until about 1832, when Lucas Chance of Sunderland, with the aid of French workmen, revived the broad-glass method, making much larger muffs that were cut cold with a diamond and opened out onto beds of glass rather than onto sand-covered iron. The resulting sheets had an area measuring from 6' to 10' square and were of vastly better quality than anything that had been made before. The Chance innovation is known as the "sheet process," distinguishing it from the earlier broad-glass making technique.

POWELL, H. J.: *Glass-Making in England.* Cambridge, Eng., 1923.

§ *GLASS BOTTLES*

See BOTTLES, Glass.

§ *GLASSES, Drinking, and Decanters*

See DRINKING GLASSES and DECANTERS.

§ *HINGES*

Contemporary lexicographers and compilers of encyclopedias agreed that there were many kinds of hinges, and, borrowing from each other, they amassed the following impressive list:

235

> *viz.* Bed, Box, Butts, Casement, *Lancashire,* and smooth filed; Casting, Chest black, *Lancashire,* smooth filed; Coach, Desk, Dovetails, Esses, Folding, Garnets, Dozen-ware-long, Dozen-ware-short, Weighty-long, Weighty-short, Lamb-heads, Port, Side-*Lancashire,* Side-smooth-filed, Side with rising Joints, *Lancashire* and smooth filed, Side with Squares, Screw, Scuttle, Shutter, *Lancashire,* and smooth filed, Stall, Trunk of sundry Sorts, Joints, *Lancashire* Dozenware, with Hooks, Dozen-ware-long, Dozen-ware-short, Weightylong, Weighty-short.

Unfortunately, the writers elected to let it go at that, assuming that no one needed to be told what these hinges looked like. Richard Neve's *Builder's Dictionary* (1736 edition), however, from which the foregoing list is taken, went on to give prices for the types that he considered the most common. They were: "butts, bed hinges, box hinges, small brass ditto, hooks and hinges, side hinges, side hinges with a square, and screw hinges."

The hinge varieties most commonly recovered from excavations are shapes now known as H, HL, T, strap, butterfly, and cock's-head. The H-hinge is presumably the equivalent of the "side hinge"; at least it is if the "side hinge with a square" means an HL-hinge. Both types were used on domestic doors, the HL being capable of carrying a greater weight than the H type. HL-hinges, for example, were used on the exterior doors of Virginia public buildings. The T-hinge was often of large size and used on the doors of barns, stables, and bulkheads, the crosspiece being anchored to the frame and the long strap to the door. The strap hinge proper (perhaps the "Dozen-ware, with Hooks") had a loop at the butt end of the strap and was seated over a pintle driven into the frame. This type was normally used for gates and doors that from time to time needed to be removed. The butterfly hinge comprised two winglike units of identical shape and was commonly used throughout both the seventeenth and eighteenth centuries for the lids of trunks and the doors of country-made cupboards. The cock's-head hinges were also used on cupboards, and these are probably what Neve meant by "Esses." They were essentially H-hinges with curling extremities ending in zoömorphic terminals that sometimes resemble a cock's head and sometimes a dragon. They are remarkably Celtic in character, and although examples are found in eighteenth-century contexts they were far more common in the seventeenth century.

While the majority were used for cupboard doors, larger examples are occasionally encountered on interior doors; some seen on the doors of English houses have been filed smooth and are kept polished, contrasting dramatically with the dark color of the wood.

Although I have yet to see an excavated example, there is little doubt that Neve's "Side with rising Joints" is an H-hinge with the interlocking loops around the pintle being slightly spiraled so that, as the door was opened, it was raised enough to ride clear of a carpet. The eighteenth-century examples of this type that I have seen in extant houses have all been of brass or bronze, as were most of the ornamental butt hinges. A bronze T-hinge retaining traces of white paint was found near the ruins of the great Virginia plantation of Corotoman, which burned in 1729, but there is no knowing where, if anywhere, in the house it was used.

D'ALLEMAGNE, HENRY RENÉ: *Decorative Antique Ironwork*. New York, 1968 (reprint of 1924 edn.).

See also FURNITURE HARDWARE.

§ *HORSESHOES and HORSE FURNITURE*

Very little serious attention has been given to the evolution of the horseshoe, possibly because it is hard to get excited about it, but more probably because there is little that can usefully be said. The published guidelines unfortunately are not always valid, but I shall summarize them here, for they are all we have. First, however, it may be helpful to mention the various parts of the shoe. The curving sides are known as the *branches* and their broad faces the *foot* and *ground surfaces*. The edges are referred to as *margins* and the ends of the branches the *heels* or, if they turn down, *calkins*. The groove close to the outer margin in which the nail holes are sunk is known as *fullering*, while any upward projection at the junction of the branches at the fore edge of the hoof is known, rather obviously, as a *toe clip*.

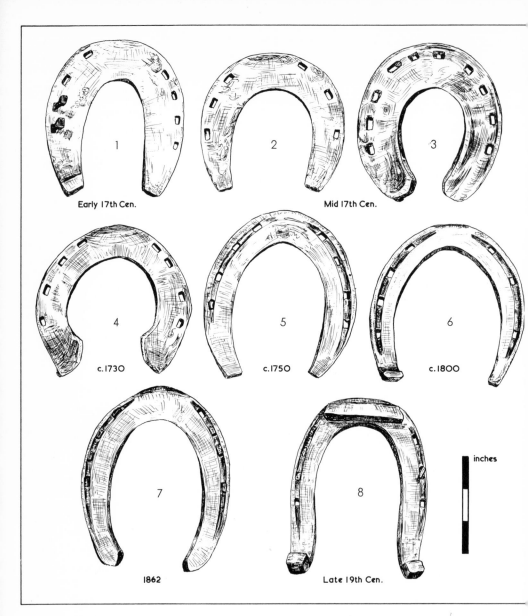

Fig. 74. Examples of iron horseshoes from dated archaeological contexts; No. 1 from London, the rest from Virginia.

It has been claimed that fullering does not appear on English shoes prior to the mid-seventeenth century, and while this may indeed be true it should be noted that at least one site in Virginia has yielded fullered shoes in a context dating no later than 1660. It is also claimed that seventeenth-century shoes have either three nail holes in each branch or three in one and four in the other, while in the eighteenth century shoes had many more nail holes, sometimes as many as ten a side. Again this may be true, but it is also true that many eighteenth-century shoes have as few as three or four holes per branch. As in the case of all handwrought objects, too much depended on the whim and training of the individual craftsman for there to be any infallible evolutionary conformity among utilitarian items. Nevertheless, like all archaeological evidence, these broad trends should be borne in mind and weighed against the many other associated clues in arriving at one's dating conclusions.

Seemingly of greater reliability is the information that the toe clip was introduced by H. Hallen, veterinary surgeon for the Inniskilling Dragoons in the mid-nineteenth century. The toe clip, incidentally, should not be confused with another nineteenth-century feature, a reinforcing bar that was sometimes welded across the fore edge of the ground surface and balanced by calkins of the same length as its thickness. (Fig. 74)

There was a tendency among shoes of the first half of the seventeenth century to spread inward at the heels, and this feature became accentuated in the second half of the century when it often created a keyhole appearance. Unfortunately, that distinctive shape is thought to have continued to the end of the eighteenth century, though I myself have yet to see it after about 1740. It is true, however, that at the end of the eighteenth century the heels became much wider apart, and many nineteenth-century shoes are entirely U-shaped, having no incurve at all at the heels. As the eighteenth century progressed, the surfaces became narrower and the shoes thicker, and those features too continued into the nineteenth century.

Occasionally one finds what appear to be half horseshoes. They are, in fact, parts of the divided branches of shoes for oxen. I can find no dating guides for these objects.

Horse furniture in general has received distressingly little attention, though it might now be possible to build up an impressive corpus of information if a study of examples from closely dated colonial sites could be made. As yet, however, most of the existing research has been devoted to medieval harness. Even more common than horseshoes on American sites (for up to the mid-eighteenth century horses traversing the coastal clays were often left unshod) are the cheekpieces of bits.

According to Chambers' *Cyclopaedia* (1728) there were only two principal types of bit then in use, namely the snaffle and curb, though there were innumerable variations of both. The snaffle bit had only vestigial cheekpieces and no other linkage but the mouthpiece itself, whereas the curb bit had elongated cheekpieces linked together with a lip strap, a chain below the chin, and sometimes a bar to hold the cheekpieces apart. (Fig. 75)

The snaffle bit generally comprised a pair of rodlike cheekpieces having a central loop for the single rein, to which was attached the usually jointed bit. When a snaffle was used in conjunction with a curb bit, the former possessed rein rings but no cheekpieces, and was then known as a bridoon. Such bits were either jointed or made in a single bar, the latter sometimes twisted. Together the curb and bridoon bits constituted a double-reined bridle called a Weymouth. The curb proper had no rein rings flanking the bit; when those were present on the cheekpieces the unit was known as a Pelham (the family name of the Duke of Newcastle, 1698–1768, who made it popular), i.e., a combination curb and snaffle.

Principal features of the cheekpieces of curb bits in the sixteenth and seventeenth centuries were elaborately cast bosses anchored with two brass rivets to the cheekpiece to conceal its junction with the mouthpiece. These bosses were molded in the form of rosettes, writhened, pierced, or elaborately chased, but in the eighteenth century they were rarely adorned with anything more than a couple of concentric grooves. However, the typical plain boss of the eighteenth century was very often plated with tin to resemble silver. A transitional form, seemingly belonging to the period c. 1680–1710, was plain save for a central nipple.

Bridle bosses are frequently found detached from their cheekpieces, but their purpose can be identified (at least in the eighteenth century) by the two pierced lugs projecting from the edges through which the rivets anchored them to the iron. (Fig. 76) Other brass bosses are found with two or more bent brass tangs projecting from their backs; those were used as ornaments for harness leathers, the largest being used on winkers. Many of these harness ornaments were tin-plated and the majority are no more than 2½″ in length, the most common having a shell over an inverted baluster that ended in a knop and nipple. Simpler forms were oval

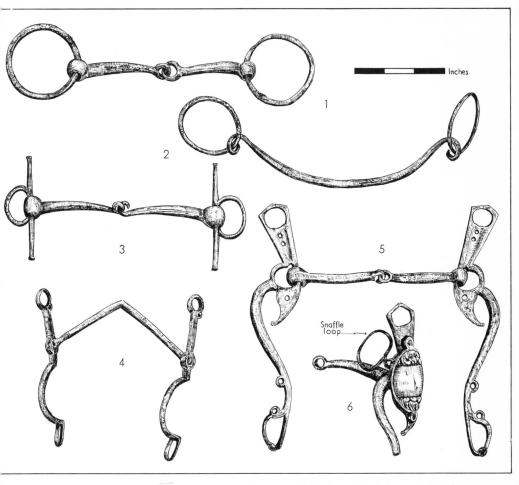

Fig. 75. Examples of 18th-century bits from Virginia. **1.** Jointed-mouthed bridoon, a type generally used in association with a curb bit; unstratified, possibly quite modern. **2.** Solid-mouthed bridoon, discarded c. 1730. **3.** Snaffle or watering bit (similar to the bridoon but with cheekpieces), discarded c. 1730. **4.** V-mouthed curb, discarded c. 1765. **5.** Jointed-mouthed curb, the most popular type used in the late 17th and 18th centuries; the small holes in the cheekpieces above and below the bit housed rivets securing ornamental brass bosses (as No. 6, and Fig. 76 [No. 3]), discarded c. 1730. **6.** Part of Pelham bit, a combination curb and snaffle, the brass boss being offset on washers to provide room for the snaffle rein loop to be attached to the cheekpiece; such cheekpieces often terminated at the bottom (not shown) in a single large ring and were linked to each other by a solid iron bar; unstratified, but almost certainly third quarter of the 18th century.

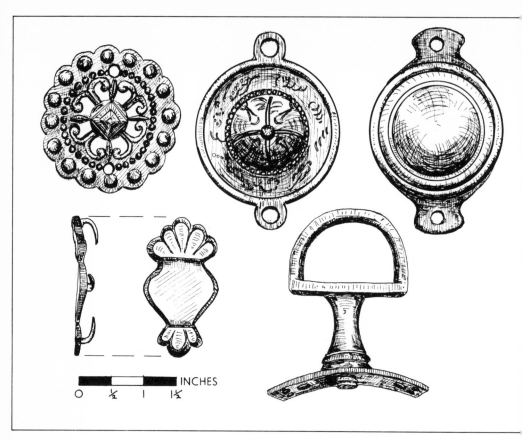

Fig. 76. Brass harness and saddle fittings. **1–3.** Bosses from the cheekpieces of curb bits—Nos. 1 and 2, 17th century; 3, 18th century. **4.** Harness-leather ornament; 18th century. **5.** Saddle terret; 18th century. All English or colonial manufacture.

or peanut-shaped, but nearly all of those that rely on form rather than embellishment can be attributed to the years 1690–1770.

If little attention has been devoted to bits, even less has been given to stirrups. In the absence of evidence to the contrary, it would seem that the earliest form found on colonial sites had a gridiron platform (i.e., an outer loop of iron surrounding a central bar), straight sides, and an oval pivoting eye for the stirrup leather. In the latter years of the seventeenth century the principal type (its origins go back at least to the tenth century) had a solid rectangular plate for the platform while the sides described what was left of a circle; the strap loop emerged from it in a shallow rectangle, with the top bar being a little longer than the width required by the sides. This slightly winglike top to the loop seems to have been popular in the late seventeenth and early eighteenth centuries. The same basic stirrup shape continued through the eighteenth century, though later in the period the sides curved less while the square-ended platform became oval. Heavy brass stirrups are often mistakenly identified as of eighteenth-century date, but it would seem that most of them belonged to the mid-nineteenth century.

Spurs occur in great variety on sites of the first half of the seventeenth century; although the majority were of iron (sometimes encrusted with silver) a few excavated examples are of silver-leafed brass, elaborately chased, and the designs filled with gold. Those spurs having large rowels generally also had elbowed shanks, but these seem to have been by no means as common as those with short, straight shanks and only small, thumbtack-sized spikes to their rowels.

Spurs are surprisingly lacking from well-dated eighteenth-century sites, but those that are known are usually of tinned brass, though much smaller than their elaborate predecessors. The dearth of iron or brass spurs in eighteenth-century contexts may perhaps mean that most spurs were of brass and that they were melted down as scrap when broken. All spurs of the seventeenth and eighteenth centuries, whether of iron or brass, terminated in figure-8 loops to which the buckles and straps were attached by thongs or rivets, but in the nineteenth century these were replaced by rectangular buckles cast as one with the spur itself, a single buckle at each end.

MURRAY, R. W.: "Dating Old English Horseshoes," *Journal of the British Archaeological Association*, 3rd Ser. (1937), Vol. 1, pp. 14–33, and Vol. 2, pp. 133–44.

§ *LOCKS and PADLOCKS*

Chambers' *Cyclopaedia* (1728) began its dissertation on locks by telling its readers that "The lock is reckoned the master-piece in smithery; a great deal of art and delicacy being required in contriving and varying the wards, spring, bolts &c." Chambers, however, listed only three types: "Those placed on outer doors are called *stock-locks*; those on chamber doors, *spring-locks*; those on trunks, *trunk-locks*, *padlocks*, &c."[1] Richard Neve's *Builder's Dictionary* (1736 edition) was considerably more explicit and listed the following varieties:

> Stock-locks plain, from 10d. to 14d. *per* Piece, or more.
> S-bitted Stock-locks, with a long Pipe, 1s. 6d.
> S-bitted and warded Stock-locks, very strong, 7s.
> Brass-locks, from 5s. 6d. to 9s.
> Brass-knob'd-locks in Iron-cases, 3s.
> Double Spring-locks, 1s.
> Closet-door-locks, 1s. 4d.
> Pad, or Secret-locks, with Slits, instead of Pipes, 1s.
> Plate-stock-locks, 3s. 8d.
> Some Ditto for half that Price.
> Plate-stock-locks in Shute,[2] 4s. 6d.
> Brass-knob'd-locks in Shute,[2] 6s. 6d.
> Iron-rim'd-locks, very large, 10s. 6d.

The most common and, as Neve shows, the cheapest of all seventeenth- or eighteenth-century door locks was the plain stock-lock, often known as the Banbury or, in America, the Bambury lock. (Fig. 77a) The parts were individually mounted in a wooden block and sealed with two strips or plates of sheet iron, one covering the wards and the other the head of the bolt. Such locks were screwed, nailed, or bolted to the doors and were less likely to be affected by wet weather than were iron-cased locks. Because there was nothing to hold the elements together once parted from their wooden block, plain stock-locks are rarely found in archaeological contexts. The metal components, however,—bolts, wards, springs, tumblers, and retaining plates—are frequently encountered, and more often than not they are improperly identified. The least locklike part (when heavily rusted) is the tumbler with its squared-P shape and occasional bolt-retaining flange immediately behind the talon. I had found these objects in contexts ranging from the second quarter of

[1] For full citation, see pp. 35–6.
[2] Probably a variant of *Chute* or *Shoot*, a trough or, perhaps in this connotation, the stock or wooden trough in which the lock was seated.

the seventeenth century well through the nineteenth, and although I had a sneaking idea that they might be parts of spring traps, for years they were classified simply as "another one of them."

The next step up from the plain stock-lock was the plate stock-lock, wherein the wards and other parts were mounted on a sheet-iron plate flanged at one end to house the head of the bolt. (Fig. 7b) The plate was then seated into the wooden stock and concealed between it and the door when the lock was mounted in position. Mr. Donald Streeter of Iona, New Jersey, one of the few people who have made a study of early locks, points out that the keys for plain and plate stock-locks differ in that for the former the shoulder of the key shank occurs at the line of the main ward cleft, while that for the plate stock-lock key is behind the entire bit and resting against the exterior of the plate when thrust through the door from the outside. (Fig. 77b, Nos. 4 and 5) There is no difference, however, between the shoulder of a plate stock-lock key and that for a metal, rim, or box lock.

The simplest of plain stock-locks had collarless wards with one or two metal strips inserted on either side of the hole, and astride which the web of the key rotated. (Fig. 77b) Keys for this type consequently have no cleft immediately below the shank; but, because neither they nor the collarless ward are well represented among excavated examples, it would seem that such basic locks were thought too simple to be safe. The vast majority of surviving plain stock-lock wards have collars around the holes and the keys have clefts to match them. (Fig. 77a, No. 6, and Fig. 77b, No. 5)

Seventeenth-century keys tended, on the whole, to be straight-shanked, though the bow often had a heart-shaped interior created by a V-shaped projection at the end of the shank. This feature continued to occur from time to time in the eighteenth century, most commonly on keys for small-drawer and trunk locks. Eighteenth-century bows were frequently thickened at the back of the loop, while the shanks were often slightly balustered immediately behind the shoulder. (Fig. 77b, No. 4)

One more component of the stock-lock should be mentioned: the keeper, or lock staple. Like the mechanism it served, the keeper was functional without being decorative, rarely more than a square-shouldered staple flattened into a bracket shape atop spikes that were driven deep into the doorframe.

In the last quarter of the seventeenth century rim locks began to be made in brass cases, eliminating the need for the wooden protective box. The new locks were attached to the door by three or four screws and were generally fitted with a safety bolt moved by a sliding handle on the surface of the plate. In the eighteenth century the handle was replaced by a slide on the underside of the box. The early brass rim locks were expensive and were often both engraved and embellished with cast details. Such locks were, of course, sold complete with a matching brass keeper that screwed to the jamb to receive both the bolt and the safety bolt. Brass rim locks of this type (though without decoration) were used on the better American doors throughout the eighteenth century, and they were fitted with either brass knobs or shouldered loop handles.

Completely spherical brass knobs are believed to have predominated in the first half of the eighteenth century and to have been followed by the oval form which was popular in mid-century. These were succeeded in the latter part of the eighteenth century by a flattened round knob, a form that continued through the nineteenth century in a variety of materials from brass to glass.

Keys for the eighteenth-century brass and iron rim locks seem to have been of forged steel, cast iron being used no earlier than the last years of that century. The date of the introduction of cast-brass keys is open to debate, at least one authority contending that they did not appear before 1840. I have yet to encounter one in a colonial context, but this negative evidence is unreliable in that scrap brass was generally remelted and therefore brass keys would not have been thrown away as frequently as would those of iron.

The majority of eighteenth-century rim locks were of iron, though closely paralleling the brass shape, and these too were usually fitted with brass handles and a brass slide for the safety bolt. But although the casing for the locks was now more substantial than it had been in the seventeenth century, the back was still open, leaving the mechanism extremely vulnerable when it was not attached to the door. It was not until the early nineteenth century that the rim lock was completely contained within a box having four sides and both a front and a back. The lock patented by James Carpenter of Staffordshire, in 1830, had a drop-forged collar welded to the sheet-iron front and nose plate to form the sides and one end,

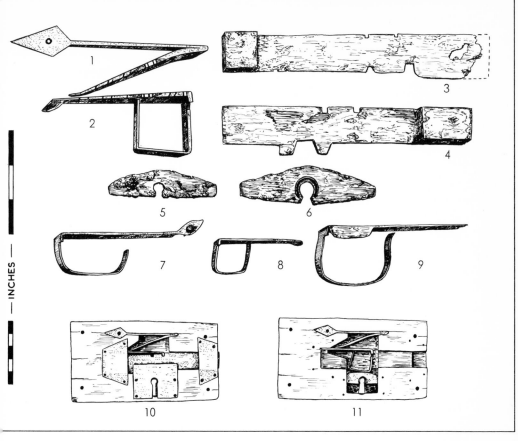

Fig. 77a. Parts of plain stock-locks. 1. and 2. Spring and tumbler from lock 10 and 11; probably 18th century. 3. and 4. Typical bolt types with characteristic upper notches; 18th century. 5. Collarless ward; mid-17th century. 6. Ward with collar; mid-17th century. 7–9. Tumblers for locks of different sizes; early, late, and early 18th century, respectively. 10. and 11. Plain stock-lock with outer iron plates *in situ,* and after removal of plates and bolt to show placement of ward, tumbler, and spring.

while the back was also of sheet iron and was screwed through to the front. The principal feature of this much-exported lock was the cast-brass or iron camb that *raised* the latch when the knob was turned rather than drawing it back. The iron keeper (edged with brass) was notched to allow the latch to be lifted free of it. The Carpenter lock is readily identified by a brass patent seal attached to the front plate bearing the legend "Carpenter and Co., Patentees." This was used on all the locks until the death of James Carpenter in 1844, at which time the firm became "Carpenter and Tildesley" and the

247

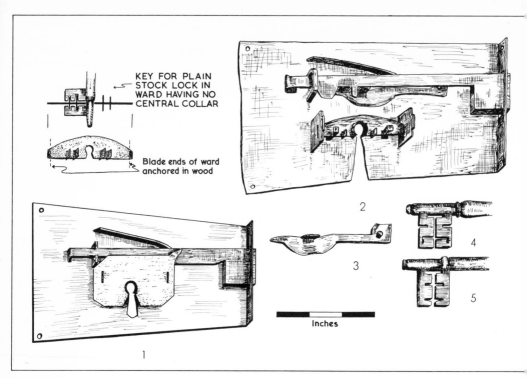

KEY FOR PLAIN
STOCK LOCK IN
WARD HAVING NO
CENTRAL COLLAR

Blade ends of ward
anchored in wood

2

3

4

5

Inches

1

Fig. 77b. Plate stock-lock parts and key types. **1.** Intact example prior to mounting in wooden case; early 19th century. **2.** Example with outer ward removed to show relationship between bolt and tumbler; 18th century. **3.** Tumbler for plate stock-lock similar to No. 2; 18th century. **4.** Web of plate stock-lock key showing position of shoulder; 18th century. **5.** Web of plain stock-lock key showing shoulder location; 18th century.

brass seals were adjusted accordingly. This firm continued in business until the late nineteenth century, though during the second half of the century Carpenter-type locks were made by a number of other companies. The true Carpenter patent seal is embossed in the center with the British royal arms, but I have recently found an apparently pirated seal having a crown in the middle and with the name spelled GARPENTER. Locks of Carpenter type were widely produced in England in the second half of the nineteenth century, notably by John Walker of Birmingham, whose locks bear a seal decorated with an American Eagle. The keepers can be of more help to the archaeologist than the locks, for these often have not only the name of the maker impressed on the brass edge strips but also the initials of the reigning monarch, i.e., GR (George IV, d. 1830); WR (William IV, 1830–7); and VR (Victoria, 1837–1901). Handles used on Carpenter-type locks were generally of brass, but no small number were of coarse "agate" pottery, the last of a once-famous Staffordshire ceramic ware.

Apart from minor improvements to the safety of the rim lock (such as the Chubb detector lock patented in 1818) no major breakthrough occurred until 1848, when Linus Yale invented the cylinder lock which is still in use today.

Padlocks are as common on excavation sites as are rim locks, and they, too, can be roughly attributed to specific periods. The common English padlock of the Middle Ages continued in use well into the eighteenth century; it was cylindrical (usually known as a barrel padlock) and its key served to compress the mechanism rather than to turn it. The principle involved two, and occasionally three, sets of leaf springs, with one arm of each welded or brazed to a base plate at one end of the cylinder. The springs then passed up through a base grill and through a matching grill in the end of the hasp. When the base plate was pushed home the leaf springs expanded, anchoring the hasp grill inside the cylinder. (Fig. 78) To release it an appropriately slotted key (resembling a right-angled wrench on the end of a flat shaft) was pushed down the cylinder from the other end, compressing the leaves of the springs and enabling the base plate to be withdrawn, thus releasing the hasp. It

Fig. 78. Barrel padlocks, iron, with hasps of shackle and sickle forms. No. 1, shown disassembled, was found in Williamsburg, Virginia, while No. 2 was excavated at Round Hill, Clavendon Parish, Jamaica; both are from mid-18th-century contexts. Length of No. 2: 3½".

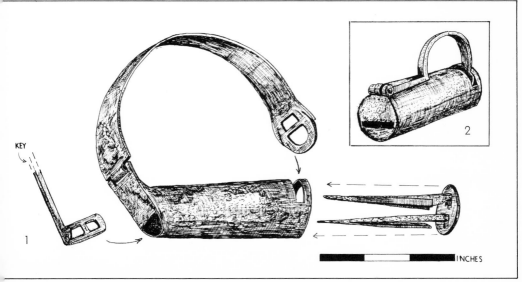

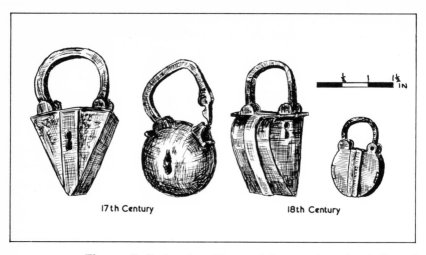

17th Century   18th Century

Fig. 79. Padlocks of sophisticated forms—triangular, ball, and half-heart—all of iron; at right a miniature lock with brass case and keyhole cover, but with iron hasp and mechanism. While the triangular and ball types have only been found in 17th-century American contexts, both shapes are illustrated a century later in Diderot's *Encyclopédie*.

was a simple device but very cumbersome in that, when open, one was left with three parts: the cylinder, the base plate with its cluster of springs, and the angled key. Nevertheless, this was one of the most long-lived and most widely used of all mechanical devices. It can be traced back in Europe to the ninth century and was still being made in the Orient a thousand years later.

Padlocks having a sliding bolt to engage the hasp were produced in Europe (principally in Germany) in the fifteenth and sixteenth centuries, but they do not seem to have reached England until the reign of Elizabeth. These improved padlocks were most frequently circular (known as ball padlocks), but some were triangular; both forms reached America in the first half of the seventeenth century, though I have seen ball padlocks in contexts dating as late as 1730. (Fig. 79, Nos. 1 and 2) The ball locks are generally about 1½″ or 2″ in diameter, while the triangular type may be up to 2½″ in body length. By the late seventeenth century, the forerunner of the familiar heart-shaped padlock had appeared; it was then broader than it was tall and may be described as bag-shaped. The cover for the keyhole was often hinged and lifted up instead of pivoting to one side as did those on later locks. (Fig. 80) As the eighteenth

250

century progressed, padlocks became taller and more pointed at the base; they also tended to become larger. Brass keyhole covers and keyhole sleeves do not seem to have been used on iron padlocks until the nineteenth century, most of them dating no earlier than 1840.

A very distinctive type of padlock fairly common in contexts of the eighteenth century appears to resemble a heart sliced down the middle. The broad curving front surface was invariably reinforced with a welded vertical strip; the keyhole was small and in the side plate, and the plate covering the top of the mechanism generally had flanges projecting beyond the body at either side. (Fig. 79, No. 3) Such locks were operated by bladed keys that freed the entire hasp (instead of being hinged at one end), which had been held closed by leaf springs attached to each end of the "U," somewhat akin to those projecting from the base plates of barrel locks. These "half-heart" locks were illustrated by Diderot, but it is unlikely that they are all of French manufacture. Examples have been found on American sites in contexts dating as early as 1730 and as late as

Fig. 80. Iron padlocks, part of a cargo of hardware recovered from a wreck in the Delaware River, on a ship that sank in the period 1770–80. The locks are exactly as found, their moving parts still operable. The left example exhibits something of the bag shape characteristic of locks of the first years of the 18th century and may, therefore, date earlier than that on the right. The latter's shape is typical of the second half of the century; its total height 4½".

1820. Although too few have been recovered for any firm dating trends to be determined, it may be noted that examples dating from the first half of the eighteenth century have vertical, braised reinforcing bands at both front and back, while those from later deposits are reinforced on the front only. These distinctive locks range in body length from 2½″ down to about ⅞″, the latter being of brass and intended for use on such things as dog collars and jewel caskets.

Small brass padlocks for boxes are often found on eighteenth-century colonial sites, the most common type being round (about the size of a quarter); others are square. In all the examples that I have seen, the back and sides were cast as one, while the front plate was attached by means of mortices that fitted around tenons projecting from the sides. (Fig. 79, No. 4)

ERAS, VINCENT J. M.: *Locks and Keys Throughout the Ages.* Amsterdam; U.S. edn. (Lips' Safe and Lock Manufacturing Co.), 1957.

§ *NAILS*

Of all the artifacts found on historical sites nails are probably the most common, but unfortunately no one has yet evolved a method of dating those that were handwrought. They were the only nails available throughout the seventeenth century and during most of the eighteenth; indeed, they continued to be used well into the nineteenth century. They varied widely in sizes and were identified as 4d., 5d., 8d., etc., a survival from the Middle Ages, when they were classified by cost, i.e., so many pence per hundred. The heads varied according to the purpose for which they were to be used, the most common being the "rose head" that generally had five hammered facets spreading out and down from a central point; others were L-headed and were used as trim and flooring nails, while another variant, also used on floors, had a flat disc head hammered over on opposite sides of the shaft and was therefore known as a T-head. (Fig. 81)

In about 1790 the first cut nails were produced—apparently an American invention—and were sliced by machine from sheet iron, though at first the heads were shaped individually by hammering. It was not until about 1815 that the head was also machine-made, at which time the nail was slightly waisted below it, a characteristic that had disappeared by c. 1830. The 1790–1820 varieties were cut in such a way that the slices caused two diagonal corners to be burred out in opposite directions, but by 1830 the cutting angle had changed and the burring occurred in the same direction at both ends of one face. A further dating clue is provided by the fact that prior to c. 1830 the fiber of the metal ran crosswise to the nails'

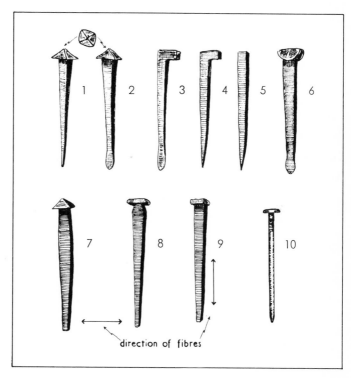

Fig. 81. Nails. **1–6.** Wrought. **7–9.** Cut. **10.** Wire. Nos. 1 and 2 have rose heads, with straight and expanded (or spatula) points; 3 and 4 are L-headed; 5, headless; 6, T-headed. Nos. 1–6 are colonial and later; 7, c. 1790–1820's; 8, c. 1815–1830's; 9, c. 1820 onward; 10, not before 1850's and probably much later.

length, causing them to snap if clenched—thus ensuring the continued need for handwrought nails. Thereafter the fibers ran lengthwise. There were really no further datable differences between nineteenth-century cut nails and those in use today.

In the mid-nineteenth century a round-shafted, steel-wire nail was perfected in Europe, and in the early 1850's wire nail-making machines were imported and set up in New York, though the products were at first confined to small brads. It was not until the last quarter of the nineteenth century that the regular sizes of wire nails were being produced in sufficient quantities to compete successfully with the well-established cut varieties.

NELSON, LEE H.: "Nail Chronology as an Aid to Dating Old Buildings," *History News* (Madison, Wis.), Vol. 19, No. 2 (December 1963).

§ *PINS, NEEDLES, and THIMBLES*

Large numbers of pins are found on historical sites, nearly all of them of brass, once tin-plated. The medieval pin was usually of iron topped by a head of solid pewter sometimes inlaid with glass or a semiprecious stone. In the sixteenth century brass pins became common but retained the large head in solid or hollow-cast brass; but by the beginning of the seventeenth century the head, though still rather large, was fashioned from a second piece of wire wrapped around the shank. The head usually consisted of three turns and was anchored by means of a blow from a treadle-operated stamp that spread the top of the shank. On occasion the blow was sufficiently hard to flatten the head at the same time. This method continued in use until the early nineteenth century, when an American, Lemuel W. Wright, secured an English patent (1824) to make a solid-headed pin that was stamped out in one process.

Seventeenth- and eighteenth-century pins vary greatly in size, ranging from lengths in excess of 5″ (hairpins) down to less than ¾″, the latter sometimes being hardly thicker than a hair. A few pins of all sizes were made from iron wire, but because of their readiness to rust and disappear in the ground, very few are found and no dating evidence is available. Along with the brass pins one sometimes finds small, tapering, brass tubes, some of which are elaborately decorated with stamped ornament. They resemble miniature dagger sheaths and were in fact containers for two pins to enable them to be carried in the pocket. It is assumed that a small number of sheaths or cases were supplied with each paper of pins. The protected-pointed safety pin was not manufactured before about 1857.

Brass hooks and eyes have been found both on archaeological sites and on surviving garments dating from the second quarter of the seventeenth century onward, though it is likely that they were in use much earlier. Also dating from the seventeenth century is a broad class of brass-wire fastenings for cloaks and other such apparel which usually consist of two lengths of brass wire hooked and pointed at the ends and held together at the midsection by a binding of similar wire. (Fig. 20, No. 8) Others took the form of a single or double hook with rings and curls of bound or woven wire (occasionally with beads incorporated into the design) overlying the midsection to create a quite elaborate broach. When found unstratified in England these fastenings have been miscataloged as Roman. Because examples have been found in association with large quantities of pins and pinners' waste on the foreshore of the River Thames, it seems likely that their manufacture was included in the trade of the pinmaker.

Needles are rarely found, for being of iron or steel and of such small size they do not survive in the ground. Occasionally, however, large needles made from brass or bone are recovered, but these were generally used for netting, tent- or rugmaking.

Brass thimbles are among the most common of the smaller domestic objects found on colonial and later sites, but so far they have received no careful study. Nevertheless, a few evolutionary pointers can be discerned, though, as with most other artifacts, the trend was gradual and there is no guarantee that all thimblemakers kept in step. It should also be remembered that thimbles must inevitably have varied in size, thickness, and coarseness of their indentations, depending upon their intended usage. Thus, the child sewing a sampler would not have used the same type of thimble as a cobbler. Nevertheless, it would seem that thimbles dating from the sixteenth and early seventeenth century were generally squat and heavy and were sometimes reinforced with an inner brass lining. They seem also to have been made from a single piece of metal, whereas, by the mid-seventeenth century, they were usually made in two pieces, the sides being fashioned from one strip brazed at the joint while the crown was made separately and joined to the wall in the same manner. The earliest examples have no decoration around the open end other than a single incised line, nor is the edge rolled or otherwise reinforced. The indentations on these early thimbles were applied unevenly and in a spiral, beginning at the open end, continuing up onto the crown, and often terminating before reaching the center so as to leave a smooth tonsurelike area at the apex. I have yet to see this last feature on an example in an archaeological context later than the third quarter of the seventeenth century. Some of the early spiral-indented examples had no crowns and were made as simple bands less than 1/2" in height. These sometimes bear a stamped maker's mark preceding the first indentation at the commencement of the spiral.

By the mid-seventeenth century very tall thimbles seem to have been popular, these being made in two parts and with the open end rolled outward or with a separate band about 1mm. in width being attached to the outside. By this time the indentations on the wall were applied in a wide strip using a multitoothed tool in place of the single punch used to impress the earlier spiral. However, the spiral treatment of the crown was sometimes used in association with the new technique. By the beginning of the eighteenth century the crowns were also pattern-stamped, the identations being in straight lines giving the top a hatched appearance. However, the spiraled crown is sometimes found on nineteenth-century specimens. It is not certain how early patterned collars were stamped around the open ends, but it seems likely that they were in use by the end of the seventeenth century, as also was the turning of thimbles to ornament them with grooves and bands at the collar and at the junction of wall and crown. There seems to be no appreciable difference between thimbles of the eighteenth century and those of the nineteenth, though all the examples that I have seen from the latter contexts are short and of light weight. Like glass beads, thimbles were used in nineteenth-century trade with the Plains Indians, and many examples have been found on Indian sites with small holes punched through the crowns enabling them to be hung on thongs over a bead as "tinklers" to ornament clothing and pouches.

LONGMAN, E. D., and S. LOCK: *Pins and Pincushions*. London, 1911.

§ *PORCELAIN, Chinese*

Although English and European porcelains are found in small quantities on colonial and Early American sites of the second half of the eighteenth century, they were not present in anything like the quantities provided by the Chinese through the India trade. Before that was established Chinese porcelain was reaching California and Mexico, presumably in Spanish ships, and is frequently found there in contexts of the late sixteenth and early seventeenth centuries, much of it the coarse, gray-cored product of Swatow in the province of Kwangtung. Just how early porcelain began to appear on English colonial sites on the American east coast is still uncertain, but numerous Ming sherds have been found in contexts dating prior to 1650. Charles I granted licenses in 1635 to a number of English merchant adventurers to trade in the Orient, but they apparently behaved so badly that the English were barred from Chinese ports from about 1640 until 1680. The first of the Navigation Acts (1651) barred the importation of Asiatic merchandise unless carried aboard English ships, and together these restrictions may have cut off the direct flow of Chinese porcelain to England almost completely in the third quarter of the seventeenth century.

Porcelain was, at least in the seventeenth and early eighteenth centuries, a fairly expensive tableware and would not have been common in the less affluent homes. Because of the small number of quality colonial homes of that period that have yet been excavated, there is no knowing how much porcelain their owners possessed. It is certainly not well represented in inventories until the second quarter of the eighteenth century. Thereafter, it seems to have become increasingly popular and available, until by the end of the century it had become one of the most common ceramic types, though the quality had declined quite appallingly.

Fig. 82. Chinese porcelain cup and tea bowls. *Top row*: left and right, decorated in underglaze blue, 17th to 18th century; center, decorated in overglaze enamels, second half of 18th century. *Bottom row*: left, can decorated in underglaze blue, mid-18th century; right, teacup with "Leeds" handle, the rim decorated with dots of blue enamel between purple lines, remains of small floral motif on side, c. 1790–1820. Ht. of handled teacup 2¾".

Chinese porcelain was made from a combination of kaolin clay and a finely ground feldspathic rock (pai-tun-tzû, or petuntse) and can be distinguished from other ceramic wares by a high-gloss glaze fused to the body and which never flaked as did its delftware imitations. In section the body ranges from pale gray to off-white, is extremely tight-grained, and the glaze clings to it in a thin, translucent line on both sides. Decoration is most commonly in underglaze blue, though in the period c. 1700–80 much of it was combined with overglaze red highlighted with gilding. Some of the designs created in these colors were very "busy," with emphasis on rosettes and compartmenting panels, and were copied from Japanese porcelains that the Dutch had made popular in Europe in the seventeenth century. Because the Japanese wares had been shipped from the port of Imari, the decorative style (be it Japanese or Chinese) has acquired that name, as, quite improperly, have other designs in comparable colors.

Like all overglaze painting on porcelain, the "Imari" red and gold becomes unstable when buried in the ground and often clings more firmly to the dirt than to the porcelain, with the result that when the fragment is lifted the overglaze decoration sometimes remains behind in the ground. When this occurs in tightly compacted dirt it is possible to photograph the transferred decoration and by reversing the resulting negative to record sufficient of the design for a drawing to be made of it. Under no circumstances should the excavator wipe his fingers across a porcelain sherd to see whether it possesses overglaze decoration, for in doing so he is liable to wipe it off. For the same reason pieces with overglaze ornament should not be washed; they should be allowed to dry naturally until the dirt can be brushed away, whereupon the surface can be sprayed with a plastic sealer, such as Krylon, to hold the decoration in place.

Much of the Chinese porcelain made for the European market (popularly and erroneously known as "Oriental Lowestoft") was decorated entirely in overglaze colors, and many a sherd that appears to be plain white, when viewed obliquely in a strong light reveals the matt lines in the surface glaze where enamels had once lain. The entirely overglaze-decorated wares are most common in the second half of the eighteenth century and often display elaborate motifs drawn from European engravings and paintings, usually encircled with chain or spearhead borders in red and gold.

Fragments decorated with large and rather blowzy pink peonies are often found in contexts of the mid- and later eighteenth century, although this, the so-called "famille rose" palette, was first used in about 1685. The flowers are often highlighted in white, and the leaves are usually a drab and washed-out green. Although this type of ornament was much used on such things as quite small vases, most of the examples found on American sites occur on heavy-bodied wares such as tureens and large dishes. The "famille rose" designs are generally informally applied without the restraint imposed by cartouches and border devices or the limitations of small-sized subjects. Those were usually handled much more delicately by painters working in pale greens ("famille verte") and black ("famille noire"), the green often being used in panels bordered with underglaze blue. Brown was also used, often as a surface wash covering the entire exterior of hemispherical tea bowls or with enameled

Fig. 83. Chinese export plate with underglaze blue decoration typical of that which provided inspiration for the English "willow pattern." Third quarter of 18th century. Diam. 9".

reserves on bowls of somewhat larger size. This technique seems to be most common in contexts of the period c. 1740–80. Also worthy of mention are those bowls and cylindrical teacups bearing decoration painted in white slip under the glaze, which, after firing, rather resembles watermarked paper. Such pieces frequently had underglaze-blue rim borders and sometimes overglaze flowers in the "famille rose" palette. Such elaborately decorated wares are never common, and those examples that I have seen have never been in colonial contexts dating before about 1740, though the technique is thought to have been developed in the last years of the Ming dynasty in imitation of earlier Sung wares that were carved beneath the glaze.

Porcelain, Chinese

In his *Observations on the Commerce of the American States* (London, 1784), Lord Sheffield reported that "East-India china is sometimes cheaper in Holland than in England. America gets the coarse kinds from St. Croix; but the consumption of china in America is inconsiderable, in comparison to that of British earthen ware; and since the improvements of the latter, it decreases daily."[3] The rather puzzling reference to St. Croix is presumably to the then-Danish West Indian island which may have traded in porcelain received from the Spanish, the Dutch, or through the Danish East India Company's "factory" at Tranquebar near Madras on the Bay of Bengal.

Toward the end of the eighteenth century overglaze-decorated Chinese porcelain made solely for the export trade declined to a point where very little craftsmanship was involved. Cups and saucers were rimmed with thin swags, wiggly lines, or dashes in black, orange, or purplish pink, sometimes flanked by dots in a thick, light-blue enamel. Decoration in the centers of saucers and on the sides of cups, jugs, and teapots was confined to small floral or foliate sprays in the same color as the border, sometimes with a cornucopia serving as a vase for the spray. Handles for this tea ware generally terminated in relief-molded foliate springs in imitation of the floral terminals on Staffordshire and Leeds creamwares. (Fig. 82) The handles themselves were sometimes double and entwined, also in the creamware manner, but although these occurred on overglaze-enameled teapots in the last quarter of the eighteenth century, they were most common on cups in the first years of the nineteenth century, then with decoration in underglaze blue.

For every piece of overglaze-decorated porcelain found on eighteenth-century sites there are a dozen or more ornamented only in underglaze blue, and as they are generally without reign marks they are virtually impossible to date with sufficient accuracy to be useful. (Fig. 83) One can only note that the later the piece the more sloppy the painting. The pseudo-Chinese "willow pattern" (*see* p. 130) did not appear before 1792 and became increasingly common in America in the early years of the nineteenth century. The earli-

[3] Sheffield, op. cit., pp. 23–4; for full citation, see fn. 7, p. 60.

Fig. 84. Typical late Chinese export porcelain plate, the decoration poorly executed in underglaze blue on a greenish-gray
body, the rim design known as "Canton"; c. 1810–35. Diam.
7¾".

:st pieces were quite well done, though the border ornaments were
overly fussy and tended to become blurred. Very soon, however, the
house, tree, boat, and bridge motif began to be applied to a heavier
body that appears greenish-gray through the glaze, roughly hatched
or scale-decorated, and the border was reduced to a wide band of
blue, roughly hatched with lines of a slightly darker blue. (Fig. 84)
This ware, so common in the first thirty years or so of the nineteenth century, is generally called "Canton," from which port it was
shipped and where, in the second half of the eighteenth century,
much of the high-quality overglaze painting for special European
orders had been executed. Slightly better quality versions of the

same late blue and white wares possessed border designs with daggers or spearheads below the inner edge, a style known as "Nanking," as opposed to those with mere swags, which are termed "Canton." In neither case were the wares made in these cities, all of them apparently having been made in the kilns of Ching-tê Chên.

Marks on excavated run-of-the-mill Chinese porcelains are few and far between, and the majority (on the undersides of bases) have no dating significance. They were, as a rule, nothing more than the painters' good wishes—a square in a circle or "cash" mark representing a coin and indicating prosperity; a counterclockwise swastika meaning long life; the Buddhist symbol of a pair of amorous fish backed by a knot, for connubial felicity; etc. (Fig. 85)

Porcelain found on American sites must belong to one or other of two dynasties, the Ming (1364–1644) or the Ch'ing (1644–1912). The reign marks usually comprised six Chinese characters, three in each of two columns, and are read from top right to bottom left. Although it is difficult to remember the individual marks, it is possible to recall enough to determine whether in fact one is looking at a reign mark at all. With the exceptions of the reigns of Ch'ung Chang (1628–43) and Chia Ch'ing (1796–1820), which only used four characters, all the reign marks begin by identifying the dynasty. The first sign at top right resembles an inverted v topped by

Fig. 85. Common marks on the bases of 18th-century Chinese porcelain. *Left*: a pair of fish over a knot, symbolic of connubial felicity. *Right*: a coin or cash mark meaning wealth. Both are in underglaze blue. Diam. of right footring $1\frac{5}{16}$".

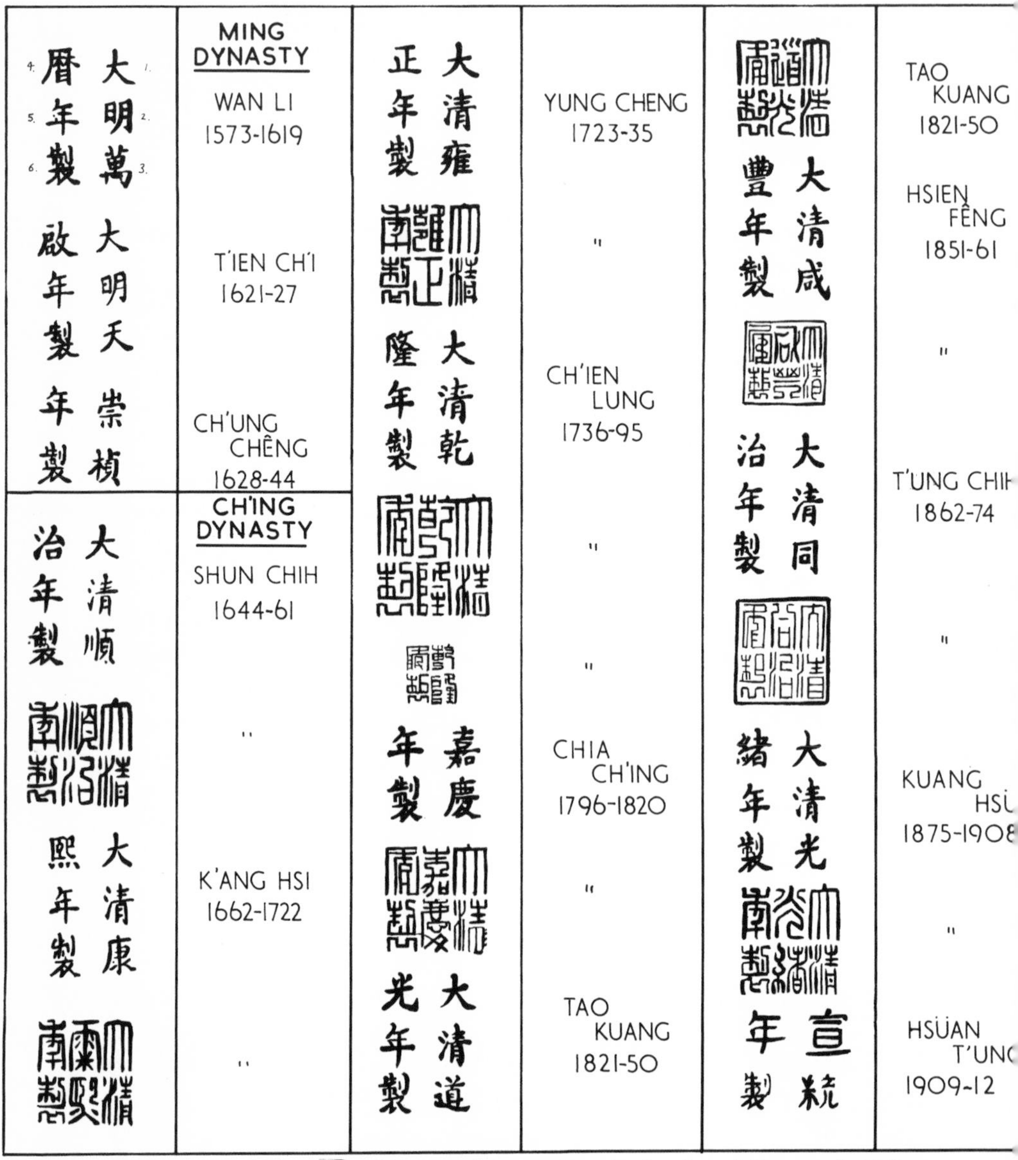

	MING DYNASTY			TAO KUANG 1821-50
4. 1. 大明萬 曆 2. 年 5. 製 6.	WAN LI 1573-1619	正 大 年 清 製 雍	YUNG CHENG 1723-35	HSIEN FĒNG 1851-61
大明天 啟年製	T'IEN CH'I 1621-27	隆 大 年 清 製 乾	''	''
崇禎年製	CH'UNG CHÊNG 1628-44		CH'IEN LUNG 1736-95	T'UNG CHIH 1862-74
治 大 年 清 製 順	CH'ING DYNASTY SHUN CHIH 1644-61		''	''
	''		''	
熙 大 年 清 製 康	K'ANG HSI 1662-1722	年 嘉 製 慶	CHIA CH'ING 1796-1820	KUANG HSÜ 1875-1908
	''	光 大 年 清 製 道	''	''
			TAO KUANG 1821-50	HSÜAN T'UNG 1909-12

Fig. 86. Chinese reign marks of the late Ming and Ch'ing dynasties, shown both in script and seal characters. They read from top right to bottom left, thus: 1. Great. 2. Ming. 3. Wan. 4. Li. 5. in the. 6. reign of. Drawing after W. Burton and R. L. Hobson: *Handbook of Marks on Pottery and Porcelain* (London, 1928).

a cross and means "Great"; the one below it resembles two square figure-8's, the right one with tails descending at either side, for Ming, or a more elaborate character with two dots at its top-left corner, for Ch'ing. The third and fourth signs give the name of the emperor, the fifth and sixth mean "in the reign of." (Fig. 86)

By no means all marks that use letters instead of symbols relate to reigns; as an example, one small bowl found on an eighteenth-century site in Williamsburg was marked as having been made for a prominent civil servant named Kao Ch'eng-yen in the second quarter of the seventeenth century.

BEURDELEY, MICHEL: *Porcelain of the East India Companies.* London, 1962.
HANNOVER, EMIL: *Pottery and Porcelain; A Handbook for Collectors* (London). Vol. 2, The Far East (1925).
PHILLIPS, JOHN GOLDSMITH: *China-Trade Porcelain.* Cambridge, Mass., 1956.
SAVAGE, GEORGE: *Porcelain Through the Ages.* Harmondsworth, Middlesex, Eng., 1954.

For English porcelain, *see* CERAMICS, British.

§ *RINGS, Finger*

It is very rarely that rings of silver or gold are found in archaeological contexts, though those of brass are not uncommon. But here, as in the case of so many of the small artifacts of the post-medieval past, little attention has been afforded them and no acceptable chronology has been established. Gold rings made from three linked strands of wire were popular in the late sixteenth century and it is reasonable to suppose that this style continued much later, probably well through the eighteenth century. Examples in brass with the central wire beaded have occasionally been found, though not, so far as I know, in dated contexts. The most common type is the simple band, convex on the outside and flat inside, which occurs on eighteenth-century sites but which is itself undatable. The only clue to distinguish between early and late examples may be the presence on the inside of poorly spelled amorous inscriptions, such as I LOVE ERVE, I LOVE V EUER, or LOVE THY TRV FRIND. These were known as "posy rings" and seem to have been dispensed rather as pins are by young people today.

Betrothal or gimmal rings were made in two or more loosely linked loops, each of which usually was adorned with a pair of clasped hands. Mourning rings were also much used in the seventeenth and eighteenth centuries and were generally of silver set with a white-enameled death's-head on a black ground. But the vast majority of rings were probably purely decorative, and it is these that are most often found on archaeological sites. Eighteenth-century examples are found comprising thin bands with relief decoration and with a small "stone" set to cover the joint of the loop. Others are plain bands with a larger setting to take two "stones," usually nonprecious and sometimes no more than faceted glass backed with foil or mercury.

Signet rings with large bezels flanked by relief ornament were not popular during the colonial period, though they became so in the latter part of the nineteenth century. On the other hand, flat bands with heavy seals (usually bearing the matrix of a crest or merchant's mark) were used throughout the period but were generally of gold.

Undoubtedly the most easily identifiable type of ring yet found on American sites are those crude brass bands with large and irregular-shaped bezels (sometimes in the form of a heart) which are very roughly engraved with Jesuit inscriptions—hearts topped by crosses or arrows, or combinations of incised initials such as BI, CB, FI, IA, IB, IM, IP, LR, LV, PI, or merely a single initial such as H, N, or T. All of these have been found at the onetime French fort and trading post of Michilimackinac on the Straits of Mackinac, which was established in about 1715. Although the rings are generally described as "Jesuit" and were doubtless sold by Jesuit traders, it is reasonable to suppose that many of them were simply trade goods premarked with likely sets of customers' initials.

OMAN, CHARLES C.: *Catalogue of Rings.* Victoria and Albert Museum, London, 1930.
PETERSON, EUGENE T.: *Gentlemen on the Frontier, A Pictorial Record of the Culture of Michilimackinac.* Mackinac Island, Mich., 1964.

§ *SCISSORS*

Although scissors were known in Europe as early as the eighth or ninth century, they were uncommon in England before the six-teenth century, their function having hitherto been served by shears. Indeed, shears were still used by some barbers in the early seventeenth century, and they continued in use for clipping sheep, trimming hedges, and similar rural duties through to the nine-teenth century. The earliest scissors had short shafts and eyes set symmetrically to the handle axis, while the blades were generally fairly narrow, pointed, and spreading slightly in the midsection. Dating from the early sixteenth century and extending through to the early seventeenth one sometimes finds scissors whose hafts are drawn out into narrow rat tails and looped outward and back onto themselves to create large, oval loops. The ends of the tails are not attached, the blades are hollow-ground and loosely anchored to-gether by means of a rivet and two large washers. (Fig. 87) More refined versions are sometimes found on colonial sites, but it would seem that the majority of scissors with drawn-loop handles that were not anchored at the ends belonged to the first half of the seven-teenth century. Another variation had extremely narrow blades worked out from a round-sectioned rod which becomes an everted haft with a compensating incurving eye at the top, the end of which was not welded to the haft. Such scissors are also believed to be of seventeenth-century date.

By the mid-seventeenth century, blades had become wider and thicker with the rivet well below the branch of the handles, and the flat area between them was often stamped with the maker's mark. Hafts were rectangular in section and the eyes were fashioned from a separate, thin strap which was generally slightly offset from the axis of the haft. The type continued into the eighteenth century; but the most common feature of scissors of the first half of that century was a broad blade which did not taper to a point but in-stead was cut at an oblique angle. Later in the century, blades were

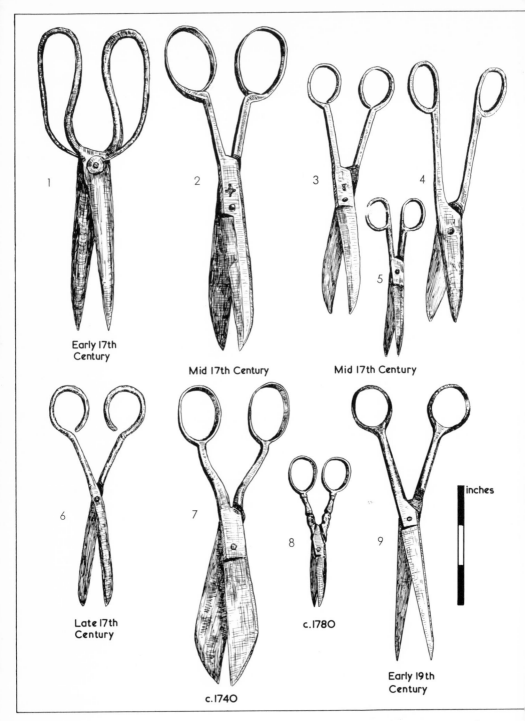

1

Early 17th
Century

2

Mid 17th Century

3

4

5

Mid 17th Century

6

Late 17th
Century

7

8

c.1780

9

c.1740

Early 19th
Century

inches

Fig. 87. Some scissor types from archaeological contexts of various dates.

268

more narrow and the hafts tended to be ornamented with knops and balusters; this was particularly true of nail and embroidery scissors. However, two pairs of regular size found in supposedly eighteenth-century contexts in Williamsburg, are embellished with hafts having openwork ornament below the eyes, and their rococo appearance would suggest a date around the third quarter of the century.

§ *SEALS, Lead*

Lead seals of various shapes and sizes are fairly common on sites once associated with trade. Very little is known about them, and until recently they have all been classified as "wool" seals. But although many of them undoubtedly related to the textile trade (being marked WORSTED REFORMED or decorated with a woolsack), others were used to secure bags of general merchandise. English examples fall into two classes, the merchants' own seals and those attached officially after excise duties had been paid. The latter are nearly always in four sections, the two central units being flat discs adorned with the portrait of the reigning monarch and with royal or county arms, while the end units comprise a lug and loop, respectively. (Fig. 88, No. 1) When used, the lug was squashed over the loop with a pair of pincers whose faces were often capable of impressing further symbols onto the lead. Because excise seals were applied in many towns, their styles differed widely. It may be noted, however, that the four sections could be round, square, or star-shaped, that those with portraits of James II or Queen Anne are most common, and that those of James I have the initials IR flanking a crowned fleur-de-lis, while those of Charles I have the letters CR flanking a crowned rose. The only examples from the reign of Charles II that cen be positively identified through being dated have no portrait but bear the initials of the sovereign beneath the royal crown. The two central units of these seals are star-shaped. The names of counties and towns are frequently spelled out (ESSEX, KENT, LANCASTER, CANTBVRI, STOWRBRIDG, etc.), and the amount of

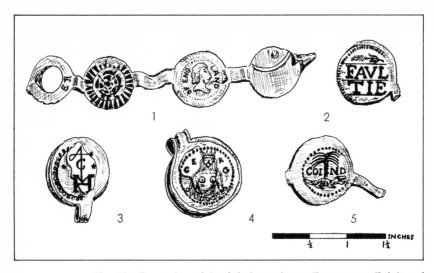

Fig. 88. Examples of lead bale seals. 1. Four-part official seal of James II. 2. Alnager's seal of uncertain date. 3. Typical merchant's seal; 17th- to 18th-century. 4. Arms of the Mercers' Company of London or perhaps the "Indian Queen" crest of Virginia; probably 18th century. 5. Emblem of the French India Company; 18th century.

duty is apparently indicated by such figures as ½, 1, 1½, 2, 3, 4, etc.

The officer whose duty it was to "look to the Assize of Woollen Cloath" was known as an alnager, or aulnegeor, and according to E. P. Phillips's *The New World of Words: Or a General English Dictionary* (London, 1671) he "hath two Seals ordained him for that purpose." His duty was not only to collect the tax but also to examine the cloth to make sure it was of the correct quality, length, and breadth. Early seventeenth-century alnagers' seals are sometimes marked SEARCHED, indicating that the material had been examined. But by the early eighteenth century the alnager's duties had been divided between three people, the searcher who checked the quality, the measurer who checked the size, and the alnager who collected the tax. One two-piece seal in my own collection bears the word FAVLTIE, but which, if any, of these officials applied it, or to what, is uncertain. (Fig. 88, No. 2)

Merchants' seals date predominantly from the eighteenth century and were made in only two sections, the pincers impressing the legend and decorative devices when the plug was squeezed over the loop. Figures presumably representing dimensions were often

270

roughly scratched on the backs. There are exceptions to prove every rule, and recent excavations in Williamsburg have yielded seals made from a rectangular strip (2½″ x ½″) with a lug at one end and a hole at the other and with the name IONAS PENEY molded in relief between them. Two examples have been found, one dated 1728 and the other 1729. Another probably later variety of seal was (and still is) used to clamp over drawstrings or wires sealing lids or bags; it is usually oval and is merely a tube of lead squeezed flat and impressed with a merchant's or official's mark. Large tubular seals approximately 1¼″ in length have been found stamped with a crown and to the right of it a large c over a Tudor rose, but although the style suggests a sixteenth-century date, their age is uncertain. Seals of one or more of the foregoing types were used by many European countries, but as most foreign goods had already passed through English ports it is likely that the seals would have been removed in transit. On the northern frontier trading posts, however, numerous French seals are found, notably those of the French India Company (established 1720), which are impressed with its arms: an alligator below a palm tree. (Fig. 88, No. 5)

PETERSON, EUGENE T.: *Gentlemen on the Frontier, A Pictorial Record of the Culture of Michilimackinac.* Mackinac Island, Mich., 1964.

§ *SHOE BUCKLES*

See BUCKLES.

§ *SILVER, Marks on English and American*

All English silver of the colonial and later periods is marked with at least four stamps comprising that of the maker (usually one or more initials), one or more town or assay-office marks, the quality mark, and the date letter. (Fig. 89) This last is, of course, the most helpful, but, as the style of the letters and the shape of the background impression represented different years for different assay offices, the reader must refer to a book on the subject to pinpoint a specific date. It is enough to note here that simple *termini post quem* can be derived from the presence of certain assay-office marks. The London mark of a crowned leopard's head was first used in 1478 (it was previously *un*crowned) and has continued until the present time, with the exception of the years 1697–1718/19 when it was replaced by a heraldic lion's head in profile. The leopard's head was also used by other assay offices (Chester, Exeter, Newcastle, and York) but always in association with their own marks. The mark of Chester was that of the City's arms, three wheat sheaves and a dagger, though between the years 1701/2 and 1778/9 it was complicated by being dimidiated or halved with three lions passant guardant on the dexter (left, as one looks at it) side. The Exeter assay office operated between 1701 and 1882/3 and had as its mark a three-turreted castle. Newcastle's mark was very similar, though the three turrets were separated; this mark began in the fifteenth century as a single castle and changed to three in about 1675, remaining until 1863/4. York had two marks, the leopard's head halved with a fleur-de-lis and a cross charged with five lions passant guardant; the office was in existence between 1423 and 1856/7. The only other major office no longer in existence is that of Norwich (1423–1697), which used both a crowned Tudor rose, and a castle (resembling a chafing dish) over a lion passant or passant guardant.

Both Birmingham and Sheffield were granted their own assay offices in 1773, the former thenceforth using the mark of an anchor and the latter a crown which, between the years 1780 and 1854, was combined with the date letter in a single punch. In Scotland, Edinburgh has been marking its silver since 1485 using a triple-towered castle rather similar to that of Exeter though differing in that all three towers stood on the same base line. Glasgow did not obtain its office until 1819, which, too, used the arms of the City as its mark, an extremely complicated one incorporating a tree topped by a bird, with a bell hanging from the sinister (right, as one looks at it) side and with a fish crossing the lower trunk. The goldsmiths of Dublin were incorporated in 1637 and issued their first date letter in 1638/9 along with the town mark, an Irish harp crowned. In 1731/2 a

Hall Mark
LONDON
Style of 1722-30

Date
Letter
1735-6

Quality
Mark
STERLING

Maker's
Mark

Fig. 89. Examples of the four classes of marks used together on English sterling silver.

second mark depicting Hibernia was added to indicate payment of a duty on plate, and it has continued to appear ever since, regardless of the fact that the duty has long been removed.

It seems that there must always be an exception to confound the rule, and the neat chronology of British assay marks is unfortunately marred by an excise duty on gold and silver that was in force from 1784 until 1890. During that time the assay offices collected the tax and substituted a stamp bearing the profile of the reigning monarch for that of the town mark. The place of origin must therefore be determined on the basis of the maker's mark or on the style of the date letter and its surrounding shield.

The next mark is that of quality, the English sterling mark being a lion passant guardant until 1821/2, when the London lion was allowed to turn its head in profile and has remained passant ever since; Birmingham followed suit in 1876, but Sheffield and Chester have retained the old position. The mark of a thistle has identified Edinburgh sterling silver since 1759/60, while Glasgow used a lion rampant until 1914/15, when it, too, adopted the thistle. There is no Irish sterling mark because all its assayed silver was automatically of sterling quality. In 1696/7 the quality of English silver was raised by eight pennyweights, and to indicate the new standard the whole lion was replaced by its head in profile and a new stamp—a seated Britannia—was added. The new increased silver content of plate remained the only approved standard until 1718/19, when the old standard (11 oz. 2 dwts. fine) was reintroduced and the old marks restored. The Britannia quality continued to be made, however, if affluent customers desired it, and the pieces were then so marked.

273

American silver of the seventeenth and eighteenth centuries was marked merely with the stamp of the maker, and it is therefore only possible to use the marks to date the pieces within the working life of known craftsmen. However, in cases where the maker is not immediately identifiable some help is to be derived from the shape and style of the mark. The earliest (c. 1670–1720) usually comprised a pair of initials over a fleur-de-lis, all within a shield. Next came the same arrangement within a heart (c. 1680–1730), in turn giving way to a simple pair of initials within an oval. That became the fashion around 1725, but by mid-century the initials (and sometimes the full name) were enclosed within a rectangle. Toward the close of the century script lettering became common, and in the early nineteenth century the names were often spread out in flowing, bannerlike stamps. Now that they were free of English restraint, American silversmiths frequently ennobled their products by adding pseudo-hallmarks. In conclusion, it is worth noting that after about 1770 those makers whose first names began with J started using that letter in place of the I (or ɪ) that had always been used before.

BUHLER, KATHRYN C.: *American Silver*. Cleveland, Ohio, 1950.

JACKSON, SIR CHARLES J.: *English Goldsmiths and Their Marks*. New York, 1964 (first pub. 1921).

THORN, C. JORDAN: *Handbook of American Silver and Pewter Marks*. New York, 1949.

§ *SPADES and HOES*

Agricultural implements are among the most common of seventeenth- and eighteenth-century artifacts, and, although they range all the way from apple shakers to watering cans, by far the most plentiful are hoes and spades. Unfortunately no thorough study has been devoted to the dating of either, and what little information has emerged from my own excavations is not well supported by extant pictorial evidence. For example, I have yet to see a wholly metal-bladed spade from a closely dated seventeenth-century context, but I have encountered numerous iron nosings for wooden blades. However, this cannot be taken to mean that iron blades were not used, for in 1565 Pieter Bruegel the Elder executed an extremely detailed drawing of gardeners at work (*Spring*) which shows two entirely metal-bladed spades. Nevertheless, the fact remains that I have yet to find one dating earlier than 1700 or a nosing dating later. The latter represented something less than a third of a spade's total blade length and was anchored to the wood by a V-shaped slot across the width of the blade and by projecting arms that gripped it at the sides. These were held in place by flanges close to the ends, as well as by two or more nails driven through the metal and into the thickness of the wooden upper blade. Such blades have been found in a mid-seventeenth-century Virginia context in various sizes, the largest 1′ in width and the smallest 5¾″. This last is thought to have been an edging spade for trimming flower beds and walkways.

The normal spade blade of the eighteenth century measured approximately 8″ x 12″, was divided at the top, and capped by flat iron shoulders that snuggled well into the instep of the foot. The shank was not cylindrical but was divided into two concave leaves. The wooden handle extended down between them into the cavity within the upper section of the blade and was held in place with nails driven through both shank and blade.

On Virginia sites of the eighteenth century the broad hoe seems to have been the most common variety, the eye always round, the socket leaning slightly forward, and the blade describing approximately one third of a circle. The most striking feature of this tool was a V- or wedge-shaped reinforcement formed over a swage and extending from the eye to about half the length of the blade. On the flat surface of this "V," the maker often stamped his initials using a rectangular die that left the letters in relief. Marked blades are far less common from seventeenth-century sites. Indeed, the broad hoe of the seventeenth century is slightly different, the blade being narrower and more closely resembling a square with its corners clipped. While all hoes were used for grubbing roots, the term is most often applied to a narrower-bladed tool whose shape is virtually triangular; the eye was the same as that for the broad hoe, but the wedge-shaped reinforcement was more slender and might better be described as a rat tail. This type of hoe was common in the seventeenth century but less so in the eighteenth.

It should be noted that the wrought-iron blade was generally reinforced with a steel cutting edge that often emerges from two hundred years in the ground in better condition than the rest of the tool. In conclusion, I should add that nineteenth-century hoe blades are generally of more even thickness, and their reinforcement, when it is present at all, is likely to be uniformly beveled.

§ *SPOONS*

See CUTLERY and SPOONS.

§ *STONEWARE, Rhenish*

At the beginning of the seventeenth century the most durable pottery available in Western Europe was the stoneware manufactured in the Rhineland, which was imported into England, and thence to America, in ever-increasing quantities. When, in 1672, an embargo was placed on the importation of "painted wares" to protect the growing English delftware industry, no such restriction was imposed on Rhenish stonewares and they continued to pour into England until late in the eighteenth century. Although Bellarmines (q.v.) had been made with ornament specifically designed for the English market as early as the reign of Elizabeth I, the majority of the seventeenth-century exports were no different from those sold on the Continent. It was not until the end of the century that virtually the entire range of exported Rhenish stonewares began to be decorated for the British trade, the first of them bearing the portrait or cipher of William III (1688–1702).

There is a tendency among collectors to call all these stonewares German, but such a grouping is misleading for some of the best pieces were made in Flanders. Indeed, it was the famous products of

Raeren near Aix-la-Chapelle that set the pace to the others, first by producing a rich brown glaze and later by learning to decorate the gray body with cobalt. Unfortunately, with the commencement of the Thirty Years' War, the products of Raeren lost their individuality and it became impossible to distinguish them from those made in other more prosperous factories of the Rhineland. The principal styles made at Raeren were tall jugs, some with tubular spouts, all elaborately mold-decorated with armorial devices, Biblical and mythological scenes (Susanna and the Elders, the Centaurs and the Lapithal, etc.), and friezes depicting tavern, market, and rural life. The most famous Raeren potter was Jan Emens; his initials are found amid the relief-molded ornaments on a surprisingly large number of pieces made between 1568 and 1594, though his long working life is believed to have spanned the years 1556–1603. Although its glory faded early, the Raeren stoneware industry struggled on as late as 1850, when the last kiln was fired.

Fig. 90. Rhenish brown stoneware in its best period. A pewter-mounted jug with benign "Bartmann" mask. Cologne, c. 1580. Jug height without lid 8½".

Farther south, on the north bank of the Rhine, was the city of Siegburg (near Bonn), which produced an unglazed gray or pale-buff stoneware throughout the sixteenth century and continuing into the seventeenth century. But its potting industry crumbled in the 1630's after being sacked first by the Spaniards (1587), then by the Elector of Brandenburg (1615), and finally by the Swedes in 1632. Although jugs and bottles of all sorts were made, the most characteristic product was a tall, tapering mug decorated almost to its full height with relief-molded contemporary figures or with Biblical stories told in numerous small panels. It is quite possible that examples of this easily recognizable ware reached America in the baggage of the earliest colonists, though I have yet to see an excavated example.

The field of Rhenish stonewares is beset with more misnomers than are its fair share, and to such dubious terms as "Bellarmine" and "German stoneware" we must add the name "Cologne ware," which had long been used by writers to describe the mottled-brown body of the typical Rhenish bearded jugs and bottles of the late sixteenth and early seventeenth centuries. The term is certainly not new, for as early as 1671 John Dwight of Fulham claimed that he had discovered the mysteries of manufacturing "Cologne ware." However, the principal authority on the subject, M. L. Solon, declared in 1892 that a scrutiny of Cologne's archives did ". . . not contain any mention of the potting trade having ever flourished in that city."[4] Nevertheless, archaeological evidence recovered during street repairs has since produced kiln wasters which demonstrate that stoneware had been made there in the sixteenth century in at least two factories and that some of the products were of high quality. Indeed, it is probable that Jan Emens was trained there. It would seem on the basis of what little evidence is available that Cologne stoneware production was devoted largely to early pale brown-glazed variations on the Bellarmine, the better-quality pieces often with a molded inscription around the girth and with classical medallions and acanthus-leaf moldings above and below. (Fig. 90) The date range of such pieces would seem to be confined to the

[4] M. L. Solon: *The Ancient Art Stoneware of the Low Countries and Germany* (London, 1892), II, 3.

Fig. 91. Rhenish gray stoneware jug, pewter mounted. Decorated with incised lines, sprigged floral ornament, and a medallion bearing the cipher of Queen Anne; the body colored with cobalt blue and the flowers with manganese purple. Grenzhausen type, c. 1702–14. Ht. 11″.

years c. 1560–1600, though other types go back to the second quarter of the sixteenth century.

Most of the so-called Bellarmines came to be attributed with reasonable certainty to kilns in the vicinity of the village of Frechen between Aix-la-Chapelle and Cologne, the potters allegedly having established themselves there after being driven out of Cologne in the early sixteenth century. If this is so, then, of course, one wonders why they were making stoneware in Cologne at the end of that century. The truth of the matter may be that a few potters returned and that most of the later products of Frechen were marketed there by Cologne merchants who then shipped them up the Rhine, thus causing foreigners to suppose that the pottery was actually manufactured in Cologne.

In addition to its vast trade in Bellarmines (variously known as *Bartmann* bottles or "Graybeards") through the later sixteenth and entire seventeenth century, the Frechen potteries also produced gray stonewares decorated in cobalt blue in the manner of Raeren

Fig. 92. Gray stoneware mugs and chamber pots with incised, stamped, sprigged, and cobalt-painted decoration, all (with one possible exception) attributable to the Westerwald district of the Rhineland. The mugs are of "3", "4", and "8" capacities, and all have GR medallions. The center example dates prior to c. 1740, but the others may run fifteen or twenty years later. Ht. of left example 6⅞". The left chamber pot is of the type common in the period 1710–65 and is decorated with alternating sprigged lions and stamped rosettes. The example on the right is slightly taller, and sprig-molded wreaths substitute for the usual rosettes. This rare form may be of Flemish manufacture and has been found in contexts of the third quarter of the 18th century; ht. 5⅜".

(as also occasionally did Siegburg); but that was a secondary consideration. It was not so much farther south in the potteries at Grenzhausen and Höhr near Coblentz that gray and blue stonewares beginning in the Siegburg and Raeren traditions were made from about 1590 on through the eighteenth century, then revived again in the nineteenth century in a conscious burst of antiquarianism. The wars and other disasters that had brought about the decline of the great factories at Raeren and Siegburg caused the most talented potters to move south to safety and new clays. Thus when the Höhr-Grenzhausen industry developed, it was launched by the most famous names in the business. So many kilns were involved, and not all of them actually in either Höhr or Grenzhausen, that the more cautious of us prefer to classify their products as Westerwald wares, naming them after the district in which both villages were located, this in spite of the fact that Solon testily asserted that the term ". . . has never come into general use, and had better, we think, be forgotten altogether."[5]

Many of the early Westerwald products were virtually identical to those made at Raeren in the first half of the century, but by the last quarter of the seventeenth century they had developed a style of their own, one that was to continue in a much-debased form through the next seventy-five years. The ornamental friezes of earlier days were abandoned in favor of elaborate floral and geometric designs achieved in a combination of extremely thin sprig molding

[5] Ibid., p. 78.

and a multiplicity of combed lines. Molded flowers would be applied and the stalks and leaves scratched or combed into the leather-hard body, the flowers then being colored in cobalt blue or manganese purple. (Fig. 91) The introduction of purple, first as a means of decorating molded ornament (and later as broad bands to be wiped around the reeded necks of jugs), was a Westerwald development that began as early as the 1660's, though it did not become common until the last quarter of the century. The earliest-recorded dated piece is a tall jug with a starlike decoration around the arms of France and is marked 1665. Solon, however, contended that a giant blue- and purple-decorated fountain jug in London's Victoria and Albert Museum may have been made as early as 1632. The earliest-dated example of blue-decorated Rhenish gray stoneware that I have seen from an American site is an incomplete oval medallion sherd from the John Hallows site (post-1644) in Westmoreland County, Virginia; it bears the legend . . .]IVS 1632 ICH BR[. . .

The carefully applied relief-molded ornament neatly embellished with manganese and outlined in cobalt did not survive long into the eighteenth century, and in the first quarter of the century the decoration was being stamped and incised (outlined in blue) around a central molded medallion bearing the cipher of the English monarch—AR, Queen Anne (1702–14), and then GR, George I (1714–27) or George II (1727–60)—beneath a crown and over a winged cherub. A few of these medallions bear the makers' initials and a date (usually 1724), but while this doubtless indicates the date at which the mold was cut it does not necessarily follow that it was also the date of the jug's manufacture. The common Westerwald jugs of the eighteenth century are virtually impossible to date with accuracy. (Fig. 92)

The majority of the GR jugs have straight, multiple-reeded necks coated with manganese, but a few possess ornamental cordoning highlighted with two bands of cobalt. As the latter style occurs on the necks of Rhenish jugs at least as early as the 1630's, it is reasonable to conclude that its presence on a GR jug is indicative of an early example, probably no later than the end of the reign of George I (1727). On the other hand, the manganese-painted neck appears on a few AR jugs, as also does the same reeded form coated with a wash of blue. The latter, however, would also appear to be a type that did not extend beyond the first quarter of the eighteenth century.

Of no dating significance (other than the fact that it does not appear on seventeenth-century examples), but useful for cataloging and descriptive purposes, was the practice of marking both jugs and mugs with capacity numbers ranging from ten to one. The figures were painted, stamped, or scratched onto the body, either in the undecorated area adjacent to the handle (Frontispiece) or at the rim. The approximate equivalents in English twenty-ounce pints are as follows:

10 = 1 gill or noggin
8 = ½ pint (or 8 Dutch "mussies")
6 = 1 pint
4 = 1 quart
3 = 2 quarts
2 = 3 quarts
1 = 1 gallon

The most common sizes are the "8," "6," and "3" on jugs and the "8" and "4" on mugs. There is some variation within the groups, but the marks were presumably only to show that the pots did not hold less than the stated quantity. On April 30, 1750, the *Boston Evening Post* carried an advertisement offering for sale "Dutch Ware, as gallon Jugs, two quart Jugs, quart and pint Mugs, Chamber Pots, etc., etc." These, therefore, would have been numbers "1" and "3" jugs and "4" and "6" mugs.

Archaeological evidences would suggest that Rhenish stonewares lost favor in England and in America in the 1760's and were no longer imported after the Revolution. It must be added, however, that English customs records show that "Pots, stone"[6] were still being imported in 1776 from Holland, though in less than half the quantity that they had been five years earlier. It should be noted that this does not mean that the stonewares were made in Holland but only that they were shipped from that country, probably from Amsterdam. In 1676, Robert Plot in his *Natural History of Oxfordshire* had referred to Bellarmine bottles (he called them "d'Alva bottles" after the then-hated Duke of Alva) as having hitherto been ". . . made only in Germany, and by the Dutch brought over into England in great quantities."

Stonewares had been shipped to England from Holland all through the first three quarters of the eighteenth century, but such imports direct from Germany were very few indeed. It is interesting to note, however, that stoneware from Flanders reappeared in British customs records in the 1770's.

Besides the reeded-necked jugs with their AR or GR medallions, Westerwald cylindrical tankards (with similar but smaller medallions) and chamber pots (q.v.) were exported to Britain and thence to the colonies in very large quantities until the Rhineland's virtual monopoly was broken by the saltglaze potters of Staffordshire, who went into the coarse jug, tankard, and chamber-pot business in a big way in the 1760's. (Fig. 37)

Solon had little to say about the products of Höhr as opposed to those of Grenzhausen, though he did indicate that it was to Höhr that the Siegburg potters had gravitated in the mid-seventeenth century, a migration that had begun in 1590—and Siegburg was

[6] Aubrey J. Toppin: "The China Trade and Some London Chinamen," *Transactions* of the English Ceramic Circle, No. 3 (1935), p. 55; abstract from the London Custom House Records.

Fig. 93. Gray stoneware storage jar, porringer, and jugs, with incised, stamped, sprigged, and cobalt-painted decoration. The storage jar and porringer may be Flemish and date from the third quarter of the 18th century, while the jugs are from the Westerwald district of the Rhineland. The small jug is of "8" capacity and, in addition to the blue decoration, is painted with manganese purple around the cordoned neck. The large jug is of "2" capacity. Both date in the period 1714–30. Ht. of right jug 10¼".

known for its plain-white or gray wares. Perhaps for this reason salt-glazed tankards and bulbous jugs of the late seventeenth century that are sprig-ornamented but not embellished with either blue or purple are generally attributed to Höhr. Even if this, too, is really a misnomer it serves a useful purpose in distinguishing this ware from the rest of the Westerwald products. A few gray jugs are found with AR medallions (Queen Anne, 1702–14), but the majority are decorated with WR ciphers or portraits (William III, 1694–1702). The body was sometimes less highly fired than the contemporary blue-decorated wares, but the sprigged floral ornaments and combed stalks are identical. It is reasonable to attribute all these pieces to the period c. 1690–1714.

Much less common than the jugs, tankards, and chamber pots are double-handled storage jars and a class of two-handled bowls rather resembling porringers, which seem to have reached the American colonies in the second and third quarters of the eighteenth century. (Fig. 93) The horizontal rolled handles of both jars and bowls are painted with cobalt, while the bodies of the jars are decorated with stamped floral devices (as on chamber pots) and the bowls with incised swags or geometric groups of stamped circles. These jars and bowls are usually of coarser quality than the regular Westerwald wares, and it is possible that they were made at some other center in the Rhineland or perhaps in a revived potting community in Flanders. Curiously enough, however, it was this coarser style that was adopted by the Early American blue and gray stoneware potters of the late eighteenth and early nineteenth centuries. It is probable, therefore, that a study of the American potters and their places of origin would help to determine the source for these mid-eighteenth-century Rhenish jars and bowls.

HANNOVER, EMIL: *Pottery & Porcelain; A Handbook for Collectors* (London). Vol. 1, *Europe and the Near East, Earthenware and Stoneware* (1925), ed. Bernard Rackham.

KLEIN, ADALBERT: *Rheinisches Steinzeug des 15. bis 18. Jahrhunderts.* Darmstadt, Ger., n.d. (c. 1950).

NoËL HUME, IVOR: "Rhenish gray stoneware in Colonial America," *Antiques*, Vol. 92, No. 3 (September 1967), pp. 349–53.

SOLON, M. L.: *The Ancient Arts Stoneware of the Low Countries and Germany.* 2 vols. London, 1892.

See also BELLARMINES; and CHAMBER POTS.

§ *TILES, Delft and Other Wares*

Here, as in the case of English tin-enameled earthenwares it is wise to spell *delftware* with a small *d*, for even those tiles made in the Netherlands were not all made at Delft; on the contrary, many were produced at Rotterdam, Gouda, Harlingen, and Haarlem, and even Dutch students have difficulty in distinguishing between them. Furthermore, from the late sixteenth century onward, Dutch and Flemish potters were making almost identical tiles in England. The products fall into two classes: flooring tiles which are about ¾" in thickness and those used for fireplaces and wall skirtings that were rarely thicker than ⅝".

I have yet to see any delftware flooring tiles among the artifacts from American excavations, but from sites of the mid-seventeenth century onward the thinner wall and fireplace varieties are well represented. In the first edition of his *Builder's Dictionary* (1703) Richard Neve wrote as follows:

> . . . there are two kinds, which I shall distinguish by the Appella-tions of Ancient and Modern: The ancient Dutch Tyles were used for Chimney Foot-paces: They were painted with some antick Fig-ures, and sometimes with the Postures of Soldiers, &c. And some-times with Compartments, and in them some irregular Flourishes; but in general they are nothing so well done (nor with so lively Colours) as the modern ones. The modern Dutch Tyles are com-monly us'd instead of Chimney-cornerstones (being plaister'd up in the Jaumbs). These Tyles seem to be better glaz'd and those that are painted (for some are only white) are done with more curious Figures, and more lively Colours than the ancient ones: But both these sorts seem to be made of the same whitish Clay as our white glaz'd Earthen Ware. The modern ones are commonly painted with Birds, Flowers, &c. and sometimes with Histories out of the *New Testament*.[7]

Neve went on to note that the "ancient" tiles measured 5¼" square and that the "modern" varieties were 6½" square, and that both were ¾" in thickness, contentions which are not borne out by the examples found in archaeological excavations. One can only sup-pose that his measurements were taken from flooring rather than chimney tiles. It is also odd that he speaks of the later, more lively colors, whereas excavations put most of the examples painted in rich maiolica colors prior to about 1640. Nevertheless, Neve's com-ments are valuable in that they mention the different designs and also confirm the existence of plain-white tiles as early as c. 1700.

Maiolica and delftware-tile making has been going on in Hol-land continuously from the sixteenth century to the present day, and variations on the early designs have been repeated again and again. In England, the first designs were painted by Dutch painters and reflected their Netherlandish training. Later, English painters copied Dutch designs simply because they were popular, while both English and Dutch tilemakers were influenced by Wan Li and later

[7] For full citation, see p. 36.

Chinese motifs. All this makes it extremely difficult to establish valid criteria for distinguishing between English and Dutch products.

Regardless of the embargoes on the importation of European delftware in the late seventeenth and eighteenth centuries, there seems to have been no halt in the flow of Dutch tiles into England and out again to the colonies. "Fine Holland Tiles" were advertised in the *Boston News-Letter* on April 23, 1716; in May, 1725, the same paper carried an advertisement for "Several Sorts of Neat Dutch Tiles." Four years later, in September, 1729, the *Boston Gazette* was a little more informative and revealed that Jacob Royalls in Union Street could provide "Very good Figured Dutch Tyle for Chimneys, to be Sold by the Dozen." The *Boston Gazette* was even more helpful in February, 1738, when Captain Stephen Richards of Queen Street, Boston, advertised "All sorts of Dutch Tyles viz, Scripture (round and square), Landskips of divers sorts, Sea Monsters, Horsemen, Soldiers, Diamond, &c." Other references to Dutch tiles occurred in the 1740's, but in June, 1761, we find the same paper advertising "English Chimney Tiles" and in February, 1762, "red & white, and blue & white English Chimney Tiles." Although there were other later references to English tiles, "Dutch" tiles were still reaching New England in 1772—providing that the word meant what it said. Casting some doubt on this is the testimony of the son of the celebrated enameler Michael Edkins, who stated that when his father began work at Bristol, he was employed at the Redcliffe delft factory "where he became a pot painter—that is, to ornament dishes, Flemish tiles for grates dairies etc., which were at that time painted by the hand with pencils made by the workmen themselves, of bristles from the noses and eyelids of oxen."[8] Presumably, therefore, the term "Flemish" meant only Flemish (or Dutch) *type*, leaving us wondering whether advertisers meant the same.

As previously noted (p. 203) the first makers of tin-enameled earthenware in England arrived at Norwich in Norfolk from Antwerp in 1567 and there established a factory for "making Gally

---

[8] Hugh Owen: *Two Centuries of Ceramic Art at Bristol* (London, 1873), p. 331 *n.*

Paving Tiles, and Vessels for Apothecaries and others, very artificially."[9] In 1570 these men, Jasper Andries and Jacob Janson, petitioned Queen Elizabeth for "House-room in or without the Liberties of *London*, by the Water-side,"[1] and it is believed that Janson moved to Aldgate in the city. Shortly thereafter, other galley-ware potters established themselves in Southwark on the south bank of the Thames. Excavations in the boroughs of what are now Southwark and Bermondsey, both east and west of Old London Bridge, have yielded evidence of tilemaking, the Bermondsey material from the vicinity of Tooley Street and Pickleherring Quay being identical to Netherlandish products of the late sixteenth and early seventeenth centuries. Further upstream in Southwark near Blackfriars Bridge digging that preceded the construction of the Bankside power station revealed many hundreds of fragments of unglazed ("biscuit") delftware tile fragments in contexts of the early eighteenth century. A few of these fragments (now in London's Guildhall Museum) retained traces of bird (?) designs penciled in blue on the unglazed ware. Perhaps forty years earlier (1671), and farther upriver, a Dutchman, John Ariens van Hamme had set up a business in the south-bank village of Lambeth for making "tiles and porcelain after the way practised in Holland."[2] Tilemaking continued at Lambeth for more than a century therafter, but no archaeological evidence has been found to show that any eighteenth-century designs were peculiar to that center.

Tiles were made in most eighteenth-century English delftware factories. The products of Bristol and Liverpool are somewhat better known than are those from London, and both centers produced designs and painting techniques that were initially their own. The most easily recognized was created at Bristol in the second quarter of the century and combined a blue-gray ground color with a thick white foliate and floral border, an effect known as *bianco*

---

[9] Stow, op. cit.; for full citation, see fn. 4, p. 203.

[1] Ibid.

[2] Quoted in Bernard Rackham: *English Pottery, Its Development from Early Times to the End of the Eighteenth Century* (New York, 1924), p. 45.

sopra bianco. The centers of these tiles were usually decorated with flowers or birds in polychrome colors. Another type attributed to Bristol made use of a manganese-stippled ground and a central scalloped reserve containing pastoral or architectural motifs in blue. The corners of these tiles were decorated with one quarter of a Tudor rose (Fig. 94, No. 20), four abutting tiles thus creating a complete rose. This type is thought to have been produced around 1740 or 1750. Also English (c. 1750–60) and probably products of Bristol or Liverpool are tiles whose corners contain quartered daisies (Fig. 94, No. 21) usually in conjunction with river, marine, or harbor scenes contained within hexagonal borders divided into lozenge-centered rectangles. A comparable eighteenth-century tile was made in Holland, but the daisy petals were more pointed and the hexagons lacked the lozenge-filled divisions. One more floral-corner device occurs on tiles attributed to Bristol; looking more like a shell than a flower (Fig. 94, No. 24), the motif occurs outlined in blue as a reserve in a manganese-stippled ground on tiles whose principal feature is a hexagonal-edged pastoral scene. The corner was derived from a Dutch carnation design occasionally used to decorate the corners of Biblical and landscape tiles in the seventeenth century (Fig. 94, No. 22) and which later occurred on Dutch reserve-decorated examples akin to the English. It would seem that the Dutch painters stippled the ends of the petals but that the English did not. (Fig. 94, No. 23)

As Figure 94 demonstrates, many of the corner designs degenerated to a point at which not even the painters could recall what they were originally meant to depict. Numbers 3–5 show what became of the fleur-de-lis after someone crossed it with a tulip, while numbers 6 and 7 and 15–19 illustrate the development of the so-called oxhead into a foliate and even-petaled device. Not illustrated is a variant of Number 15 wherein the dot-terminaled loops have been turned into eyebrows and the dots themselves into eyes, thus deftly converting the design into a human face. This occurs on a group of manganese-decorated Biblical tiles found near the Pickleherring Quay kiln in London, which presumably date from the late seventeenth or early eighteenth century. It is tempting (though probably dangerous) to claim them as products of the Bermondsey kilns.

It is evident that English tile painting in the eighteenth century was less accomplished than it was in the Netherlands, particularly when trees were depicted. On Dutch tiles the foliage was invariably treated in a careful and natural manner, but on English tiles the leaves are often applied as horizontal bars, either brushed or sponged, across a trunk shaped from a single vertical line. Just as frequently, English trees more closely resembled small whirlwinds speeding across the countryside. This rather alarming effect has been attributed to Bristol in the period c. 1750–65, and it occurs both on tiles whose scenes are confined within circles and on those that cover the entire surface. Another, rather more creditable English painting technique developed in Liverpool, where tiles were decorated with flowers and birds in pastel colors—slate blue, olive green, orange, and violet—the petals and feathers outlined and veined in black or brown. The so-called "Fazackerley" palette seems to have been first used to decorate delft tableware around 1750 and continued for some fifteen or twenty years thereafter. Comparable colors (with the addition of yellow and dull red) were also used at Bristol.

Undoubtedly the best-known of Liverpool's delftware tiles are those decorated with overglaze transfer prints by Messrs. Sadler and

Fig. 94. Some corner designs on delftware tiles. The majority of the styles are Dutch, but Nos. 9, 15–21, and 24 occur on English examples. Design nomenclature as follows: 1. and 2. Fleur-de-lis. 3–5. Fleur-de-lis/tulip. 6–8. "Oxhead" and variants. 9. Wan Li. 10. and 11. Trinity. 12–14. "Bug" or "Spider's-head." 15. and 16. "Oxhead"/foliate. 17–19. Foliate (derived from "oxhead," in turn developed from fleur-de-lis). 20. Tudor rose. 21. Daisy. 22–4. Carnation. Approximate dating: Nos. 1–4, 9, and 10, first half of 17th century; 5, 7, 8, and 11, mid-17th century; 6 and 12–14, second half of 17th to 18th century; 15, late 17th to mid-18th century; 16–19 and 23, first half of 18th century; 22, late 17th century; 20, 21, and 24, mid-18th century. Nos. 1 and 3 are polychrome; 2, 4–14, 19, and 21–3, blue; 15–18, blue or purple; 20 and 24 (occasionally 23), blue with purple stipple. Note that many of the 18th-century Dutch designs had longer lives than are suggested here, but they did not reach the British American colonies. Approximately half size.

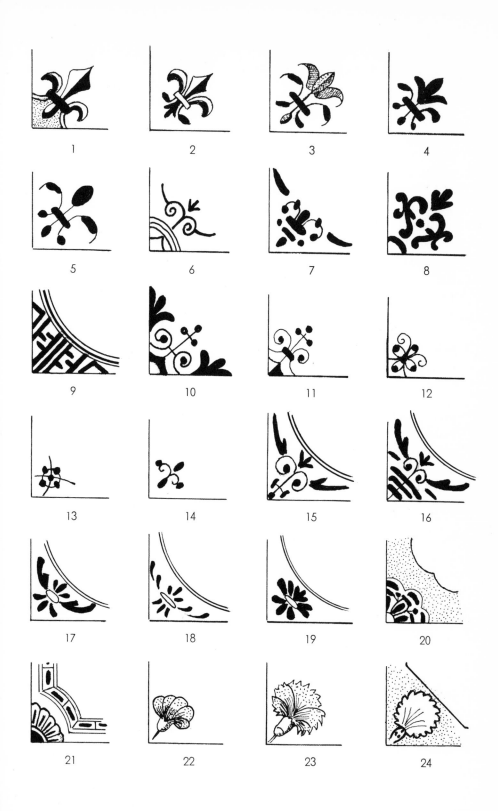

1   2   3   4

5   6   7   8

9   10   11   12

13   14   15   16

17   18   19   20

21   22   23   24

Green in the third quarter of the eighteenth century. The decoration was executed in black or brick red, using motifs adapted from contemporary engravings of chinoiserie and pastoral scenes and designs depicting popular theatrical personalities. Sadler and Green, who claimed to be able to print twelve hundred tiles in six hours, had opened their Printed Ware Manufactory in 1756 and then applied for a patent wherein they stated that they had invented the printing process and already had six years' experience.

So much, then, for decorative features that can point to a delft tile's being of English origin. In the absence of evidence to the contrary, it must be supposed that the vast majority of tiles found on American sites were made somewhere in the Netherlands, and we must be content to try to locate them in *time*, if not *geographically*. Corner devices, some of which have already been mentioned (Fig. 94), can be helpful, there being those whose advent can be fairly accurately dated.

The majority of tiles found on American sites of the seventeenth century are distinguished by their large, unadorned white areas, the decoration being confined to a single figure or a group of human figures in the centers, invariably in blue, and, at Jamestown, with oxhead and "bug" corner ornaments similar to those in Figure 94, Numbers 6 and 12. Figure-decorated tiles of this type (often with the figures of diminutive size) were popular in the third quarter of the seventeenth century; by the last quarter, the figures were larger, often equestrian, and new designs depicting ships, mermaids, and sea monsters became common, tending to fill up more and more of the plain background areas.

The comparatively small number of sites of the seventeenth century that have been excavated in America naturally has a strong bearing on the extent of our knowledge of the use of tiles in early colonial homes. So far as I know, not one polychrome example of the first half of the seventeenth century has yet been recorded, though it is perfectly reasonable to suppose that they were used. The earliest polychrome patterns are likely to have been geometric in the medieval manner, but these were soon followed by central motifs of tulips in vases and by designs of animals or soldiers enclosed within circles or diamond-shaped borders. Corner devices were frequently derived from the fleur-de-lis (Fig. 94, No. 1) or from the Wan Li lattice (Fig. 94, No. 9), which the European painters never quite mastered.

By the end of the seventeenth century, designs contained within double concentric circles became common and remained so for about sixty years. They were painted in blue or purple and depicted ships, harbors, shepherds, milkmaids, and landscapes. Equally popular (as Neve noted; *see* p. 286) were the Biblical scenes, the majority of which were painted in purple. A set of rather similar character, but depicting the story of the Popish Plot of 1678, is in the Victoria and Albert Museum and has been tentatively attributed to John van Hamme's Lambeth factory (*see* p. 288). The majority of roundel-decorated tiles thought to be English possess foliate corner devices (Fig. 94, Nos. 17–19) rather than the oxhead or bug forms common on Dutch tiles of the same general types.

Although Biblical scenes were invariably contained within roundels, this was not true of pastoral or seascape designs which, in the mid-eighteenth century, often stretched from edge to edge across the midsections of the tiles, still retaining the corner devices which were then no more helpful to the whole than spandrels on a clock that had lost its dial.

Delftware remained the sole material out of which decorative tiles were made until the third quarter of the eighteenth century. They were subsequently produced in large numbers in creamware, and Wedgwood's c. 1810 manuscript catalog offered them in sizes measuring 8″, 7″, 6″, 5″, and 4″ square. As early as 1769 (September 17) Wedgwood wrote to his partner Bentley telling him that Lady Gower would "build a dairy on purpose to furnish it with Cream Couler if I will engage to make Tiles for the Walls."[3] Later, on November 4, 1776, he wrote noting that "The rising fashion of furnishing Baths, Dairys &c with Tiles, must stop their exportation into Russia for some time."[4]

When discussing the decoration of creamware, the often-unreliable Simeon Shaw stated that workmen were recruited "from Bristol, Chelsea, Worcester, and Liverpool, where Tiles had long been

[3] K. E. Farrar, ed.: *Letters of Josiah Wedgwood, 1762–1772* (London, 1903), I, 277–8.
[4] Ibid., II, 210; Wedgwood to Bentley.

made of Stone Ware and Porcelain; and who had been accustomed to enamel them upon the white glaze, and occasionally to paint them under the glaze."[5] I have yet to hear of porcelain or stoneware tiles being found in America, but there are examples of white relief-molded salt-glazed stoneware tiles in American collections. Some saltglaze tiles, notably "a Heron fishing, and a Spewing-Duck fountain,"[6] were attributed by Shaw to Wedgwood and to a date shortly after 1760. Other animal and farmyard designs are represented among surviving specimens.

In conclusion, it may be worth recalling that the use of tiles as dating evidence for the archaeological contexts in which they are found can be extremely misleading. Unlike domestic pottery, once installed in a home they were likely to remain there until the building was destroyed, and consequently their date of manufacture could be far removed from that of their descent into the ground. Conversely, they are not necessarily valid clues to the date of construction of a building in whose debris they are found, for new tiles were often added to already-old houses.

De Jonge, C. H.: *Oud Nederlandsche Majolica en Delftsch Aardewark.* Amsterdam, 1947.
Korf, Dingeman: *Dutch Tiles.* New York, 1964.
Lane, Arthur: *A Guide to the Collection of Tiles.* Victoria and Albert Museum. London, 1960.
Ray, Anthony: *English Delftware Pottery in the Robert Hall Warren Collection, Ashmolean Museum.* London, 1968.

See also DRUG POTS, JARS, and PILL TILES.

§ *TILES, Roofing*

Clay roofing tiles were in use in colonial America from the earliest years onward, and through both the seventeenth and eighteenth centuries the most common variety was rectangular, measured

[5] Shaw, op. cit., p. 179; for full citation, see fn. 8, p. 119.
[6] Ibid., p. 183.

about 10″ x 6″ x ½″, and had two nail or peg holes at one end through which they were anchored to the roof lathes. For greater security a strip of mortar was often wiped across the midsection of each row so that the noses of the next course up would be discouraged from lifting in high winds. In addition to the plain tiles, interlocking S-shaped pan tiles are found on eighteenth-century sites. These pan, crooked, or Flemish tiles generally measured 1′ 2½″ x 9½″ and were clipped at top-right and bottom-left corners; they had no nail holes but were hung on the lathes by means of a rectangular lug on the top edge of the underside of each. Similar lugs occur at one end of plain tiles made by the Moravians at Bethabara in North Carolina in the second half of the eighteenth century; they also occur on tiles used to roof the thermal bath house near the *soufrière* on the island of St. Lucia, a building erected on orders from Louis XVI of France in 1785.

Both the plain and pan tiles had to be capped at the ridge, and both made use of a simple semicircular ridge tile. Other more elaborate types were available for dormers, lying in the valleys of roofs, and for covering hips and corners. Unfortunately, no dating is possible; indeed it is virtually impossible to tell the difference between an eighteenth-century ridge tile and the imbrex tiles used in Roman times. While it is true that cyprus and pine shingles were much used on colonial roofs, the constant fear of fire made clay tiles highly desirable for use on brick buildings, and archaeological evidence indicates that many more were used than is often supposed.

Although the discovery of fragmentary rectangular roofing tiles can prompt one to conclude that a nearby building was thus roofed, it is worth remembering that the same type of tile was sometimes used for paving, in the construction of bake ovens, and in bonding courses for stone walls. The quantity and distribution of mortar on the fragment will sometimes indicate whether or not it had been used for roofing.

§ *TOBACCO PIPES and SMOKING EQUIPMENT*

The English kaolin tobacco pipe is possibly the most valuable clue yet available to the student of historical sites, for it is an item that was manufactured, imported, smoked, and thrown away, all within a matter of a year or two. Fortunately the shape of the pipe's bowl underwent an easily recognizable evolution that had begun before the start of the seventeenth century and was still going on well through the nineteenth century. In addition, pipes were extremely cheap (selling in 1709 for as little as two shillings a gross), thus making them available to all economic levels of colonial society. They were as expendable as cigarettes, though vastly more durable, ensuring that their fragments survive in the ground in prodigious quantities.

The Indian habit of smoking tobacco by means of a device formed "like a little ladell"[7] became fashionable in England in the 1570's, and by the early seventeenth century the clay pipe had become commonplace. The earliest types, those of the late sixteenth century, were very short-stemmed, some being no more than 1¾″ in length, though the average was about 3½″. By the third quarter of the seventeenth century the average stem length was between 11″ and 12″, and by the end of the century many were a little longer still. Lengths of 13″ or 13½″ seem to have been common during the first half of the eighteenth century (Frontispiece), though advertisements referred to both short- and long-stem pipes. In the second half of the eighteenth century a few pipes were made with stems of enormous length, 2′ and more (popularly termed "churchwardens," a name coined in the nineteenth century), while others

---

[7] Adrian Oswald: "English Clay Tobacco Pipes," *The Archaeological News Letter* (London), Vol. 3, No. 10 (April 1951), p. 153; quoting from William Harrison's *Great Chronologie* of 1588.

reverted to an earlier and more manageable size and were no more than 9" or so from heel to mouth. Boston newspapers carried advertisements offering "long London Tobacco Pipes" in 1716 and 1742, "Boxes of short Pipes" in 1761, "long and short Pipes" the next year, and "long and midling Pipes" in 1763. More helpful was the advertiser in the *Boston Gazette* (May 28, 1764) who offered his customers "glaz'd 18 inch London Pipes per Box," but whether these were considered long or extra-long remains anybody's guess.

It should be noted that as a rule the length of the stem had no bearing on the size of the bowl, but it did have a very considerable influence on the size of the hole that passed through it. This was made with a wire that was pushed down the solid stem while it was still supported in the mold. When the stem was short, a fairly large hole could be made by using a thick wire, but when the stems became longer and the wire had further to travel a thick wire was more liable to stick through the side than was a thin. In consequence, therefore, smaller wires were generally used as the stems became longer. This, at least, is the theory, though it is possible to find wires of differing thickness in use in the same period by the same maker. (*See* p. 300.) There is no denying, however, that the holes in pipe stems became smaller and smaller through the seventeenth century and on into the second half of the eighteenth, a fact first noticed by Mr. J. C. Harrington of the United States National Park Service. In September 1954, after a careful study of many thousands of pipes both in America and in England, Harrington published a chart showing the percentages of different diameters (gauged in sixty-fourths of an inch) represented among well-dated

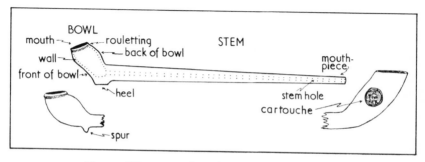

Fig. 95. The parts of a tobacco pipe.

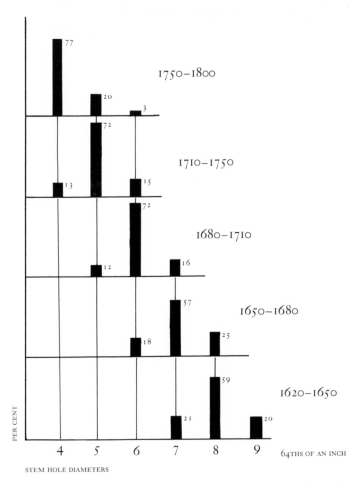

Fig. 96. Chart showing variations in hole diameters through the stems of clay tobacco pipes.

English pipes in five successive time periods from 1620 to 1800. (Fig. 96)

At first, what has come to be known as the "Harrington Theory" was received with considerable merriment among pundits of the pipe, but it soon became apparent to those who took the trouble to test the chart that there was a good deal of truth in it—though Harrington himself had made it very clear from the start that he considered the sampling too small and that much refinement would be necessary when more groups of archaeologically datable pipes became available for study. He also pointed out that associations of only twenty or thirty pipes would probably be insufficient to produce an accurate answer.

So far as I know, no real effort has yet been made to redefine Harrington's date brackets, though much new information has been unearthed in the past decade. However, Dr. Lewis Binford produced a straight-line regression formula based on the Harrington chart enabling a mean date to be arrived at for any assemblage of stem fragments, be it large or small. That formula is as follows:

$$Y = 1931.85 - 38.26X$$

Y being the mean date for the group, 1931.85 the theoretical date when the stem hole would disappear altogether, 38.26 the number of years between each sixty-fourth-of-an-inch decrease, and X being the mean hole diameter for the group. This last is arrived at by first determining the diameter of the bore of each fragment (using a set of wood drills of graduated sizes), multiplying the number of fragments by the number of sixty-fourths, next adding together the total of fragments of all sizes and then all the products, and dividing one into the other, carrying the answer to three places of decimals. Thus:

Hole diameter	Fragments	Product
7/64	35	245
6/64	79	474
5/64	50	250
4/64	20	80
	184	1049 = 5.701

Extremely helpful though this is, it is still based on Harrington's original chart, and the question remains as to how accurate his dates really are.

In the course of excavations in Williamsburg in the summer of 1963 a large quantity of broken pipe stems was found tramped into the ground to make a walkway, all undoubtedly laid down at the same time and most of them the products of a single maker, for nearly 150 bowl fragments bore the initials RM astride the heels. There were, in all, approximately 12,000 stem fragments, and on the basis of other archaeological and historical evidence it was deduced that they were deposited in the early 1740's. Using the Binford formula and taking arbitrary samplings from the collection, the following results were obtained:

No. of Pipes	*Formula date*
19	1726.38
35	1738.09
54	1733.67
105	1733.29
129	1742.09
290	1736.59
295	1740.55
296	1738.26
383	1737.74
591	1739.79
932	1740.55
1111	1740.55
4746	1741.70
9272	1740.55
11164	1740.55

It will be seen, therefore, that although 295 fragments produced a "correct" date of 1740.55, five pieces less put it four years earlier, while one more put it two years less. It was not until 932 fragments were used that a more or less consistent answer could be relied upon. Nevertheless, the very fact that the Harrington-Binford system produced a date for the pipe fragments within ten years of that suggested by other means demonstrates its valuable contribution to historical-archaeological studies. Unfortunately, however, its range of acceptable accuracy seems to be restricted to the period c. 1680–1760, with the probability of error increasing rapidly as one moves away from that bracket in either direction. The following short list of samples from sites of various dates will serve as an illustration:

No. of fragments in deposit	Formula date	Date deduced on other evidence
90	1631	1645–53
924	1636	1645–60
300	1622	1650–60
648	1698	1690–1700
91	1709	1702–10
17	1731	1725–35
271	1751	1745–60
121	1758	1750–65
213	1767	1760–70
485	1747	1762–72
290	1753	1770–80
772	1747	1775–80
51	1755	1775–90
168	1751	1817–20

Although the large quantity of fragments needed to produce a consistent date was present in none of these instances, it is significant that within the period of reliability even quite small groups of stem fragments were capable of producing useful answers, whereas beyond it even the larger groups could provide no greater accuracy than could the small. It should be noted that the foregoing examples show the pipe-dating discrepancies falling consistently earlier than that provided by other evidence. It might be argued, of course, that even a thirty-year tolerance might be helpful in enabling the novice to get a broad idea of the era to which his site belongs, though when I ventured to make this point a lady archaeologist of my acquaintance retorted that if the excavator was unable to pin his site down to such a bracket through his knowledge of other artifacts, he had no business to be digging it.

Among the fallacies nurtured by earlier students of the pipe was the belief that the reason so many stem fragments are found is because smokers passed the pipe from mouth to mouth in the Indian fashion, each smoker breaking a piece off the stem to give himself an unsullied mouthpiece. Broadly speaking, this is nonsense. Pipes were carefully tapered so that the lips easily closed over them, and consequently the removal of more than 2″ or 3″ would have defeated that purpose. Furthermore, broken pipes are found whose fractured stem has been carefully filed or ground down to shape a new mouthpiece. It is extremely unlikely, therefore, that a smoker would have been satisfied to smoke a jagged-ended, thick-mouthed pipe. The obvious explanation for the prevalence of stem fragments on colonial sites is that pipes were long and fragile, and when dropped or knocked broke into numerous pieces. With this said, however, I must note that Colonial Williamsburg owns a mid-eighteenth-century pair of steel ember tongs (*see* p. 309) having three semicircular notches on the inner faces of the arms just above the pads, which, when the tongs are closed, create three circular holes of two sizes that could well have been used to break very small pieces from the mouthpieces of clay tobacco pipes. On the other hand, the notches could be purely decorative. Before leaving the matter of mouthpieces, I should mention that some were coated with a brown or green lead glaze for a distance of about 1″, while others were dipped for a similar distance into red wax—presumably having first had a plug placed in the hole. Both glazing and waxing appear to have been an eighteenth-century innovation and were by no means common.

Prior to Harrington's study of stem holes, the dating of tobacco pipes had relied on the evolution of the bowl form, and for the seventeenth century this is still the most reliable guide. However, as was demonstrated when more than 12,000 stem fragments were found together in Williamsburg, bowls are comparatively scarce, for the stem fragments were accompanied by only 800 bowls, the stem of each pipe therefore theoretically breaking into fifteen pieces.

The first study of bowl evolution (on which nearly all others have been based) was published by the English archaeologist Adrian Oswald in 1951. Figure 96 demonstrates the development of the bowl through the seventeenth into the nineteenth century in a somewhat simplified form.

The shapes were dependent on the mold makers, and each pipe-maker had his own molds. Although the forms followed the same

Fig. 97. A simplified evolutionary series of English clay tobacco pipes, plus examples of locally distributed American types. Nos. 1–24 are English; 25 and 30, American of uncertain provenance; 26–8, Virginian; 29, North Carolinian.

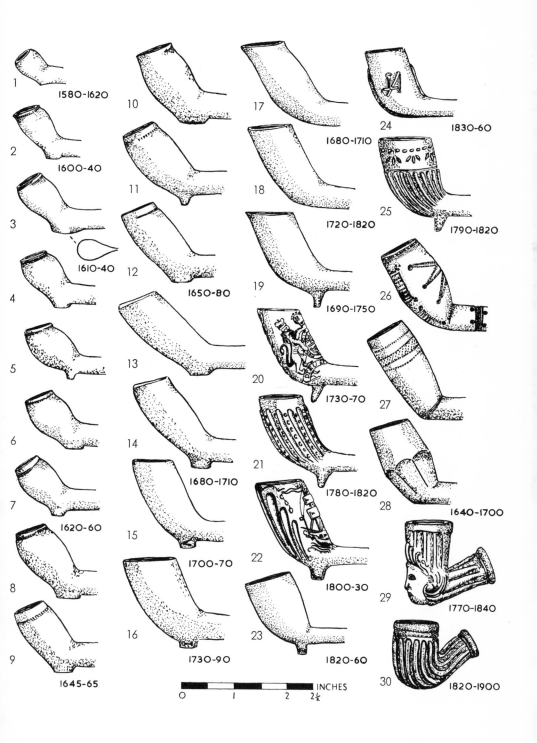

1   1580–1620

2   1600–40

3

     1610–40

4

5

6

7   1620–60

8

9   1645–65

10

11

12   1650–80

13

14   1680–1710

15   1700–70

16   1730–90

17

     1680–1710

18   1720–1820

19   1690–1750

20   1730–70

21   1780–1820

22   1800–30

23   1820–60

24   1830–60

25   1790–1820

26

27

28   1640–1700

29   1770–1840

30   1820–1900

INCHES

0   1   2   2½

general evolutionary trends, it is clear that the pipes made at Chester or Broseley differed from those produced in Salisbury and that the latter were not the same as those made in Bristol—unless the manufacturers happened to buy their molds from the same maker. When one reaches the nineteenth century, decorative bowls were extremely common, and while I have illustrated three examples of styles attributable to different periods I make no pretense that they are adequately representative of the entire class.

There is, unfortunately, a great deal that we do not yet know about the so-called evolution of bowls and stems, and there is reason to suspect that present stylistic and dating criteria have been oversimplified. According to Randle Holme's *An Academie or Store House of Armory & Blazon* (c. 1682) there were then no fewer than ten pipe types, for which there were "seuerall Molds for seuerall fashions as. Lark heele pipes, Flat heele pipes, Round bolls or head, Long Bolls, Long shanks, Midle shanks, Short shanks or ends, Wrought pipes in the head and shank, Smooth pipes, [and] Gleased pipes."[8] The last two almost certainly refer to styles of finishing after removal from the mold; i.e., burnishing and glazing. It would appear that in the latter part of the seventeenth century there were three stem lengths, long, middle, and short, a revelation which casts doubt on the validity of the theory that the stem-hole wire (or "Shanking Wyer" as Holme called it) became progressivly smaller as stems grew longer. Holme's "Lark heeles" were probably what we term *spurs* (e.g., Fig. 97, No. 11), while his "Round bolls" are paralleled by my example in Figure 97, Number 10, and the "Long Bolls" by Number 12. As for the "Wrought pipes in the head and shank," they were almost certainly those with relief decoration.

In addition to the evidence of stem holes and bowl shapes, pipes may also be dated through the correct identification of makers' marks. Here again Adrian Oswald's published work provides the fullest available information. In the first half of the seventeenth century, marks were generally stamped on the flat base of the heel and took the form of initials, full names, or occasionally a rebus. In the third quarter, marks were less common, but they became plentiful again in the last quarter of the century. At this time they were normally reduced to two initials, one on either side of the heel or

[8] Holme, op. cit., p. 271; for full citation, see fn. 1, p. 37.

spur, or occasionally more fully on the back or side of the bowl in incised circles or relief-molded cartouches. These last are particularly characteristic of Bristol pipemakers. The side cartouches extended into the first quarter of the eighteenth century, but the heel-flanking initials as well as the back circles went right on through the eighteenth and nineteenth centuries. By about 1690, Bristol pipemakers were producing pipes without either heels or spurs (apparently in imitation of the traditional Indian styles) for export to the American colonies. Some of these were embossed with the makers' initials on either side of the bowl base. Although such plain bowls continued to be made until the latter years of the eighteenth century, the majority of marked examples belong to the years c. 1690–1730.

Makers' initials are also found straddling the stem, running around it as part of ornamental bands, and stamped in circles on the top—all occurring in the first half of the eighteenth century. In the second half, and on through the nineteenth century, one often finds Liverpool, Glasgow, and Irish makers' names in rectangles stamped on one side of the stem and that of the town along the other.

Stems were sometimes decorated with large, multiple, diamond-shaped fleur-de-lis stamps, a style most popular in the mid-seventeenth century. Toward the end of the century and into the early 1700's, Chester pipemakers decorated stems with bands of ornament that sometimes included spiral fluting and cartouches containing tavern signs or the arms of the City of Chester. The most striking stem decoration yet encountered comes from a mid-eighteenth-century site in Delaware where fragments of two pipes were found coated with a thin brown slip around multiple, irregular reserves exposing the white pipeclay beneath and creating a dramatic, though none-too-pleasing, polka-dot effect.

A few English pipe bowls of the seventeenth century were decorated with groups of raised dots in the shape of trees or bunches of grapes, while on rare occasions the fronts of the bowls were pinched and pared into the shape of a human face. Decorative bowls became much more common in the eighteenth century, a considerable number of them being molded with the arms of the monarch or with the crest of the Prince of Wales. Because the British royal arms appear not only on pipes, but on slipware pottery, on coins, tokens, etc., engraved on glass, and molded on iron firebacks, it may be useful to enumerate the changes made to the royal arms in the seventeenth, eighteenth, and early nineteenth centuries.

From 1403 to 1603, when James I became king, the arms were divided into four quarters (reading from top left to bottom right) comprising the three fleur-de-lis of France in the 1st and 4th and the three lions passant guardant (leopards) in the 2nd and 3rd. From 1603 until the flight of James II, the charges of the previous arms were compressed into the 1st and 4th quarters, while the 2nd received the lion rampant of Scotland and the 3rd the harp of Ireland. With the accession of William III the arms of Nassau were added as an escutcheon on the center of the shield, these arms comprising a lion rampant with rectangular billets around it. From 1702 to 1707, until the union with Scotland, the Stuart arms were restored in the form established in 1603. But after the Union and until the death of Queen Anne, the three leopards of England shared the 1st and 4th quarters with the lion of Scotland, while the fleur-de-lis occupied the 2nd quarter and the Irish harp retained the 3rd. In 1714, with the accession of Hanoverian George I, quarters 1 to 3 remained the same, but the 4th was divided into four elements to accommodate the arms of the Electorate of Hanover. These comprised: (1) two Brunswick leopards; (2) a Luneberg lion rampant surrounded by hearts; (3) (below) a Westphalia running horse; and (4) in the center an escutcheon charged with the crown of Charlemagne. There were no further changes until 1801, when the Hanoverian arms of the 4th quarter were moved onto a central escutcheon surmounted by the Elector's cap and replaced by the three English leopards which then appeared in both the 1st and 4th quarters, the lion of Scotland ousting France from the second quarter. Another minor change occurred in 1815 when the Elector's cap was replaced by a crown in keeping with Hanover's change from electorate to kingdom. Because Queen Victoria could not succeed to the kingdom of Hanover, the Hanoverian escutcheon was removed in 1837, thus creating the simplest royal arms since the death of Elizabeth I. There have been no changes since.

The majority of armorial tobacco-pipe bowls bear the 1714–1801 Hanoverian arms, but a few have been found bearing the post-Union arms of Queen Anne. So many ornamental devices were used in the nineteenth century that it is likely (though I have not seen one) that the Victorian arms were also used. The arms of London were frequently borrowed in that period, those being a shield charged with a cross and with the sword of St. Paul in the 1st quarter.

Pillar-molded or gadrooned bowls became popular in England and America in the late eighteenth century and continued into the nineteenth, but by mid-century English styles had become much more adventurous and the bowls were decorated with arms and crests of counties, with the insignia of Freemasonry or of the Royal Order of Buffaloes, with figures of soldiers or of ships. Sometimes the whole bowl was cast in the shape of a barrel or even a boot.

In addition to English pipes, a small number of Dutch specimens are found on eighteenth-century American sites, most of them in Florida and the Gulf States but some of them in other areas during the Revolutionary War. These Dutch pipes have somewhat egg-shaped bowls very often with evidence of vertical paring on the sides, thin walls, narrow stems, and generally highly burnished buff surfaces. Makers' marks are stamped on the backs of the bowls, on the bases of small heels, or on either side of spurs, nearly always in diminutive letters or minuscule shields of arms. Equally small pictorial marks were impressed on the bases of the small heels, among them a fish, a windmill, a milkmaid carrying two buckets, and a figure whom the Dutch describe as the "lady of easy virtue." The thin stems are often elaborately molded with fleur-de-lis, rosette, and foliate motifs, and the name GOUDA (their principal place of manufacture) is frequently included in the embossed decoration.

A few French pipes are found on early Federal sites and may be identified by the superior quality of their molded bowls, which may be shaped as faces, figureheads, or other elaborate devices. Pipes made either in the United States or for the American trade occur in large quantities in the first quarter of the nineteenth century, usually with pillar-molded or gadrooned lower bowls with broad collars above adorned by thirteen stars.

Large numbers of locally made pipes occur on Virginia sites from the second quarter to the end of the seventeenth century, some of them of great elaboration involving the use of blended clays to produce "agate" effects and employing stamps and rouletting wheels to create various impressed devices. Many of the latter are distinctly Indian in character, giving rise to the strong possibility that they were made by the Indians and smoked by the colonists. By mid-century, cruder copies of the plain English pipes were also produced in Virginia and New England, but as no positively identified kilns have yet been found we do not know exactly where or by whom they were made. It may also be noted that very crude hand-rolled, red-clay copies of late-seventeenth-century English pipes (though with stamped ornament) are found in appropriate contexts in Jamaica. It is reasonable to suppose that the continuing exploration of early sites in others of the erstwhile British colonies will produce more evidence of local pipemaking.

Similar studies are needed in the area of nineteenth-century pipemaking in America. Until recently it was assumed that the so-called Indian-head pipes with reed stems were unknown before the early 1800's, but excavations at the Moravian settlement site at Bethabara in North Carolina have revealed similar bowl types (Fig. 96, No. 29) in a potter's waster pit dating at least as early as 1771. No doubt other such surprises are in store for us.

As well as pipes of clay, a few were of metal. There are silver examples dating from the second quarter of the seventeenth century whose stems unscrew in the middle for portability; but the majority of metal pipes belong to the latter part of the eighteenth century, when they were made of either iron or brass. They are said to have been designed for travelers and huntsmen, for whom the clay pipe was too fragile. However, the metal pipes could be painful if jolted into someone's eye, and they were not widely used. Nevertheless, fragments have been found in American excavations. In addition, the remains of a pewter pipe of uncertain date were found at Jamestown.

Supplying the smoker with fuel for his pipe proved to be one of history's most influential endeavors, and the changes wrought by it have left their mark on the world in which we live. While it would be possible to write an entire book on the artifacts, from anchors to wire, that were employed in the service of tobacco, we are here only concerned with those that kept the pipe going during the actual smoking process. Next to the weed itself, the fire was the most important accessory, coupled, of course, with a means of bringing the two together. While lighting one's pipe from a candle was probably the most convenient method (e.g., Hendrick Terbrugghen's

Boy lighting a Pipe, 1623), the embers from domestic hearths were frequently used, picked up by a pair of long steel tongs, the ends resembling those of ordinary fireplace tongs but the handles separate above a pivot with a spring between them to hold the ember-seizing pad ends together. Such tongs were used in both the seventeenth and eighteenth centuries, and some have removable tampers and even whistles as terminals. Dated examples occur from the late seventeenth to the mid-eighteenth century.

Much smaller tongs, also with spring grips, were often used, generally through the seventeenth and into the early eighteenth century. They were normally about 3¼″ long and of steel or brass. The ember-seizing ends were almost pointed and together somewhat resembled the beak of a heron. The two arms were linked and pivoted in the same manner as their larger counterparts, the thicker of the two having a small spring against which the other pressed. These tools are frequently found broken, at which times the thicker of the two arms often resembles a miniature ice skate, an appearance partially derived from the flat disc at the handle end. The other handle also ended in a disc, though turning outward and intended for use as a pipe tamper. This small, and by no means rare, tool has rightly been described as a "smoker's companion," but more often than not it fails to be identified or is classed as a surgical instrument.

In the seventeenth century the embers into which the small tongs were dipped were generally contained in earthenware braziers or chafing dishes and were stood on the table. However, the same kind of burner was used as a heater for wooden foot warmers, the boxes being open, or having a door in one side and holes or slots in the top. Good examples of both types are to be seen in seventeenth-century Dutch paintings, notably Jan Miensz Molenaer's *Tavern of the Crescent Moon* (before 1668), Jan Steen's *Twelfth Night* (1688) and *Welcome for the Visitor* (before 1679), and Cornelis de Man's *The Chess Players* (before 1706). The pottery braziers were of two shapes, the most common being roughly triangular with three short legs and a single looped or cylindrical handle. These are generally of lead-glazed red earthenware, and both ware and handle types are clearly shown in two of Molenaer's paintings, the already cited *Tavern of the Crescent Moon* and *Peas-*

ants in the Tavern. The second and more elaborate type of brazier comprised a bowl with a slotted or punctured bottom over a hollow pedestal foot, the latter generally having a triangular aperture in the side to encourage an upward draft. One such foot in "Metropolitan" slipware was found at Jamestown and, being decorated, was clearly not intended to be hidden in a foot warmer. Smokers' braziers were also made in more expensive and ornamental materials, such as brass and even silver gilt. An example of this chafing dish type is shown in Willem Pietersz Buytewech's *A Merry Party* (about 1615). Small sheet-brass braziers with a turned wooden handle attached to one side were common in the eighteenth century. They generally stood on a cast-brass collarlike foot, made in at least two sections and decorated with patterns of circular holes and crescents. Parts of these feet are found on American archaeological sites of the mid-eighteenth century—and are generally classed as *unidentified*.

Next to the means of lighting his pipe, the smoker's most important tool was the tamper or stopper. These were commonly of brass, and from at least as early as 1660 they were cast with elaborately ornamental handles. (Fig. 98) Close dating is not always as easy as it looks, for the designs were frequently retrospective; for example, a profile of Charles I would have been popular in the reign of Charles II, while a coin mounted on the handle might already have been old (and therefore interesting) when it was so used. The best clue to an early date is provided by the size of the tamper itself, for those that were of small diameter (Fig. 98, No. 1) fitted small bowls—and small bowls were generally early. A sophisticated type appeared in the early eighteenth century (and continued through it) in the form of a closed-ended tube topped by a signet ring; the tube served both as a tamper and as a case for a pocket corkscrew attached to the ring handle.

Sometimes mistaken for a corkscrew is another smoker's aid, this one in the shape of a miniature steel hatchet. Attached to the handle end was a double "corkscrew" resembling the "worm" for extracting debris from gun barrels; it served a comparable purpose in extracting plugged tobacco from pipe bowls. At the other end of the tool was a small blade with an unsharpened edge to break up tobacco without cutting it, while behind, at what might be termed

Fig. 98. Brass pipe tampers. 1. Amorous couple; third quarter of 17th century. 2. Profile of Charles I; late 17th or 18th century. 3. Nude boy; 17th or 18th century. 4. Hand with pipe, probably early 19th century. 5. Handle in the shape of a Queen Anne coin; early 18th century (?). Ht. of No. 1: 3".

the poll of the hatchet, was a round-sectioned tamper sometimes decorated with multiple collars and grooves. The small diameter of the tampers suggest that these tools may date from the seventeenth rather than the eighteenth century, but unfortunately I know of no examples from dated archaeological contexts.

Tobacco boxes fall into two classes, those used to carry it around on one's person and those to keep it in the home. Pocket boxes are sometimes impossible to distinguish from large snuffboxes, and cheap varieties of both were made of tin, pewter, and brass. Copper boxes with brass lids having stamped and engraved decoration were made in the Netherlands throughout much of the eighteenth century and are identified by the presence of Dutch inscriptions describing designs of ships, harbors, towns, and convivial or Biblical scenes. The majority of such boxes were oblong, but the earliest examples seem to have been oval with both top and bottom of brass. (Frontispiece)

Nonportable tobacco boxes used in the home and in taverns or other public buildings were most commonly of lead, usually with poorly defined cast decoration (tavern scenes, shields of arms, etc.) on the sides; they had removable lids and a press inside to keep the tobacco tight and away from the air. These boxes were often gaily painted, particularly in the early nineteenth century. The archaeologist who finds scraps of lead with molded, paneled ornament would do well to consider the possibility of its having been part of a tobacco box. They were also made in iron, brass, and pewter. In the nineteenth century brown stoneware jars with flat lids were widely used, some of the more elaborately decorated jars coming from the Rhenish potteries of Nassau in the Rhineland as part of their Gothic revival.

Although clay tobacco pipes were relatively cheap, tavern keepers who provided them for their customers were wont to re-use them as long as they remained unbroken. In the interests of hygiene they baked used pipes in what were known as "kilns," iron racks comprising three hoops held together by horizontal straps and with a suspension ring in the mid-section of the second hoop. Slung in this rack, the pipes were baked over the kitchen fire or sealed in the bread oven. Iron feet in the form of bent lengths of strapping were usually attached to the bottom horizontal strap so that once cleansed, the pipes and rack could be stood beside the hearth to cool. Thus skeletal iron tubes found in excavations may well have been pipe "kilns." It is worth remembering that such items listed in household inventories do not necessarily mean that the owners manufactured pipes!

BINFORD, LEWIS R.: "A New Method of Calculating Dates from Kaolin Pipe Stem Fragments," *Southeastern Archaeological Conference Newsletter* (Cambridge, Mass.), Vol. 9, No. 1 (June 1962), pp. 19–21.

HARRINGTON, J. C.: "Dating Stem Fragments of Seventeenth and Eighteenth Century Clay Tobacco Pipes," *Quarterly Bulletin* of the Archeological Society of Virginia (Richmond), Vol. 9, No. 1 (September 1954).

LINDSAY, J. SEYMOUR: *Iron and Brass Implements of the English and American House.* Rev. edn. London, 1964.

MOJZER, MIKLOS: *Dutch Genre Paintings in Hungarian Museums.* English edn. Budapest, 1967.

NOËL HUME, AUDREY: "Clay Tobacco Pipe Dating in the Light of Recent Excavations," *Quarterly Bulletin* of the Archeological Society of Virginia (Richmond), Vol. 18, No. 2 (December 1963), pp. 22–5.

OSWALD, ADRIAN: "English Clay Tobacco Pipes," *The Archaeological News Letter* (London), Vol. 3, No. 10 (April 1951), pp. 154–9.

————: "The Archaeology and Economic History of English Clay Tobacco Pipes," *Journal of the Archaeological Association* (London), 3rd Ser., Vol. 23 (1960), pp. 40–102.

————: "The Evolution and Chronology of English Clay Tobacco Pipes," *The Archaeological News Letter* (London), Vol. 7, No. 3 (September 1961), pp. 55–62.

PAWSON, MICHAEL: "Clay Tobacco Pipes in the Knowles Collection," *Quarterly Bulletin* of the Archeological Society of Virginia (Richmond), Vol. 23, No. 3 (March 1969), pp. 115–47.

§ *TOYS*

In the seventeenth and eighteenth centuries, and earlier still for that matter, the word *toy* meant not only a plaything but also a trifle, a small article of little intrinsic value. Thus such items as buttons, cheap jewelry, and odds and ends that today one might buy at a notions counter in an American store could be classed as toys, as could pottery ornaments, money boxes, and the knicknacks and gewgaws sold at fairs and now collected under the category of *fairings*. I am here concerned, however, only with toys in the sense of children's playthings.

The majority of eighteenth-century toys were miniature versions of well-known objects whose dating criteria can generally be applied to them. This is particularly true of dollhouse furnishings in pottery, glass, pewter, and occasionally silver. Delftware potters made miniature bowls and dishes, but the ware did not lend itself as easily to them as did white-saltglaze stoneware. The latter was much used for this purpose in the period 1730–65, and, as might be expected, it was followed by similar dollhouse items in creamware. Miniature wine glasses are rare, but there is a good range of early-eighteenth-century examples in the Victoria and Albert Museum,

Fig. 99a. Clay and metal toys. 1. White-pipeclay lion, cast in poorly matched two-piece mold; probably 16th century. 2. Red-pottery dog, presumably cast in a two-piece mold though no mold marks are visible, face and legs largely missing, decorative chain collar around the neck; late 16th or early 17th century. 3. Watch in hollow-cast pewter; 18th century. 4. Lead-and-tin-alloy soldier cast from an elaborately detailed two-piece mold, the two halves of which were slightly different, stand and horse's feet missing; German, c. 1760–80. 5. Pewter whistle with drilled wooden "pea"; late 18th or 19th century. 6. Brass pistol of matchlock type, moving parts missing; late 16th or early 17th century.

all said to have been made in Holland and to have been part of the furnishings of Queen Anne's dollhouse.

Guns have been dear to the hearts of boys ever since the bullet challenged the arrow, and some of the best toy guns were being made as early as the reign of Elizabeth I. They were cast either in pewter or brass in the style of the pre-wheel lock pistols of the mid-sixteenth century. It seems that the brass examples (Fig. 99a, No. 6) were intended to fire, for their barrels and touchholes were fully drilled. A serpentine cock was mounted in front of the pan to take the fuse and was linked to a lever below the stock, which, when turned, thrust the fuse into the pan. However, it seems likely that if the toy guns were fired, it would have been much safer to have simply touched a match into the pan, ignoring the mechanism. Just how late these toys were made is open to speculation. Since neither the wheel lock nor the flintlock could be made in a working form that small, it may be that the miniature matchlock gun remained popular long after the fullsize mechanism became obsolete.

Small cannon made in both iron and brass are found on American archaeological sites of the eighteenth century and these, too, have drilled barrels and touchholes. It has been suggested, however, that they may not be toys at all but signal or sundial guns originally mounted on stands with a burning glass over them and oriented so as to cause the touch powder to ignite at a given time. Signal devices of this kind were used aboard ships in both the seventeenth and eighteenth centuries, but it is stretching the imagination rather far to make such an identification on the evidence of a barrel alone.

Figurines made in two-piece molds from colored clay were pop-

314

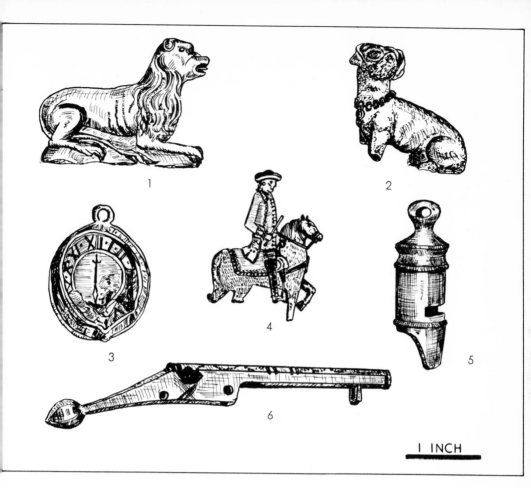

ular in the seventeenth century. Examples occur in white, gray, red, and blue, and in shapes ranging from crudely modeled animals to people whose clothes and features are shown in great detail and with remarkable fidelity. Examples in my own collection from the river Thames include an emaciated lion in pipeclay, a beautifully modeled redware dog with an Elizabethan-style collar around its neck (Fig. 99a, Nos. 1 and 2), and the torso of a blue cherub holding a dove. The finest example I have discovered, however, came from a test excavation on the land site at Port Royal in Jamaica where a truncated figure of a Caroline gentleman was found in the debris of a fire that swept the unlucky town in 1703. (Fig. 99b) While I have yet to see figures of this type dating from the eighteenth century, they are to some degree paralleled by those cast in white saltglaze in the 1740's and 1750's. Among the latter are small dogs, birds, and female figures. These last are generally rather crudely modeled, their costumes being more lifelike than their features. Some of them are embellished with spots of brown slip on their eyes and nipples—suggesting that they were intended for the amusement of older children.

Wooden dolls can be traced back to remote antiquity, and pottery examples with movable arms and legs were popular in Greece in the 4th century B.C. There are some of these in the British Museum, along with a Roman rag doll of the 3rd century A.D. Wooden figures were the commonest dolls available in the sixteenth, seventeenth, and eighteenth centuries, the later heads of wax or wood being fleshed out with gesso and enamel. By the mid-eighteenth

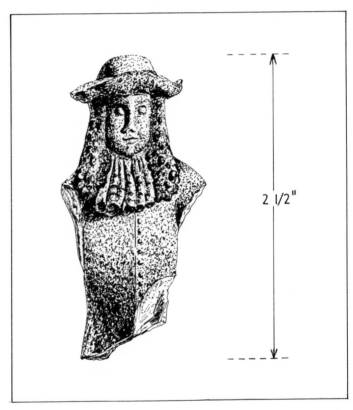

2 1/2"

Fig. 99b. Head and body of man wearing clothes popular in the 1680's, cast in pipeclay from a two-piece mold, the ware now dark gray possibly caused by fire damage. It was found in the debris of that part of Port Royal, Jamaica, which burned in 1703.

century, glass eyes were being added, and examples were advertised by colonial shops. Delftware dolls with mortice-hinged arms and legs were made in the eighteenth century, but their exact date and place of origin remain uncertain. By the early nineteenth century papier mâché dolls were being made, usually with wax-coated faces. Other composition bases were introduced during the first half of the century, and gutta-percha began to be used in about 1850.

The most common of all relics of Victorian childhood to be recovered from American historical sites are the heads, arms, and legs of German (Thuringian) "china" dolls. Opinions differ alarmingly as to the date range of these items, but the continuing researches of Miss Elizabeth Coleman of the Newark Museum suggest that dolls with porcelaneous heads and limbs were rare before 1860 and that the vast majority date no earlier than the 1880's. The earliest of these hollow glazed heads were made from clay pressed into the two halves of a mold and subsequently luted together. In the late 1860's the heads were beginning to be slip-cast, the technique leaving no mold marks on the inside and causing the interior contours to follow more closely those of the exterior. The earliest heads were generally well painted with flesh tones and black hair, the curls of which were fairly regularly molded. The first of the slip-cast heads were usually somewhat flat on the cranium with a minimum of hair modeling. In the 1880's, the black or blond hair became more exuberant and bushed out above the ears; the modeling of the features was often of excellent quality, the larger dolls exhibiting such details as pierced ears. The 1890's hair style was quickly simplified into a coiffure that bushed out all over, and these, generally black-painted, were made from the 1890's through to the 1930's with little discernible change. All these heads were sewn to the textile bodies by means of pierced saddle-shaped shoulders.

Along with the glazed and painted porcelaneous heads were comparable types in glazed but unpainted porcelain, while others were in bisque. In 1845 a Staffordshire factory invented Parian ware, a marble-like body that took well to intricate molded detail and which is said by some authorities to have been much used in the manufacture of dolls in the third quarter of the nineteenth century. While I have seen this ware used for ornamental figurines, it would seem that the vast majority of doll parts found on nineteenth-cen-

317

tury American sites are of German manufacture, with Japanese products becoming plentiful in the present century. The latter are invariably of slip-cast bisque, usually with tinted flesh colors. In its best period, however, this fabric is German rather than Japanese and dates back to the 1870's.

The most frequently encountered doll parts are the legs, the majority extending no further than the knee and anchored to the body by threads sewn around a groove at their tops. The larger examples were hollow-cast, but the smaller and more common legs were solid, usually with a blue or brown garter close to the top of the calf. These colors, in association with bulbous calves, date from the 1880's right through to the 1930's. They generally have brown-glazed, or blue- or black-painted boots with heels, the later nineteenth-century examples often exhibiting molded buttons. Earlier legs dating from the 1860's and 1870's had smaller and more naturalistic calves, and the boots were flat-heeled. It has been suggested, on the evidence of the boot shape, that these may date back to the period c. 1815–40, but it is more likely that they actually belong to the period c. 1855–70. The earliest of the heeled boots, incidentally, were often more brightly and carefully colored (in green, red, and yellow, etc.) than were those on the later, thick-calved variety.

Arms were generally fairly straight and were anchored in the same manner as the legs. They were rarely colored, the best—and usually earlier—examples having the thumbs clearly defined. The earliest of all, dating from the mid-nineteenth century had a clenched fist with a hole through it to take a stick. The latest and cheapest were those solid hands akin to spatulas with mere grooves to suggest fingers, and those continued well into the present century.

Not all porcelaneous heads had cloth, wood, or composition bodies; some were cast in one with ceramic bodies having fixed or movable limbs, in which case the arms and legs were extended to shoulders and thighs, which were pierced and attached to the bodies by wires that passed through holes in the torso. This type, in tinted bisque, dates back at least to the 1870's and has continued through to the present century. It is important, however, to note that the limbs were straight and "adult" to the end of the nineteenth century, but became bent and naturalistically "infant" starting in 1909.

It is hard to determine where a doll ends and a figurine begins, but a transitional type, solid-cast, with fixed legs and wired arms, became common in the last decades of the nineteenth century. Mold marks down the sides of the body were roughly pared away to enable the arms to swing. Many of these figures are bald-headed, and it should be noted that some authorities have suggested that hairless pates (to be covered by wigs) are the earliest of the glazed and bisque heads. Another variation of the same type of figure, with a hole through the shoulders for the arm wire, but with carefully molded braided hair and bonnet, is usually attributed to the last decades of the nineteenth century, though an example found in a cemetery in northern Turkey has been thought to be a relic of the Crimean War.

Before leaving dolls and figurines, a word must be said about those with both arms and legs cast immovably in the mold. Although all too little is known about the date ranges of such objects, it is tentatively concluded that those that are hollow and press-molded date from the second half of the nineteenth century and that those made by the slip-casting method were made after 1900. It is also believed that examples with divided legs are liable to be earlier than are those with legs joined all the way to their feet. Many of these figures have incised numbers on their backs indicating their size. The same is true of arms and legs and also of some porcelaneous heads. Roman numerals occur on some of the limbs of the last decades of the nineteenth century.

However, all these observations are based on little hard fact and much supposition. Porcelaneous dolls and doll parts were made in numerous factories, in many sizes, and at a variety of prices. Consequently, it is dangerous to attempt a chronological series of dating criteria based on the assumption that regardless of place, size, or price, they all developed in step with each other.

Relics of games are by no means rare, though it is often impossible to be sure whether they should be classified under *games* or *gaming*. Among them are bone and pottery dice, loo fish in mother-of-pearl, ivory billiard balls, counters in all those materials, and dominoes in combinations of bone and wood. The same problem applies to whistles, most of which are of pewter; those of miniature size were almost certainly children's toys, but when they are larger it depends on who blew them to determine whether or not they were tooted for fun. Of all musical toys, the jew's-harp is archaeo-logically the most common, and the majority that I have recovered date from the eighteenth century. Some were of iron with steel or brass reeds, while others were brass with steel reeds; but like so many of the small artifacts of colonial America, no one has given them much thought.

Lead (or rather tin and lead-alloy) soldiers were first produced in Germany in the eighteenth century, at which time manufactur-ing was centered in the cities of Nuremberg and Augsburg. They were two-dimensional and had no moving parts, but the quality of the mold engraving was usually extremely high. The example shown in Figure 99a, Number 4 dates from the period 1760–80, and even after more than a century on a tidal river foreshore every detail of his dress facings, weapons, and harness can be clearly seen, as can the hairs on the horse's hide. This particular warrior seems to be holding a marshal's baton, and the casting of one side of his face bears a faint and perhaps accidental resemblance to Frederick of Prussia, who was a military hero in England during the Seven Years' War.

Marbles are found on many colonial sites, though none that I have seen are of marble. The majority are of plain-gray or brown clay, though some are "agates" made from the mixing of two clays of different colors, generally gray and a reddish brown. Glass mar-bles seem to have become common in the nineteenth century.

Wooden tops have a lengthy history, but being of an organic material readily subject to decay in the ground, one does not expect to find them on archaeological sites. Nevertheless, what one expects and gets are not always the same, and four tops were found in a well on the home site of George Washington's father-in-law, John Custis. They were thrown away in about 1790, were lathe-turned, and spun on iron pegs driven into the tapered ends. One of the Custis site tops retained traces of red paint and it is quite possible that all were originally gaily colored.

Perhaps the simplest and most ubiquitous of toys was the whirligig, a serrated-edged disc with two holes through the middle and mounted on a loop of string. By twisting the string and then pulling the ends tight the disc could be made to saw the air, creat-ing a buzzing noise. The toy's simplicity tends to ensure its anonymity, but although the majority were made from uninformative bits of scrap metal they were sometimes made from copper coins or datable fragments of filed pottery. I have not seen a seventeenth-century example, but they seem to have been popular in the eighteenth century and have been found in both town and plantation excavations. They also occur on military camp sites of the Revolutionary period.

CARSON, JANE: *Colonial Virginians at Play*. Williamsburg Research Studies, Williamsburg, Va., 1965.

COLEMAN, DOROTHY S., ELIZABETH A., and EVELYN J.: *The Collector's Encyclopedia of Dolls*. New York, 1968.

HODGSON, MRS. WILLOUGHBY: "Late Seventeenth and Early Eighteenth Century Toys and Dolls' Clothing," *The Connoisseur*, Vol. 48, No. 192 (August 1917), pp. 193–202.

§ WIG CURLERS

These small pipeclay objects are among the most distinctive of eighteenth-century artifacts and seem to have been used in the colonial home as well as in the barbers' and wigmakers' shops. The majority are between 2½″ and 3″ in length, expanding toward the ends and then incurving quickly to flat extremities which are often impressed with the initials IB or WB, generally under a crown and sometimes over a dot. I have found examples of these marks (but never any others) on both English and American sites. The matrices vary considerably, and those that are poorly cut or badly impressed can be misread as IR or WR and so have led some writers to claim that the curlers were made under royal patents from James II and William III. I have found no evidence that that was so, and there is no doubt that when clearly stamped the R's become B's. It is strange, however, that these are the only initials to occur on the curlers, for such marked examples are found in no small numbers on sites dating between c. 1700 and 1780. As it is generally supposed that curlermaking was a sideline of the tobacco pipemakers, it is surprising that we do not find as many initial variations on

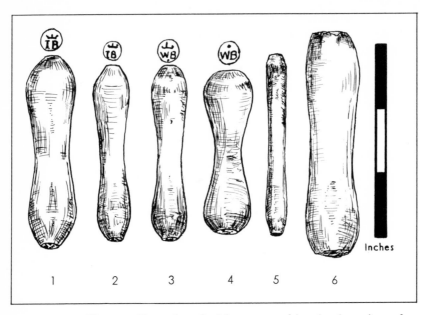

Fig. 100. Examples of 18th-century white-pipeclay wig curlers, the marks somewhat enlarged.

curlers as on pipes. It should also be noted that the presence of the same letters on curlers of different lengths and whose shapes range from very slightly expanded ends to heavy dumbbell profiles implies that they were not intended to identify specific types.

The purpose of these curlers was almost the same as that of women's rollers today. The curls of a new wig, or of one being dressed, were rolled in strips of damp paper around the clay curlers, the weight of which served to pull the hair downward against the block over which the wig was seated. In addition to the average sizes mentioned above, a few longer and thicker curlers are found, the proportions varying to cater for curls of differing size and tightness. The finished curl was tied around the curler with a piece of rag, after which the whole wig was baked, sometimes in a nearby baker's oven. The same baking process was also afforded to individual curls when a wig was being made. In either case, the paper used to wrap them was often derived from old newspapers, and in the course of baking the dampened ink was sometimes transferred— letter by letter—to the white curler, where it remains to this day.

322

Care should therefore be taken in washing wig curlers lest such printing should inadvertently be destroyed. In other instances the curlers may have become discolored at the ends while remaining white in the waisted central area that was protected by the paper and hair. Thus, it is possible to determine the approximate width of the curls for which a curler had been used.

These objects vary considerably in quality from the carefully shaped and polished IB and WB varieties, through almost-straight rods sloppily trimmed at the ends, to three-inch fragments of tobacco-pipe stems ground at both fractures. A quantity of the crudely made rods (along with one WB) was found on Edward Charlton's barber-shop site in Williamsburg in a context of about 1770–5. This type has yet to be found in earlier archaeological groups.

Like so many once-common objects of the seventeenth, eighteenth, and even the nineteenth centuries, the evolution of the wig curler has become lost in the gray fog of time and our knowledge of it stems almost entirely from the fruits of archaeology. As yet it remains a very limited knowledge, for no one has attempted a thorough study of the role of the curler in eighteenth-century life. It is possible that research into wigmaking techniques may reveal names and purposes for the different shapes and sizes, and from this we may perhaps learn the date ranges during which certain types were used. Alternatively, that same information may emerge from a tabulation of all the examples found in dated archaeological contexts. If patents were granted or applied for, records of them may be found in the English *State Papers, Domestic,* or perhaps in eighteenth-century newspaper advertisements. Illustrations may exist in genre paintings or humorous engravings. Admittedly, cursory examination of the wig-curler evidence has failed to produce any flashes of inspiration, but many people had spent much time studying clay tobacco pipes without ever realizing that the sizes of the stem holes had anything important to tell them.

INDEX

In the interests of both brevity and clarity, the index has been restricted to objects and, in certain significant cases, the names of their makers and the places of their manufacture. Exceptions do occur, however, in relation to the introductory chapter, which differs from the body of the book in that it deals as much with ideas as it does with artifacts.

As a general rule, unimportant references have been omitted, as have all proper names relating to the ownership or discovery of objects. Similarly, the donors of information are not cited unless their names have since become particularly associated with that information. Thus, for example, Mr. Hugh de S. Shortt, the provider of helpful but little-known data on rumbler bells, is not included, but Mr. J. C. Harrington, the pioneer of pipe-stem dating, is cited under "pipes, tobacco, Harrington theory," his name being firmly associated with that process.

The indexed artifacts are throughout assumed to be of either English or British colonial origin unless otherwise stated. In cases where other nationalities are specified under a main object heading, those that are English are thus identified. It should be noted, however, that as all too little is yet known about the products of Scotland and Wales, the word "English" might be more safely read as "British."

Index

beads, shell, 54
bedpans, earthenware, 150
Bell, Samuel, potter, 123
Bellarmine bottles, 55–7, 76, 277–9, 283; English, 112
Bellarmino, Cardinal Roberto, 55
bell glasses, 225–6
Bellingham, John, glassmaker, 186
bells, 58; rumbler, 58–9
Bennington (Vermont) pottery, 101
Bentley, Nathaniel ("Dirty Dick"), 31–2
billiards: balls, 319; table, 25
bin labels, delftware, 210
bits: bridoon, curb, Pelham, and snaffle, 240–1
"black Basaltes," 121
Blaikley, William, closets of, 29–30
bodkin, 37
Bolsover, Thomas, of Sheffield, 90, 184
Bonnin and Morris, porcelain makers, 11, 100
bosses: bridle, 240–2; harness, 240–242
bottles, ceramic: American stoneware, 80, Bellarmine, 55–7, 76, 112, 277–9, 283; blacking, 78–9; "d'Alva," 283; delftware, 76; English brown stoneware, 78–9, 112; ink, 78–9; manufacturers of English, 79
bottles, glass, case, Dutch, 62, 69; case, English, 202; case, French, 69–70; Coca-Cola, 47–8; liquor, 60–71; manufacture of, 20–1; patent medicine, 73–5; pharmaceutical, 72–5; see also seals, glass
Bouffioulx stoneware, 148
bowls: annular ware, 133; Astbury ware, 122
box, tobacco, 111–12
brassfounding, 11–15
braziers, earthenware, 309–10
brick bonds, 83–4
brickmaking, 80–1
bricks, 80–4; American, 82; English, 81–2; Flemish, 83; sizes of, 81
Britannia metal, 184
Buckingham, Duke of, 186
buckles: baldric, 88; belt, 86–7; dress, 84–7; hat, 86; knee, 85–6; shoe,

84–7; spur, 85, 87, 243
Buckley earthenware, 132, 135
bullet, evolution of, 221
bullet molds, 222
Burroughs, James, bellfounder, 59
buttonmaking, American, 92
buttons, 88–93; Continental Army, 92; lead, 174

cabinetmakers' guides, 37
caldrons, 176-7
cames, glaziers', 234
candles, 97–8
candlesticks: creamware, 97; crude earthenware, 97; delftware, 96; metal, 18, 93–5; saltglaze, 96; slipware, 105; see also chambersticks
casters, furniture, 231
cat, agateware, 26
Caveat emptor, 16
ceramic terminology, 34
ceramics: *see ware and object entries*
chafing dish, metal, 310
chamber pots: coronation, 150; creamware, 148; crude earthenware, 146; delftware, 146–7; Metropolitan slipware, 149; pearlware, 148; Rhenish stoneware, 148–9, 281; scratch blue, 118, 149–50; slipware, 103, 149; white saltglaze, 118, 147, 149–50
chambersticks, 96–7
Chance, Lucas, glassmaker, 235
chargers, delftware, 108
chocolate pot, copper, 29
clasps, books, 232
clockmakers, American, 13–14
clocks: bracket, 151–3; case fittings, 152–3; lantern, 9, 151; spandrels for, 12–14, 152; weight for, 9, 152
closestool pan, earthenware, 150
clouded ware, 123
coins: American state, 169; colonial, 167–8; Commonwealth pewter, 156–7; Elizabethan silver, 154; English copper, 155–63; forgeries, 156–7, 162–3; gun money, 165; Irish copper, 156–7, 164, 166; Scottish copper, 156–7,

Ivor Noël Hume was born in London, studied at both Framlingham College and St. Lawrence College in England, and served during World War II in the Indian Army. In 1949 he joined the staff of the Guildhall Museum in London as an archaeologist. He moved to Colonial Williamsburg as chief archaeologist in 1957 and eight years later became director of the Department of Archaeology. Since 1959 Mr. Noël Hume has been an honorary research associate of the Smithsonian Institution; he is also a fellow of the Society of Antiquaries of London and vice president of the British Society for Post-Medieval Archaeology. Mr. Noël Hume is the author of *Here Lies Virginia; 1775: Another Part of the Field*; and has recently published *Historical Archaeology*, a companion work to this volume. He lives in Williamsburg with his wife, who is also an archaeologist and writer.

A NOTE ON THE TYPE

The text of this book was set on the Linotype in a type face called Baskerville. The face is a facsimile reproduction of types cast from molds made for John Baskerville (1706–75) from his designs. The punches for the revived Linotype Baskerville were cut under the supervision of the English printer George W. Jones.

John Baskerville's original face was one of the forerunners of the type style known as "modern face" to printers—a "modern" of the period A.D. 1800.

The book was composed and bound by The Haddon Craftsmen, Inc., Scranton, Pa., and printed by Halliday Lithograph Corporation, West Hanover, Mass.